Intelligent Image and Video Interpretation:

Algorithms and Applications

Jing Tian
Wuhan University of Science and Technology, China

Li Chen
Wuhan University of Science and Technology, China

Managing Director:	Lindsay Johnston
Editorial Director:	Joel Gamon
Production Manager:	Jennifer Yoder
Publishing Systems Analyst:	Adrienne Freeland
Development Editor:	Austin DeMarco
Assistant Acquisitions Editor:	Kayla Wolfe
Typesetter:	Lisandro Gonzalez
Cover Design:	Jason Mull

Published in the United States of America by
Information Science Reference (an imprint of IGI Global)
701 E. Chocolate Avenue
Hershey PA 17033
Tel: 717-533-8845
Fax: 717-533-8661
E-mail: cust@igi-global.com
Web site: http://www.igi-global.com

Library of Congress Cataloging-in-Publication Data

Intelligent image and video interpretation : algorithms and applications / Jing Tian and Li Chen, editors.
     pages cm
  Summary: "This book covers all aspects of image and video analysis from low-level early visions to high-level recognition, highlighting how these techniques have become applicable and will prove to be a valuable tool for researchers, professionals, and graduate students working or studying the fields of imaging and video processing"--Provided by publisher.
  Includes bibliographical references and index.
  ISBN 978-1-4666-3958-4 (hardcover) -- ISBN 978-1-4666-3959-1 (ebook) -- ISBN 978-1-4666-3960-7 (print & perpetual access) 1. Image analysis--Research. 2. Image processing--Research. 3. Artificial intelligence--Research. 4. Digital images--Research. 5. Digital video--Research. I. Tian, Jing, 1979- II. Chen, Li, 1977-
  TA1637.I476 2013
  621.36'7--dc23
                              2012051548

British Cataloguing in Publication Data
A Cataloguing in Publication record for this book is available from the British Library.

All work contributed to this book is new, previously-unpublished material. The views expressed in this book are those of the authors, but not necessarily of the publisher.

Editorial Advisory Board

List of Reviewers

Table of Contents

Detailed Table of Contents

    Saurabh Upadhyay, Banaras Hindu University, India
    Shrikant Tiwari, Banaras Hindu University, India
    Sanjay Kumar Singh, Banaras Hindu University, India

This chapter presents an intelligent video authentication algorithm using a support vector machine, which is a non-linear classifier and its applications. It covers both kinds of tampering attacks, spatial and temporal.

    Lee Hao Wei, Sunway University, Malaysia
    Seng Kah Phooi, Sunway University, Malaysia
    Ang Li-Minn, Edith Cowan University, Australia

This chapter reviews audio-visual speech recognition processes and relevant techniques with a specific focus on feature extraction and classification for both audio and visual processing.

    Xin Xu, Wuhan University of Science and Technology, China
    Li Chen, Wuhan University of Science and Technology, China
    Xiaolong Zhang, Wuhan University of Science and Technology, China
    Dongfang Chen, Wuhan University of Science and Technology, China
    Xiaoming Liu, Wuhan University of Science and Technology, China
    Xiaowei Fu, Wuhan University of Science and Technology, China

In image and video sequence analysis, human activity detection and recognition is critically important. This chapter provides a comprehensive review of the recent advances in human activity recognition. Various methods for each issue are discussed to examine the state of the art.

    Chun-Yan Zeng, South China University of Technology, China
    Li-Hong Ma, South China University of Technology, China
    Ming-Hui Du, South China University of Technology, China
    Jing Tian, Wuhan University of Science and Technology, China

This chapter reviews typical sparsity known greedy algorithms as well as emerging blind sparsity greedy algorithms. Furthermore, the algorithms are analyzed in structured diagrammatic representation and compared by exact reconstruction probabilities for Gaussian and binary sparse signals.

    Ji-Hye Kim, Sogang University, Korea
    Ji Won Lee, Sogang University, Korea
    Rae-Hong Park, Sogang University, Korea
    Min-Ho Park, PIXTREE, Korea
    Jae-Seob Shin, PIXTREE, Korea

This chapter proposes a pre-processing method of motion-adaptive edge-preserving smoothing and detail enhancement for H.263 and H.264 video in which temporal and spatial edges are used to define a region of interest.

    Yonghao Xiao, South China University of Technology, China & Foshan
        University, China
    Weiyu Yu, South China University of Technology, China & Soochow
        University, China
    Jing Tian, Wuhan University of Science and Technology, China

Image thresholding segmentation based on Bee Colony Algorithm (BCA) and fuzzy entropy is presented in this chapter. The fuzzy entropy function is simplified within a single parameter. The BCA is applied to search the minimum value of fuzzy entropy function for obtaining the optimal image threshold.

Chapter 7

Jingyu Hua, Zhejiang University of Technology, China
Wankun Kuang, Zhejiang University of Technology, China

This chapter provides a comparative study of the conventional lowpass filtering approach, then proposes an improved method based on learning method, where pixels are filtered by five edge-oriented filters, respectively, facilitated to their edge details. Furthermore, the differential evolution particle swarm optimization algorithm is exploited to refine those filters.

Chapter 8

Maofu Liu, Wuhan University of Science and Technology, China
Huijun Hu, Wuhan University of Science and Technology, China

The image shape feature can be described by the image Zernike moments. This chapter pinpoints that the high dimension image Zernike moments shape feature vector can describe more details of the original image, while it has too many elements making trouble for the next image analysis phases.

Chapter 9

*Sheng Ding, Wuhan University, China & Wuhan University of Science
and Technology, China*
Li Chen, Wuhan University of Science and Technology, China
Jun Li, Wuhan University of Science and Technology, China

This chapter addresses the problems in hyperspectral image classification by the methods of local manifold learning methods. With a proper selection of parameters and a sufficient number of features, the manifold learning methods using the k-nearest neighborhood classification results produce an efficient and accurate data representation that yields higher classification accuracies than conventional linear dimension reduction methods for the hyperspectral image.

Preface

This book is focused on a fundamental and challenging research area—Image and Video Interpretation—and it covers all aspects of image and video analysis from the low-level early vision to the high-level recognition and interpretation in image and video data. These techniques have received increasing attention due to their potential in numerous real-world applications, such as visual communications, computer-assisted biomedical imaging, and video surveillance. For example, a video surveillance system exploits a set of spatially distributed video sensors, each of which is equipped with a video camera to capture, transmit, and process visual information about a scene. Such capability has led to massive research efforts devoted to research challenges in the design of a system for collection and dissemination of video data and the development of algorithms for processing and meaningfully interpreting the data collected. The above trend has motivated us to propose this book with the aim to consolidate recent research achievements that address broad changes in both theoretical and applied aspects of image and video interpretation.

This publication aims to consolidate state-of-the-art research achievements that address broad changes in both theory and application of image and video interpretation. It can serve as an important reference in image and video processing for academicians and researchers.

The target audience of this book is composed of professionals and researchers working in the fields of image and video processing in various disciplines. The book can also serve as an important reference for upper-level undergraduate and graduate students studying this subject by helping both academic lecturers and students to understand the state-of-the-art techniques in image and video interpretation. In addition, this book will stimulate new research activities and inspire more researchers endeavoring in this area.

This publication has received overwhelming responses and received high quality submissions from several countries. All submissions were peer-reviewed by at least two independent reviewers. In the end, only 9 chapters were included in this publication.

We close by thanking the authors for their submissions, reviewers for their constructive comments, editorial staffs of IGI Global Press for guiding us through the whole process.

Jing Tian
Wuhan University of Science and Technology, China

Li Chen
Wuhan University of Science and Technology, China

Acknowledgment

This work was supported by National Natural Science Foundation of China (No. 61105010), Hubei Provincial Natural Science Funds for Distinguished Young Scholar of China (No. 2010CDA090), Program for Outstanding Young Science and Technology Innovation Teams in Higher Education Institutions of Hubei Province, China (No. T201202), Key Project of Chinese Ministry of Education (No. 210139), Wuhan Chen Guang Project (No. 201150431095).

Chapter 1
Intelligent Video Authentication:
Algorithms and Applications

Saurabh Upadhyay
Banaras Hindu University, India

Shrikant Tiwari
Banaras Hindu University, India

Sanjay Kumar Singh
Banaras Hindu University, India

ABSTRACT

With the innovations and development in sophisticated video editing technology, it is becoming increasingly significant to assure the trustworthiness of video information. Today digital videos are also increasingly transmitted over non-secure channels, such as the Internet. Therefore, in surveillance, medical, and various other fields, video content must be protected against attempts to manipulate them. Video authentication has gained much attention in recent years. However, many existing authentication techniques have their own advantages and obvious drawbacks; we propose a novel authentication technique that uses an intelligent approach for video authentication. This book chapter presents an intelligent video authentication algorithm using support vector machine, which is a non-linear classifier, and its applications. It covers both kinds of tampering attacks, spatial and temporal. It uses a database of more than 4000 tampered and non-tampered video frames and gives excellent results with 95% classification accuracy. The authors discuss a vast diversity of tampering attacks, which can be possible for video sequences. Their algorithm gives very good results for almost all kinds of tampering attacks.

DOI: 10.4018/978-1-4666-3958-4.ch001

1. INTRODUCTION

Visual information has always had a great role in our society, as well as in history as today. Its control is always being very significant for the individuals, organizations and for countries too. It can express from a very tiny moment of our life to the history of the universe. In contrast to early days of human society, today we can transmit the information thousands of kilometers within a couple of seconds. This makes a great impact on the development of our society. In today's digital era, communication and compression techniques facilitate sharing of multimedia data such as image and video (Upadhyay, Singh, Vatsa, and Singh, 2007). With the wide-spread availability of sophisticated and low-cost digital video cameras and the pervasiveness of video sharing websites, digital videos are playing a more important role in our daily life. Since digital videos can be manipulated maliciously, their authenticity cannot be taken for granted. Although it is fact that tampering with a digital video is more complex and challenging task than tampering with a single image, but today's elegant and sophisticated video editing technology makes it easier to tamper with videos. The increasing sophistication of computing devices and its equipment has made digital manipulation of video sequences very easy to perform. Ensuring the trustworthiness and integrity of a digital video has posed considerable challenges. This is because of one of the significant properties of digital data, i.e., a copy of digital multimedia data behaves the same as the original one.

1.1. Necessity of Video Authentication

In some of the video applications, the authenticity of video data is of much interest such as in video surveillance, forensic investigations of digital videos, law enforcement, and content ownership (Upadhyay, Singh, Vatsa, and Singh, 2007). For example, in court of law, it is significant to establish the trustworthiness of any video that is used as evidence. As in another scenario, for example, suppose a motionless video recorder for surveillance purpose, is positioned on the pillar of a railway platform to capture every activity on that platform along a side. It would be quite simple to remove a certain activity, people or even an event by simply removing a handful of frames from this type of video sequences. On the other hand it would also be feasible to insert, into this video, certain objects, people taken from different cameras and in different time. These are the instances where modifications are not tolerated. Thus video authentication is a process which ascertains that the content in a given video is authentic and exactly same as when captured. For verifying the credibility of received video content, and to detect malicious tampering attacks and preventing various types of forgeries, performed on video data, video authentication techniques are used.

1.2. Related Works

In past few years, watermarking and digital signatures have been widely used for the purpose of video authentication. Different techniques have their own advantages and shortcomings. In fact, fragile watermarking and digital signatures are the two commonly used schemes for authentication (Peng & Hong, 2001). Fragile watermarking embeds the authentication data into the primary multimedia sources, while digital signature stores the authentication data separately, either in user defined field, as like, in the header of MPEG sequence, or in a separate file (Peng & Hong, 2001). Moreover there has also been worked on intelligent techniques for video authentication (Upadhyay, Singh, Vatsa, and Singh, 2007; Singh, Vatsa, Singh, and Upadhyay, 2008). Intelligent authentication techniques use learning based techniques for authentication purpose. Apart from these digital signature, fragile watermarking, and intelligent techniques, some other authentication techniques are also introduced by researchers, which are specifically designed for various cases of malicious attacks.

2. VIDEO TAMPERING

A continuous video data $V_c(x,y,t)$ is a scalar real valued function of two spatial dimensions x and y and time t, usually observed in a rectangular spatial window W over some time interval T. If $M(x, y, t)$ is modification vector then the tampered video $B_c(x, y, t)$ would also be a scalar real valued function of spatial dimensions x and y and time t as follows:

$$B_c\left(x, y, t\right) = M\left(x, y, t\right) + V_c(x, y, t)$$

When the content of information, being produced by a given video data is maliciously altered, then it is called tampering of video data. It can be done for several purposes, for instance to manipulate the integrity of an individual or to deceive any one by producing fake information through tampered video. Since a wide range of sophisticated and low cost video editing software are available in the market that makes it easy and less expensive to manipulate the video content information maliciously, it poses serious challenges to researchers to be solved.

2.1. Video Tampering Attacks

There are several possible attacks that can be applied to modify the contents of a video data. Formally a wide range of authentication techniques have been proposed in the literature but most of them have been primarily focused on still images. However the basic task of video authentication system is to prove whether the given video is tampered or not but in several applications, due to large availability of information in video data, it may be more significant if the authentication system can tell where the modifications happened (It indicates the locality property of authentication) and how the video is tampered (Peng & Hong, 2001). On considering these where and how, the video tampering attacks can have different classifications. A lot of works have been done that briefly address the classification based on where (Upadhyay, Singh, Vatsa, and Singh, 2007; Peng & Hong, 2001). And some papers address the classification based on how (Dittman, Mukharjee and Steinbach, 2000). In general finding where the video data is altered is more efficient than to find out how the how data is tampered. When a video is being recorded by a video recording device, it captures the scene which is in front of the camera lens, frame by frame, with respect to time. Number of frames being captured by video recording device in a second, depends on the hardware specification of the device. Thus a video can be viewed as a collection of consecutive frames with temporal dependency, in a three dimensional plane. It refers to the regional property of the video sequences. When a malicious modification is performed on a video, it either attacks on the contents of the video (i.e. visual information presented by the frames of the video), or attacks on the temporal dependency between the frames of the video. Therefore based on the regional property of the video sequences, we can broadly classify the video tampering attacks into three categories: spatial tampering attacks, temporal tampering attacks and the combination of these two, spatio-temporal tampering attacks (Peng & Hong, 2001). They can be further classified into their subcategories.

2.1.1. Spatial Tampering

In spatial tampering malicious alterations are performed on the content of the frames (X-Y axis). The operations which are performed as a tampering attack in spatial tampering are cropping and replacement, morphing, content (object) adding and removing, in the frames of the video etc (Peng & Hong, 2001). These attacks can be efficiently performed with the help of any professional video editing software for example *Photoshop*, etc.

2.1.2. Temporal Tampering

In temporal tampering malicious manipulation is performed on the sequence of the video frames. The focus is on the temporal dependency of the video. Temporal tampering attacks are mainly affecting the time sequence of visual information, captured by video recording devices. The common attacks in temporal tampering are frame addition, frame removal, and frame reordering or shuffling in the video.

2.1.3. Spatio-Temporal Tampering

Spatio-temporal tampering attacks are the combination of the both kinds of tampering attacks: spatial and temporal tampering attacks. Frame sequences are altered and also visual contents of the frames are modified in the same video. The authentication system should be able to identify both kinds of tampering attacks.

All these tampering are further classified into their subcategories. Spatial tampering can be in effect either at block level or at pixel level. In both the cases, the objects of the frames of the video are altered.

Further, the objects of the frames are classified into two categories: Foreground objects and Background objects. The foreground objects are those, which are captured as individual elements, excluding the background, in a frame. And the background object is the background part of the frame excluding all of the foreground objects. The different pieces of visual information shown in the frames of the video are altered in spatial tampering. Basically, the contents of the video frames are treated as objects. Based on these objects and their classification the spatial tampering can be further classified as shown in Figure 1.

2.1.3.1. Object Removal Attack

In object removal attack of the spatial tampering, the objects of the frames of the video are eliminated. This kind of tampering attack is commonly performed where a particular person wants to hide his/her presence in a certain sequence of frames. With this kind of attack he /she may disappear in a specific time domain, recorded

Figure 1. Spatial tempering classification

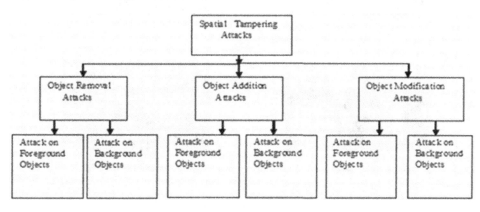

5

in the video, and with the help of this, he/she can easily prove his/her absence in any event which has been recorded by video recording device, as shown in Figure 2.

2.1.3.2. Object Addition Attack

An object or set of object is inserted in a frame or in a set of frames of the video in object addition attack of spatial tampering. In any video, which can be treated as evidence, an additional object can be pasted in a frame or set of frames, with the help of sophisticated video editing software to mislead the investigation agencies as well as court of law. With the help of this kind of attack, one can prove his/her presence in any event of the pre-recorded video, as shown in Figure 3.

2.1.3.3. Object Modification Attack

In object modification attack of the spatial tampering, an existing object of the frame(s) can be modified in such a way that the original identity of that object is lost, and a new object may be in appearance, which is completely different from the original object. The object modification attacks can be existed in many prospects of the given video. For instance, the size and shape of any existing object may be

Figure 2. Example of object removal attack: (a) shows object removal attack with foreground object, where a small device is removed from the original frame in tampered frame; (b) shows the object removal attack with background object. Here a small object on the right side of the wall is eliminated from the original frame in tampered frame.

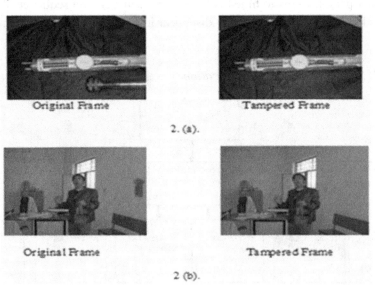

2. (a).

2 (b).

Figure 3. Example of object addition attack. In original frame of (a) two persons are there as major foreground objects, while in tampered frame of (a) an additional person as a foreground object is added. In tampered frame of the (b), not only a foreground object is added but also an additional wall as a background object, in the middle of the frame, is added.

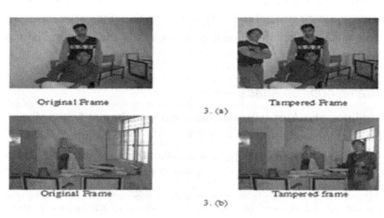

changed, the color of the object may be changed or it may be discolored, and with the help of additional effect the nature of the object and it's relation with other objects also may be changed. It depends upon the intention. In fact it is very hard to detect and locate this kind of attack of spatial tampering for authentication systems, since these attacks are performed at pixel level. The authentication systems should also be robust enough to differentiate this kind of attack with the normal video processing operations. Figure 4 shows a typical example of object modification attack where the face of a person has been changed in such a way that the person's face, which is introduced in the altered frame, is completely different from the face of the person in original frame.

Figure 4. Example of object modification attack. The face of the person in original frame is modified in tampered frame, in such a way that the new face of the person cannot be identified as the same as in original frame.

7

Besides spatial tampering, temporal tampering attacks have also sub classifications. Temporal tampering attacks are specific to video applications and can be performed at scene level, shot level and frame level, but the primary focus is on attacking the temporal dependency of the frames of the video. This kind of tampering attack basically affects the sequencing of video frames. We call it 'Third dimensional (dimension with respect to time) attack' on the video sequences. Therefore based on this third dimensional attack we can classify the temporal tampering attacks into following subcategories.

2.1.2.1. Frame Addition Attack

In frame addition attack of temporal tampering, additional frames from another video, which has the same statistical (height and width of frames) and dimensional (number of frames per second) properties, are intentionally inserted at some random locations in a given video. This attack is intended to camouflage the actual content and provide incorrect information (Upadhyay, Singh, Vatsa, and Singh, 2007). A typical example of the frame addition attack is shown in Figure 5.

2.1.2.2. Frame Removal Attack

In frame removal attack of temporal tampering, the frames of the given video are intentionally eliminated. In this kind of tampering attack frames or set of frames can be removed from a specific location to a fixed location or can be removed from

Figure 5. Example of frame addition attack. In first row, the original frame sequence from frame 6 to frame 16 has been shown. After attack, the second row of the frames shows the altered frame sequence in which a new frame is inserted between frame 6 and frame 16 and frame 16 becomes frame 17.

different locations. It depends upon the intention. Commonly this kind of tampering attack is performed on surveillance video where an intruder wants to remove his/her presence at all. Figure 6 shows a typical example of frame removal attack.

2.1.2.3. Frame Shuffling Attack

In frame shuffling attack of temporal tampering, frames of a given video are shuffled or reordered in such a way that the correct frame sequence is intermingled and wrong information is produced by the video as compared to original recorded video. Figure 7 shows a typical example of frame shuffling attack where two frames are shuffled.

2.2. Levels of Tampering Attacks

In addition of these types of tampering attacks, tampering can be done at different levels in video sequences.

2.2.1. Scene Level

When the tampering attacks are performed at scene level then a whole scene of the video sequence is manipulated in such a way that, not even the scene itself is modified but also in reference to the given video the scene of that video is modified. It means spatial and temporal both kinds of tampering can be done at scene level.

Figure 6. Example of frame removal attack. The first row of this figure shows the original frame sequence with frame 14, frame 22, and frame 30. In second row of the frame sequence, which shows the tampered frame sequence with frame removal attack, frame 22 is eliminated from the video and hence frame 30 becomes frame 29.

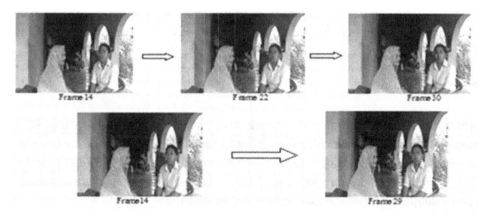

Figure 7. Example of frame shuffling attack. The first row of this figure shows the original frame sequence with frame 13, frame 20, and frame 26. After the frame shuffling attack, the original frame sequence is tampered as shown in second row of the figure where the positions of frame 13 and frame 26 have been changed.

2.2.2. Shot Level

In shot level tampering a particular shot of the given video is modified in reference to the given video. In shot level tampering a shot can be added or removed from the video. It can also be performed with all kinds of tampering attacks.

2.2.3. Frame Level

When frames of the given video are maliciously modified, then it is called tampering at frame level. Frame removal, frame inserting, and frame shuffling are the common tampering attacks that can be performed at frame level. In other words, temporal tampering attacks are commonly performed at frame level.

2.2.4. Block Level

In block level tampering, tampering attacks are performed on the blocks of the video frames. The content of the video frames are treated as blocks on which the tampering attacks are applied. Blocks (a specified area on the frame of the video) can be cropped and replaced, morphed or modified in any way in block level tampering. Spatial tampering attacks are commonly performed at block level.

2.2.5. Pixel Level

In pixel level tampering contents of the video frames are modified at pixel level. This is the smallest level in video sequences at which tampering attacks can be performed. The video authentication system should be robust enough to differentiate the normal video processing operation and pixel level tampering, since many normal video processing operations are performed at pixel level. Spatial tampering attacks are commonly performed at pixel level.

All these levels of tampering show the different aspects of tampering.

3. AUTHENTICATION TECHNIQUES

By definition, authenticity means sometimes "as being in accordance with fact, as being true in substance," or "as being what it professes in origin or authorship, as being genuine"[1]. Another definition of authentication is to prove that something is "actually coming from the alleged source or origin"[2]. A video authentication system ensures the integrity of digital video and verifies that whether the given video has been tampered or not. But in most of the cases, especially in the court of law, it may be more beneficial if the authentication system can tell where the tampering happens and how the video is tampered. A typical video authentication system is shown in Figure 8. For a given video, authentication process starts with feature extraction. After that, with a specific video authentication algorithm, the authentication data H is generated using the features f of the video. This authentication data H is encrypted and packaged with the video as a signature or alternatively it can be embedded into the video content as a watermark. The video integrity is verified by computing new authentication data H` for the given video. The new authentication data H` is compared with decrypted original authentication data H. If both are matched, the video is treated as authentic else it is considered as tampered video. An ideal video authentication system, to be effective, must support to the properties such as sensitivity to malicious alteration, localization, and self recovery of altered regions, robustness to normal video processing operations, tolerance against some loss of information, compactness of signature, sensitivity against false intimation and computational feasibility. In fact in addition to having robustness against benign operations, an ideal video authentication system must make a given video resistant against all possible attacks and must verify whether a given video is tampered or not. Benign operations are those video processing operations that do not modify its content semantically such as geometric transformations, image enhancements, and compression. Once the verification is done for the given video, it would be useful to find where and how the tampering has been done.

Figure 8. A typical video authentication system

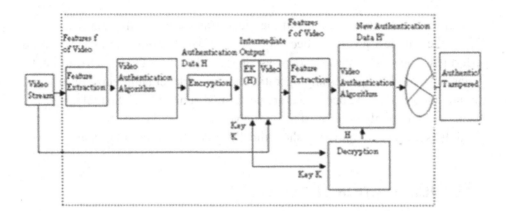

However, based on the objectives of authentication, an authentication system can be categorized as complete verification and content verification. Techniques that are proposed for complete verification consider that the multimedia data, which have to be authenticated, have to be exactly the same as the original one. Content verification is a characteristic of multimedia data authentication.

3.1. Classification of Authentication Techniques

In past few years, watermarking and digital signatures have been widely used for the purpose of video authentication. Different techniques have their own advantages and shortcomings. In fact, fragile watermarking and digital signatures are the two commonly used schemes for authentication.

Fragile watermarking embeds the authentication data into the primary multimedia sources, while digital signature stores the authentication data separately, either in user defined field, as like, in the header of MPEG sequence, or in a separate file (Peng & Hong, 2001). Moreover there has also been worked on intelligent techniques for video authentication (Upadhyay, Singh, Vatsa, and Singh, 2007, Singh, Vatsa, Singh, and Upadhyay (2008). Intelligent authentication techniques use learning based techniques for authentication purpose. Apart from these digital signature, fragile watermarking and intelligent techniques, some other authentication techniques are also introduced by researchers, which are specifically designed for various cases of malicious attacks. Basically video authentication techniques are broadly classified into four categories: Digital signature based techniques, watermark based techniques, intelligent techniques, and other authentication techniques. Figure 9 represents a tree structure of authentication techniques which have been commonly proposed for the purpose of video/image authentication.

Figure 9. Tree structure of authentication technique

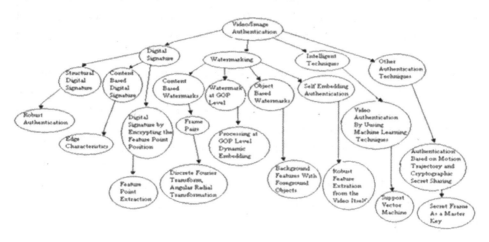

3.1.1. Digital Signature

Integrity of multimedia data can be greatly verified by digital signature. For the authentication of multimedia data, it was first introduced by Diffie and Hellman in 1976 (Diffie and Hellman, 1976). For the purpose of authentication, digital signatures can be saved in two different ways. Either they can be saved in the header of the compressed source data, or it can be saved as an independent file. Further, they can be produced for verification. In the prospective of robustness, since the digital signature remains unchanged when the pixel values of the images/videos are changed, they provide better results. In the digital signature authentication, the digital signature of the signer to the data depends on the content of data on some secret information which is only known to signer (Wohlmacher, 1998). Hence, the digital signature cannot be forged, and the end user can verify a received multimedia data by examining whether the contents of data match the information conveyed in the digital signature. In fact, digital signature can be used to verify the integrity of multimedia data which is endorsed by the signer.

In Lin and Chang (1999), two types of robust digital signatures are used for video authentication in different kinds of situations. The first type of authentication signature is used in situation where the GOP (Group of Pictures) structure of the video is not modified, after transcoding or editing processes. The situation, where the GOP structure is modified and only the pixel values of picture will be preserved, a second type of digital signature is used.

In another work, video authentication is done by generating digital signatures for image blocks and using them as watermarks (Celik, 2002). In this approach local-

13

ization packet, watermark insertion is done via LSB modification of pixel values. As compared to Mobasseri and Evans (2001) where video tampering is identified through an analysis of watermark sequencing, here (explicit) block ID's are used for this purpose.

The Johns Hopkins University Applied Physics Laboratory (APL) has developed a system for authentication of digital video (Hopkins). The authentication system computes secure computer generated digital signatures for information recorded by a standard digital video camcorder. While recording, compressed digital video is simultaneously written to digital tape in the camcorder and broadcast from the camera into the Digital video authenticator. In this authentication system, video is separated into individual frames and three unique digital signatures are generated per frame—one each for video, audio, and (camcorder) control data—at the camcorder frame rate.

Here the key cryptography is used. One key, called a "private" key is used to generate the signatures and is destroyed when the recording is complete. The second a "public" key is used for verification. The signatures that are generated make it easy to recognize tampering. If a frame has been added it would not have a signature and will be instantly detected and if an original frame is tampered the signature would not match the new data and it will be detected in verification process.

In digital signature based video authentication schemes, different features are used for different applications. Dittman (Ditmann, Steinmetz, & Steinmetz, 1999) and Queluz (1998) used the edge/corner of the image as the feature to generate the digital signature. They claimed this feature is robust against high quality compression and scaling but the problem is that the signature generated based on the edge is too long, and the consistency of the edge itself is also a problem. Formally digital signature based authentication techniques are able to detect regions that have been tampered, but often they are too fragile to resist incidental manipulations. For this type of incidental manipulations structural digital signature (Lu and Liao, 2003) can be used for image authentication. This approach makes use of an image's content to construct a Structural Digital Signature (SDS) for image authentication. The characteristic of the SDS is that it can tolerate content preserving modifications while detecting content changing modifications. In this approach (Lu and Liao, 2003), many incidental manipulations which can be detected as malicious modifications in other digital signature verifications or fragile watermarking schemes, can be ignored.

In the scenario of a station streaming video over network, it is significant for the audiences to have guarantees that the video stream they are watching is indeed from the station. Schemes that are used for this purpose can prevent the malicious parties from injecting commercials or offensive materials into the video streams. Actually, this problem has been covered in information security called streaming signing (Gennaro and Rohatgi, 1997, Park, Chong and Siegel, 2002), which is an extension from message signing by digital signature schemes which are able to both protect the integrity of the message and prevent the signer's repudiation.

In another technique, a separate authentication code is written in (Su, Chen and Chang, 2009) from the blocks of the video frames. Here the authors Po-Chyi Su, Chun Chieh Chen and Hong Min Chang use the approach of scalar/vector quantization on the reliable features. Once the authentication code is written, it is transmitted along with the video. Thus the authenticity of the given video content can be checked by matching the extracted feature with the transmitted authentication code. The authentication code chosen by authors is sensitive to malicious modifications of video data. The proposed work also considers two classical false detection tests. These are false alarms and misses. In the situation of former false detection test the authentication scheme wrongly signals a happening of tampering while the normal video processing operations are there. In the later situation, false detections are related to misses of detection after an actual tampering on video content has been performed. This work is resilient to lossy compression procedures, while the tampered regions on the video frames can be located if malicious attacks were applied (Su, Chen and Chang, 2009).

Navjit Saikia and Prabin K. Bora present a scheme for video authentication in Saikia and Bora (2007) that generates the Message Authentication Code (MAC) for a Group Of Frames (GOF) using coefficients from the last but one high pass band at full level of temporal wavelet decomposition. This digital signature based scheme uses temporal wavelet transform for the generation of message authentication code. After the extraction of GOFs from the video, these GOFs are recursively decomposed into high pass band up to a certain level using temporal wavelet transform. At this level the high pass band consists of two frames. In the signature generation process, these frames are divided into some blocks of fixed sizes. These blocks are randomly mapped on to a set of groups, using a mapping key in such a way that each group contains equal number of blocks. With the transform coefficients and these groups of blocks, a set of linear combination values is evaluated for each frame in the high pass band. And with these sets of linear combination values, message authentication code (MAC) is obtained for the GOF. In the signature verification process, the distances d ($MAC_{i,1}$, $MAC`_{i,1}$) and d($MAC_{i,2}$, $MAC`_{1,2}$) are calculated where d is any distance measure and { $MAC_{i,1}$, $MAC_{i,2}$ } is the MAC of GOF of the original video and {$MAC`_{i,1}$, $MAC`_{i,2}$} is the MAC of corresponding GOF calculated at receiver site. Here the GOF of the video would be authentic if these two distances are below some predefined threshold values, otherwise tampered. When all GOFs in it are found authentic then the given video is declared as authentic video. This authentication scheme would be advantageous for spatio-temporal manipulations, since it is effective for spatial tampering as well as for temporal tampering.

3.1.2. Watermarking

Watermarking always remains a significant issue for solving authentication problems regarding digital multimedia data, in past few years. A wide variety of watermark based authentication techniques have been proposed by various researchers in literature. However watermarking techniques can be used for authenticating various multimedia data, but most of the work has been done for image and video authentication. Based on the application areas, watermarking can be classified in different categories (Dittman, Mukharjee and Steinbach, 2000). Beside to ensure the integrity of the digital data and recognizing the malicious manipulations, watermarking can be used for the authentication of the author or producer of the content. Watermarks can be embedded with the multimedia data, without changing the meaning of the content of the data. The advantageous feature with the watermarks is that, they can be embedded without degrading the quality of multimedia data too much. Since the watermarks are embedded in the content of video data, once the data is manipulated, these watermarks will also be modified such that the authentication system can examine them to verify the integrity of data. In (Guerrini, Leonardi and Migliorati, 2004), authors describe the use of video authentication template, which uses a bubble random sampling approach applied for synchronization and content verification in the context of video watermarking. The authentication template is introduced in order to ensure temporal synchronization and to prevent content tampering in video sequences (Guerrini, Leonardi and Migliorati, 2004).

Basically in past few years, an increasing use of digital information in our society and availability of very sophisticated and low cost video editing software creates problems associated with copyright protection and authentication. One of the main advantage of digital world is that here perfect copying is performed easily. That causes severe security related issues. The owners or producers of information resources are being worried of releasing proprietary information to an environment that appears to be lacking in security (Queluz, 2001). On the other hand, with the help of powerful video editing software one can challenge the trustworthiness of digital information.

In Queluz (2001), M. P. Queluz presents the generic models with labeling and watermarking approaches for content authentication, in which existing techniques for content authentication are described and compared. In labeling based approach authentication data are written in separate file (Queluz, 2001), while in watermarking based approach the authentication information is embedded in the frames. In this labeling-based authentication system, features C and C` are extracted from the original and modified pictures respectively as according:

$$C = f_c(I), \quad C' = f_c(\hat{I})$$

In order to assure the authenticity of the label content, it is signed in a trustworthy way, that is, the label is encrypted with a private key (K_{pr}). The label content is produced as:

$$L = EKpr \ (C, C_I)$$

where C_I is optional information, say *Complementary Information*, about the frame and its author, assigned by an author society. Besides image-dependent features, the label can also convey this information. In the authentication system, the corresponding public key Kpu is used to decrypt the label, producing:

$$C, C_I = EKpu(L)$$

Moreover in (Queluz, 2001) M. P. Queluz presents two classical image features for image/video content authentication. The first image feature is concerned with second order image moments. It has a less computational requirement with small memory, which makes it more advantageous computational feature. The second feature relies on image edges and it takes the problem of image/video authentication from a semantic, higher level point of view (Queluz, 2001). In image moments feature, for a two dimensional continuous function *f(x, y)*, the moments of order (p+q) is defined as:

$$m_{pq} = \int_{-\infty}^{+\infty}\int_{-\infty}^{+\infty} x^p y^q \, f(x,y) \, dx \, dy \quad for \ p,q = 0,1,2,$$

For a digital image the above equation would be as follows:

$$m_{pq} = \sum_i \sum_j i^p j^q f(i,j)$$

where $f(i,j)$ represents image color values at pixel site (i, j). Moments are usually normalized dividing it by the image total mass, defined as. He also presents a brief comparison of labeling approach with watermarking for tamper detection, which is independent of applications where they can specifically be implemented. The video authentication techniques using the watermarking approach have wide dimension in the literature.

In Liang, Li, and Niu (2007), Chang-yin Liang, Ang Li and Xia-mu Nin proposed a video authentication system which is robust enough to separate the malicious attack from natural video processing operations with the cloud watermark. The authentication system in Liang, Li, and Niu (2007) first of all splits the video sequence into shots and extracts the feature vector from each shot. Then the extracted feature is used to generate watermark cloud drops with a cloud generator (Liang, Li, & Niu, 2007). Here, for robustness, a con tent based and semi fragile watermark is used for authentication. In this authentication technique, DCT coefficients are evaluated firstly by partially decoding the given video. After watermarking the video is encoded again (Liang, Li, & Niu, 2007). Invariable features of the video are selected for content based watermarking. The watermarks are then embedded back into DCT coefficients of the video. The extracted watermarks are compared with the features derived from the received video, to check the authenticity of the given video.

Figure 10 shows a video authentication system that uses watermark to verify the integrity of the video. In this system, the given video is first segmented into objects. According to spatial content of the video, feature extractor extracts the feature of the video.

After feature extraction, watermark generator generates the watermark according to features and embeds the watermark into video. At the receiving site, video encoder extracts the watermark from the video. If this watermark matches the original watermark, the given video is claimed as authentic. However attacks on watermarks may not necessarily remove the watermark (Johnson, 1999), but can disable its readability. Image/video processing operations and transforms are commonly employed to create and apply watermarks on the multimedia data. These techniques can also be used to disable or overwrite watermarks. Multiple watermarks can be placed in an image and one cannot determine which one is valid (Craver, Memon, Yeo, & Yeung, 1998).

Figure 10. A watermarking-based authentication system

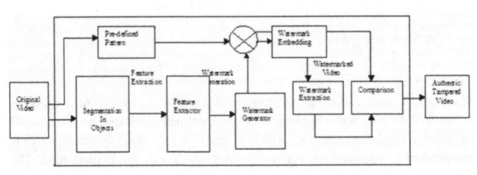

In Mobasseri and Evans (2001), the proposed algorithm explains the frame-pair concept where one video frame would watermark another frame downstream based on a specific sequencing and a key. Basically in this approach three points are there: First the watermark is derived from the video itself, therefore cannot be pirated. Second, if video frames are taken out, it is possible to identify their locations by simply monitoring the breaks in authentication key sequence. And third, video frames that are removed could actually be recovered because frame pairs contain copies of other frames disguised as watermarks. In this approach unless both frames are removed, frame restoration is possible. Watermarking can also be used for the authentication of compressed video (Cross & Mobasseri, 2002). Here the watermarking of compressed video (Cross & Mobasseri, 2002). is done by identifying label carrying VLCs in MPEG-2 bit stream. In this approach, every bit in the watermark payload is compared with the LSB of the current label carrying VLC. If they are the same, the VLC remains unchanged, if they are not, the LSB is replaced by the watermark bit. The embedded watermark may be used for the authentication of video and protection against tampering.

For the authentication of MPEG video, authentication data can be embedded at the Group Of Pictures (GOP) level (Peng & Hong, 2001). Since it is almost infeasible to embed information in all pictures of a video clip or embed all the information for each picture in a video clip, Dynamic Embedding for each picture in a digital video can be adopted (Peng & Hong, 2001). In this approach, current GOP's authentication data (bits) are embedded into next GOP. Basically this approach has three advantageous features. First, by making each watermarked GOP dependent upon other GOP, the problem of watermark counterfeiting becomes computationally impossible and thus reduces the chances of success for the attackers. Second, for MPEG video, if watermark is added in I picture in a GOP, it results in drift errors for the following P or B pictures in the same GOP. If the video quality requirement is in demand, the drift errors should be corrected, the correction could cause the changes of the authentication bits and thus need to re-add the watermark in I picture. This will cause dead loop. Therefore, it would be advantageous to embed the authentication data at the GOP level. Third this operation is causal and saves much memory to store a GOP's data.

For the investigation of the authenticity of uncompressed video signal, the quality of digitization process is considered significantly (Geradts & Bijhold, 1999). The way the A/D conversion is done is important for the result. For this purpose the histogram of gray values can be checked. Previously Lin et al (1999) and Peng et al (2002) have worked on compressed domain schemes that are robust against transcoding and editing operations. For computing the signature, Lin (1999) used the difference in DCT coefficients of frame pairs. Since the value of DCT coefficients can be modified keeping their relationship preserved, it is vulnerable to counterfeiting attacks. Peng (2002) used DC-DCT coefficients as features to build watermark.

An object based watermarking scheme for video authentication is proposed by Dajun et al (2003) They use background features to embed the watermark into foreground objects to establish a relation between background and the foreground of a video. Here the raw video is segmented into foreground objects and background video the watermark is generated by using the features extracted from both the foreground and background. The watermark is then embedded into foreground objects, so that a secure link between foreground objects and the background is created. At the receiving end, integrity between the foreground objects and the background can be verified by comparing two sets of codes: one is the watermark extracted from the objects and the other is regenerated from both the received object and the background. If these two sets of codes are the same, then the video is claimed as authentic.

A more robust authentication scheme for scalable video streaming by employing Error Correction Coding (ECC) in different ways (Sun, He, Zhang and Tian, 2003) has also been produced. This scheme achieves an end - to-end authentication independent of specific streaming infrastructure. Actually this scheme is an extension from Sun, Chang and Maeno (2002) where a semi fragile authentication framework, for images in terms of ECC and public key infrastructure, is used.

In another work, a semi fragile object based authentication solution is produced for MPEG 4 video (He, Sun, & Tian, 2003). To protect the integrity of the video objects /sequences, a content based watermark is embedded into each frame in the Discrete Fourier Transform domain before the MPEG 4 encoding. A set of Angular Radial Transformation (ART) coefficients are selected as the robust features of the video objects. Error Correction Coding (ECC) is used for watermark generation and embedding. The main difference between the frame based video application and the object based video application lies in the utilization of the shape information.

In a self embedding authentication system (Martinian, Wornell, and Chen, 2005), a robust and important feature of the video is extracted and embedded in to the video at the sending site; the detector retrieves this original feature from the watermark and compares it with the feature extracted from the received video to determine the authenticity of the video. If the difference exceeds a threshold, the received video will be claimed as un-authentic video.

3.1.3. Intelligent Techniques

Intelligent techniques for video authentication use database of video sequences. The database comprises authentic video clips as well as tampered video clips. As in Upadhyay, Singh, Vatsa, and Singh (2007), the authors proposed an intelligent technique for video authentication which uses inherent video information for authentication, thus making it useful for real world applications. The proposed algorithm in Upadhyay, Singh, Vatsa, and Singh (2007) is validated using a database of 795 tampered and non tampered videos and the results of algorithm show a classification accuracy of 99.92%. The main advantage of intelligent techniques is that they do not require the computation and storage of secret key or embedding of watermark. The algorithm in Upadhyay, Singh, Vatsa, and Singh (2007) computes the local relative correlation information and classifies the video as tampered or non-tampered. Performance of this algorithm is not affected by acceptable video processing operations such as compression and scaling. Here the algorithm uses Support Vector Machine (SVM) for the classification of the tampered and authentic videos. SVM (VN, 1995) is a powerful methodology for solving problems in non-linear classification, function estimation and density estimation (Singh, Vatsa, & Noore, 2006). In fact, SVM is a non linear classifier that performs classification tasks by constructing hyper planes in a multi dimensional space and separates the data points in different classes. This algorithm (Upadhyay, Singh, Vatsa, and Singh, 2007) is performed in two stages: (1) SVM training and (2) Tamper detection and classification, using SVM. In SVM training, the algorithm trains the SVM by using a manually labeled training video database, if the video in the training data is tampered, then it is assigned the label -1 otherwise the label is +1 (for the authentic video). From the training videos, relative correlation information between two adjacent frames of the video is computed, with the help of corner detection algorithm (Kovesi, 1999). Then relative correlation information *RC* is computed for all adjacent frames of the video with the help of:

$$RC = \frac{1}{m}\sum_{i=1}^{m}L_i$$

where Li is local correlation between two frames for i=1,2,...m. and m is the number of corresponding corner points in the two frames. The local correlation information RC is computed for each video and the *RC* with the label information of all the training video data are provided as input to the SVM. With this information of all the video in video database the SVM (VN, 1995) is trained to classify the tampered and non tampered video data. Output of SVM training is a trained hyper plane with classified tampered and non tampered video data. In Singh, Vatsa, Singh, and Upadhyay (2008), authors integrate the learning based support vector machine classification (for tampered and non-tampered video) with singular value decomposition watermarking. This algorithm is independent of the choice of watermark and does not require any key to store. This intelligent authentication technique embeds the inherent video information in frames using SVD watermarking and uses it for classification by projecting them into a non-linear SVM hyper plane. This technique can detect multiple tampering attacks.

3.1.4. Other Authentication Techniques

Apart from digital signature, watermarking and intelligent techniques, various other techniques are there for authentication purpose of digital video in the literature. In Yan and Kankanhalli (2003), an authentication scheme for digital video is introduced which is based on motion trajectory and cryptographic secret sharing (Yan and Kankanhalli, 2003). In this scheme, the given video is firstly segmented into shots then all the frames of the video shots are mapped to a trajectory in the feature space by which the key frames of the video shot are computed. Once the key frames are evaluated, a secret frame is computed from the key frames information of the video shot. These secret frames are used to construct a hierarchical structure and after that final master key is obtained. This master key is used to identify the authenticity of the video. Any modification in a shot or in the important content of a shot will be reflected as changes in the computed master key. Here trajectory is constructed, using the histogram energy of the frames of the video shot. For a particular video shot, in Figure 11, vertical axis indicates the histogram energy of each frame of the shot and the horizontal axis marks the frame number in the shot. A polyline belonging to the video shot is drawn which is a motion trajectory. This figure also shows the process of key frames extraction from the video shot. The starting frame S and the last frame E of the trajectory are connected to each other. Then a distance d between each frame point and this line is computed by using:

$$d = \frac{|Ax + By + C|}{\sqrt{A^2 + B^2}}$$

where d is the distance from a point (x,y) to the straight line $Ax + By + C = 0$.

After that, the point at the maximum distance from the line is chosen and the corresponding frame is declared as one of the key frames in this shot. Once the key frames are computed these are utilized to compute the secret frame by extrapolation as shown in Figure 12.

Here the x coordinate indicates the locations of the key frames for the purpose of computing the polynomial for secret sharing and the y coordinate indicates the value of the pixels of each frame (Yan and Kankanhalli, 2003). Now an interpolating polynomial $f(x)$ is computed by using key frames as follows.

Figure 11. Frames with their histogram energy for a video shot

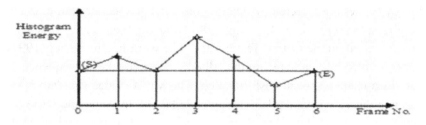

Figure 12. Secret frame extrapolation

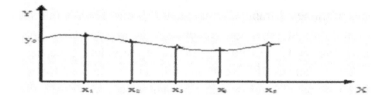

$$f(x) = \sum_{j=1}^{n+1} \prod_{i=1}^{n+1} \frac{x - x_i}{x_j - x_i} I_j$$

This is Lagrange interpolation formulation where the x_i position refers to each key frame and I_i is the pixel value of the key frames. By using this equation and extrapolation a frame at $x = 0$ is computed, which is regarded as the secret key. Considering the set of secret keys as another set of shares, the master key frame is computed for that particular video. With this scheme any video can be authenticated by comparing its computed master key with the original master key. This comparison can be performed by using the general cosine correlation measure given by:

$$sim = \frac{I_O \cdot I_N}{|I_O \cdot I_N|}$$

where I_O and I_N are the original master key and the new master key considered as vectors. The similarity value would be in the range [0, 1] and if *sim* = 1, the two master keys would be the same, however if sim = 0, the two master keys would be different. Here the authors also claim that if the similarity value is high then the video has undergone benign transformations. But if the similarity value is low, then the video must have undergone some significant tampering. In Latechi, Wildt, and Hu, the key frames are selected by deleting the most predictable frame. In the approach of reference (Zhao, Qi, Li, Yang, 2000), the key frames are extracted from a video shot based on the nearest feature line. The work in Quisquater (1997) authenticates a video by guaranteeing the edited video to be the subsequence of the original video using a special hash function. The MPEG video standard is one of the most popular video standards in today's digital era. In Wang and Farid (2007) Weihong Wang and Hany Farid have been worked on MPEG video standard(MPEG-1 and MPEG-2) in this paper they specifically show how a doubly compressed MPEG video sequence introduces specific static and temporal statistical perturbations whose presence can be used as evidence of tampering. In a MPEG video sequence, there are three types of frames: *I*-frame, *P*-frame and *B*-frame. Each with different level of compression occurs in a periodic sequence in the MPEG video. Amidst all the frames *I*-frames are the highest quality frames of the video sequence, which are usually encoded by standard JPEG compression scheme. In the *I*-frame, compression is achieved at spatial level by reducing spatial redundancies within a single frame (Wang & Farid, 2007). Temporal redundancies are concerned with *P*-frames arcos the frames of video sequence. For achieving double MPEG compression, *I*-frames of the MPEG video sequence are compressed twice. For this purpose when the frames are double quantized with different step size, there is a significant difference in their histogram. When the step size decreases in image quantization, some bins in the histogram are empty while in greater step size some bins of the histogram contain more samples than their neighboring bins (Wang & Farid, 2007). In both cases of double quantization, periodicity of the artifacts is introduced in to histograms. This artifact would be used as evidence of double compression and hence tampering. In temporal analysis, addition or deletion of frames from a video sequence and re-encoding the resulting sequence, results in a large motion error between consecutive *P*-frames of the video, since they originated from different GOPs. Moreover, this increased motion error would be periodic, occurring throughout each of the group of pictures following the frame deletion or addition. Periodic spikes in the motion error indicate tampering (Wang & Farid, 2007).

In Farid (2006), Hany Farid describes three techniques to expose digital forgeries in which the approach is to first understand how a specific form of tampering disturbs certain statistical properties of an image and then to develop a mathematical algorithm to detect this perturbation. These are Cloning, Lighting and Retouching. In Cloning, a digital image is first partitioned into small blocks of the regions. The blocks are then reordered so that they are placed a distance to each other that is proportional to the differences in their pixel colors (Farid, 2006). Since it is statistically unlikely to find identical and spatially coherent regions in an image, therefore their presence can be used as evidence of tampering. In lighting approach, the direction of an illuminating light source for each object or person in an image is automatically evaluated by some mathematical techniques. The retouching technique exploits the technology by which a digital camera sensor records an image, for detecting a specific form of tampering.

A robust video authentication system should tolerate the incidental distortion, which may be introduced by normal video processing such as compression, resolution conversion, and geometric transformation, while being capable of detecting the intentional distortion, which may be introduced by malicious attack. There has also been some work for scene change detection of video sequences in the literature.

3.2. Limitations of Existing Video Authentication Techniques

There are different challenges with the existing watermark and digital signature based video authentication approaches. However there is no issue related with the size of authentication code in digital signature based video authentication techniques, but if the location where digital signature is stored is compromised then it is easy to deceive the authentication system. On the other hand, fragile watermarking algorithms perform better than algorithm based on conventional cryptography (Hauzia & Noumeir, 2007). Fragile and semi fragile algorithms show good results for detecting and locating any malicious manipulations but often they are too fragile to resist incidental manipulations. Moreover embedding the watermark may change the content of video, which is not permissible in court of law (Upadhyay, Singh, Vatsa, and Singh, 2007). In other techniques, most of the authentication techniques are established for specific attacks. Moreover, existing algorithms are also affected by compression and scaling operations.

4. PROPOSED METHODOLOGY

Keeping in mind all those limitations, we are going to propose an intelligent video authentication technique, which does not require computation and storage of any key or embedding of any secret information in the video data. Our proposed video authentication algorithm computes the statistical local features information in digital video frames and establishes a relationship among the frames. A Support Vector Machine (SVM) (VN, 1995) based learning algorithm is then used to classify the video as tampered or non-tampered. The proposed algorithm uses inherent video information for authentication, thus making it useful for real world applications.

4.1. Support Vector Machine

Support Vector Machine, pioneered by Vapnik (VN, 1995), is a powerful methodology for solving problems in nonlinear classification, function estimation and density estimation (Singh, Vatsa, & Noore, 2006). The main idea of a support vector machine is to construct a hyper plane as the decision surface in such a way that the margin of separation between two classes of examples is maximized. It performs the classification task by constructing hyper planes in a multidimensional space and separates the data points into different classes. SVM uses an iterative training algorithm to maximize the margin between two classes (Upadhyay, Singh, Vatsa, and Singh, 2007; Singh, Vatsa, & Noore, 2006). The mathematical formulation of SVM is as follows:

Let be the training sample of N data vectors, where x_i is the input pattern for the example and d_i is the corresponding desired response. It is assumed that the pattern (class) represented by the subset $d_i = +1$ and the pattern represented by the subset $d_i = -1$, are linearly separable. The equation of generalized decision function can be written as:

$$f\left(x\right) = \sum_{i=1}^{N} w_i \varphi_i\left(x\right) + b = W \bar{\varphi}\left(x\right) + b$$

where $\varphi_i\left(x\right)$ is a nonlinear function representing hidden nodes and

$$\bar{\varphi}\left(x\right) = \left[\varphi_1\left(x\right), \ \varphi_2\left(x\right), \ldots \varphi_N(x)\right]^T$$

and b is a bias. To obtain a non-linear decision boundary which enhances the discrimination power, the above equation can be rewritten as:

Here $K\left(x, x_i\right)$ is the nonlinear kernel that enhances the discrimination power and $\propto_i$ is the Lagrangian multiplier (Upadhyay, Singh, Vatsa, and Singh, 2007). Basically a nonlinear SVM uses a kernel function $K\left(x, x_i\right)$ to map the input space to the feature space so that the mapped data becomes linearly separable. One example of such kernel is the RBF kernel

$$K\left(x, x_i\right) = exp\left(-\gamma x - x_i^{\ 2}\right), \quad \gamma > 0$$

where x and x_i represent the input vectors and γ is the RBF parameter (Upadhyay, Singh, Vatsa, and Singh, 2007). Additional details of SVM can be found in (VN, 1995).

4.2. Proposed Video Authentication Algorithm

As mentioned above the common tampering attacks on a video data are spatial and temporal tampering attacks, which include object addition, object removal, object modification, frame removal, frame addition, and frame shuffling. Our proposed algorithm gives excellent results for temporal tampering attacks. However, the proposed algorithm can handle all types of malicious attacks. Since we are using SVM based learning and classification technique, it can also differentiate between attack and acceptable operations.

The concept of the proposed algorithm is shown in Figure 13. The proposed video authentication algorithm computes the statistical local features information between two consecutive video frames.

Here we take the absolute difference of every two consecutive video frames. The average object area and entropy of difference frames are used as statistical local features information. They are worked here as the basis for SVM learning. This information is computed locally using statistical tools and then classification is performed using support vector machine (VN, 1995). Based on the functionality, the proposed algorithm is divided into two stages: (1) SVM Learning and (2) tamper detection and classification using SVM.

4.3. SVM Learning

SVM learning is the first step of the proposed algorithm, so that it can classify the tampered and non-tampered video data. For this purpose, a database of 20 tampered and non-tampered video clips is used. In SVM learning a kernel is trained. Training is performed using a manually labeled training video database. If the video in

Figure 13. Block diagram of the proposed video authentication algorithm

27

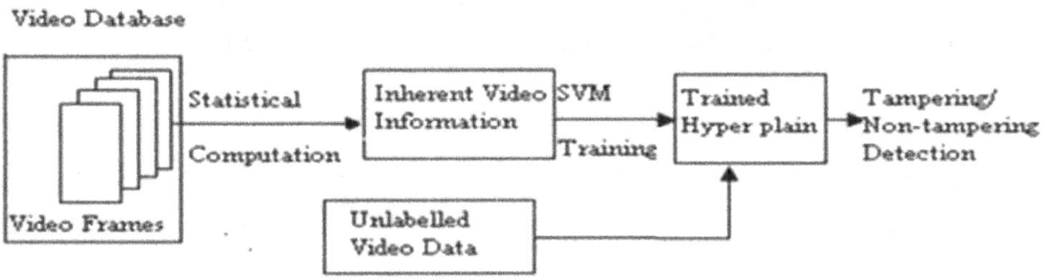

the training data is tampered, then it is assigned the label 0 otherwise (if it is not tampered) the label is 1. From the training videos, statistical local information (Average object area and Entropy) are extracted. This labeled information is then used as input to the SVM which performs learning and generates a non-linear hyper plane that can classify the video as tampered and non-tampered. All these steps involved in the training of the kernel are explained in the Learning Algorithm.

4.3.1. Learning Algorithm

1. **Input:** Labeled training video frames.
2. **Output:** Trained SVM with a non-linear hyper plane to classify tampered and non-tampered video data.
3. **Algorithm:**
   a. Individual frames are obtained from the different tampered and non tampered video data.
   b. The difference frames of all the video data are obtained by taking absolute difference between every two consecutive frames. In absolute difference, we subtract each pixel value in second frame from the corresponding pixel value in the first frame.
   c. All these difference frames are converted into binary frames.
   d. The total number of objects in first binary difference frame and their area are calculated. Then the average object area and the entropy of the first binary difference frame are computed statistically.

If the area of an object in a binary frame is a_i then the average object area of the binary frame A would be

$$A = \frac{1}{N}\sum_{i=1}^{N} a_i$$

where N is the total number of objects

If the average object area and entropy of a binary frame are A_i and E_i then the statistical local information of all the binary difference frames of different tampered and non tampered video data of the video database would be defined as

$$SL = \sum_{i=1}^{m} [A_i, E_i]$$

This statistical local information is a column vector of size where m is the total number of binary difference frames extracted from all the tampered and non tampered video of the video database.

Steps 1-6 are performed on all the labelled training video frames and the statistical local information SL is computed for each binary difference frames of different videos.

    e.   Statistical local information and labels of all the training video frames are given as input to the Support Vector Machine.

    f.   In the learning process the SVM kernel [10] is trained to classify the tampered and non tampered video data. Output of this training is a trained hyper plain with classified tampered and non tampered video data.

4.4. Tamper Detection and Classification

We now explain the proposed tamper detection and classification algorithm. Input to this classification algorithm is a video data of which authenticity needs to be established. As performed in SVM learning algorithm, statistical local information of all the binary frames of the given video is computed and the trained SVM is used to classify the video. The proposed algorithm uses the dynamically adoptive threshold value to decide whether the given video frame is tampered or not. It automatically selects a threshold value with the help of learning database, for declaring any binary difference frame as a tampered frame. If the SVM classifies the input video as tampered then the location of tampering is computed. The tamper detection and classification algorithm is described below.

4.4.1. Tamper Detection and Classification

1. **Input:** Unlabelled video frames.
2. **Output:** Classification result as tampered and non-tampered video data.
3. **Algorithm:** Using steps 1-7 of the SVM learning algorithm, the statistical local information SL for the input video is computed.
    a.   This statistical local information of the input video data is projected into the SVM hyper plane to classify the video as tampered or non-tampered. If the output of SVM is one for all of the difference frames of the input video then the given video is authentic otherwise it is tampered.
    b.   If any of the frame of given video is classified as tampered then we determine the particular frames of the video that have been tampered.
    c.   Plot the statistical local information SL (average object area and entropy) of difference frames of all the adjacent frames of the video.

    d.   Local values showing the maximum deviation in the plot are the values corresponding to the tampered frames.

    e.   Plot the trained SVM classifier which shows the support vectors for the training video data

5. EXPERIMENTAL RESULTS AND DISCUSSION

The proposed algorithm shows very good results for both kinds of attacks, spatial and temporal tampering attacks. We have shown the results for all kinds of tampering attacks of temporal tampering and also for spatial tampering.

5.1. Results for Temporal Tampering Attacks

Figure 14a shows the plot of average object area values as statistical local information for the first 105 frames of a tampered video in frame addition attack. The plot shows that the average object area values of the binary difference frames regarding frames 6th, 11th, 14th, and 17th are significantly higher compared to the average object area values of other binary difference frames. Since frames 6th, 11th, 14th, and 17th are common video frames and lead to higher average object area values, these are detected as tampered frames. In the similar way Figure 14b shows the plot of entropy values as statistical local information for the first 105 frames of the tampered video sequence. Here again the entropy values of binary difference frames regarding frames 6th, 11th, 14th, and 17th are significantly higher, compared to entropy values of other binary difference frames. Henceforth from this plot also frames 6th, 11th, 14th, and 17th are detected as tampered video frames.

In the similar manner, Figure 15a shows the plot of average object area values as statistical local information, for the first 105 frames of a tampered video in frame removal attack. The plot shows that the average object area values of all the binary difference frames are in zigzag form. It means that the average object area value of every second binary difference frame of the video is significantly higher as compared to the average object area value of previous binary difference frames. Therefore, every second frame of the given video is a tampered frame. We dropped here 20 frames for frame removal attack, as in place of every frame, frame is inserted. Figure 15b shows the plot of entropy as statistical local information for the same 105 frames of the tampered video in frame removal attack. This plot also express that every second frame of the given video (in first 150 frames) is tampered. Frame shuffling is also a kind of temporal tampering in which the frame ordering is altered. The proposed algorithm gives good results for frame shuffling attack.

Figure 14. (a) Plot of average object area as statistical local information of a tampered video sequence in which 6th, 11th, 14th, and 17th frames is tampered subjected to spatial tampering attack; (b) plot of entropy as statistical local information of a tampered video sequence in which 6th, 11th, 14th, frame is tampered subjected to spatial tampering attack

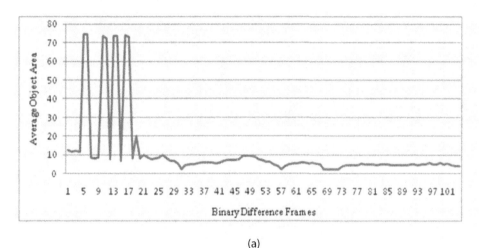

(a)

(b)

Thus with the help of these plots we can say that our proposed algorithm gives very good results for all kinds of temporal tampering attacks.

5.2. Results for Spatial Tampering Attacks

For spatial tampering, we have modified the spatial content of the frames of the video with the help of professional software and created the tampered videos for our

Figure 15. (a) Plot of average object area as statistical local information of a tampered video sequence in which every second frame is tampered subjected to frame removal attack; (b) plot of entropy as statistical local information of the same 105 frames of the tampered video sequence in which every second frame is tampered subjected to frame removal attack

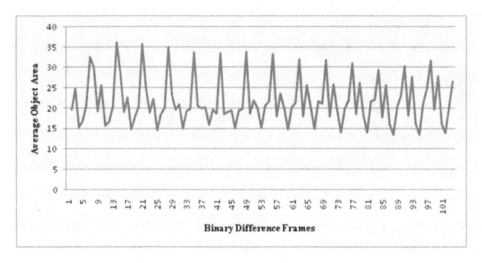

(a)

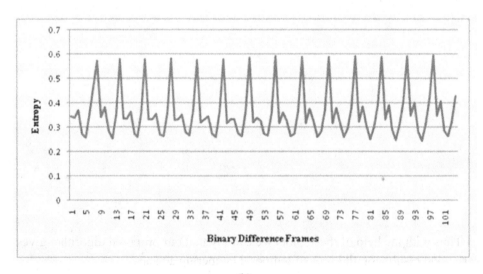

(b)

video database. These tampered videos include almost all kinds of spatial tampering attack. Figure 16a shows the plot of average object area values as statistical local information for the 66 frames of a tampered video in spatial tampering attack. In this figure the average object area values of 2nd, 10th, 21st, and 32nd binary difference

Figure 16. (a) Plot of average object area as statistical local information of a tampered video sequence 2nd, 10th, 21st, and 32nd frame is tampered subjected to spatial tampering attack; (b) plot of entropy as statistical local information of a tampered video sequence 1st, 10th, 21st, and 32nd frame is tampered subjected to spatial tampering attack

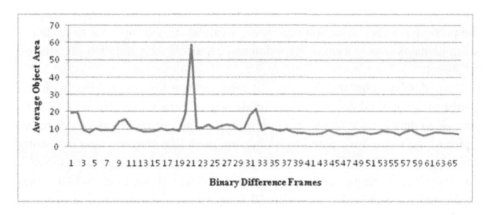

(a)

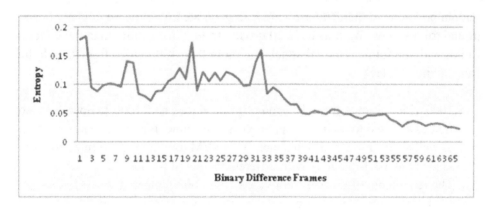

(b)

frames are comparatively higher than the average object area values of other binary difference frames. Therefore, the frames regarding 2nd, 10th, 21st, and 32nd binary difference frames are declared here as tampered frames.

In the similar way, Figure 16b shows the plot for entropy as statistical local information for the same 66 frames of the spatially tampered video. Here again the 2nd, 10th, 21st, and 32nd binary difference frames shows the higher entropy values. Therefore the frames regarding 2nd, 10th, 21st, and 32nd binary difference frames are again declared as tampered frames.

Thus with the help of these graphs one can easily analyze that the proposed intelligent algorithm for video authentication gives very efficient and accurate results for both kinds of tampering attacks; spatial and temporal.

5.3. Validation of Proposed Algorithm

The proposed tamper detection algorithm is validated by using a video database, which contains twenty videos. Experimental protocols for validation process are as follows:

Video database contains 20 originally recorded non-tampered videos with 350 frames each captured at 23 fps. The frame size of each video clip is 720×576. This video data is used as the ground truth. For each of the 20 videos different copies of the video are created by subjecting them to different video tampering attacks. In the database, for frame removal attack, 10 copies are created for each video in which 20 frames have been dropped at different positions and 10 copies are created for each video in which 50 frames have been dropped at different position. For the frame addition attack, an additional video other than the 20 videos in the database is chosen. Frames of this additional video are inserted at random positions in the database videos to generate 20 tampered copies of each ground truth videos. We thus have 20 ground truth videos, more than 4000 video frames with the frame removal attack and more than 4000 video frames with the frame addition attack.

1. 1000 video frames from 10 ground truth videos and 1000 tampered video frames are used to train the support vector machine, for frame removal attack as well as for frame addition attack. This SVM training is performed for both kinds of attack separately with different tampered frames.
2. The remaining 10 ground truth videos and 1000 tampered video frames are used as the probe database to determine the performance of the proposed algorithm.

The performance of the proposed video authentication algorithm is evaluated with this experimental protocol.

All of the computations are performed using the hardware configuration of Pentium ® Dual-Core CPU 2.20 GHz computer with 2 GB RAM under MATLAB programming environment. The RBF parameter used in the proposed algorithm is computed empirically using the training video frames. The best suited value of RBF parameter (γ) among 1 to 5 is 3. The value of $\gamma = 3$, gives the maximum classification accuracy. We therefore used $\gamma = 3$ for classification on the probe data.

The results given in Table 1 summarize the performance of the proposed video authentication algorithm. For authentic video frames and video frames subjected to the frame addition attack of temporal tampering, our algorithm gives the result with maximum accuracy and yields 100% correct classification. For frame removal attack, a classification accuracy of 90% is obtained. For frame removal attack our algorithm misclassified twenty tampered frames out of 200 tampered frames, because the object movements in the binary difference frames were very small. For spatial tampering attacks, the proposed algorithm gives the result with 85% accuracy and misclassifies thirty tampered frames out of 200 tampered frames. Thus the overall classification accuracy of the proposed algorithm is 95%.

According to steps 3-5 of our tamper detection algorithm, the SL values, obtained from video frames, are analyzed. This analysis gives the specific frames that have been altered. These results show the efficacy of our proposed video authentication algorithm for all kinds of tampering attack of temporal tampering and spatial tampering. This algorithm also successfully determined the modified frames among the non-tampered video frames.

We also compared the performance of the proposed video authentication algorithm with the motion trajectory based video authentication algorithm (Yan and Kankanhalli,, 2003), proposed by Wei-Qi Yan et al. Table 2 depicts a theoretical comparison of both algorithms. Motion trajectory based algorithm (Yan and Kankanhalli, 2003) is fast and simple but unable to detect spatial tampering attacks (object addition, removal, and modification in a frame). It also gives poor results in frame removal attacks of temporal tampering, when only three or four frames are dropped (in case of twenty-frame removal). It also gives unsatisfactory results in frame removal attack of temporal tampering, when object movements within consecutive frames of the video, are very less.

Table 1. Classification results of the proposed video authentication algorithm for tampered and non tampered video frames

Tampering Attacks	Total Number of Video Frames	Number of Correctly Classified Frames	Classification Accuracy (%)
Non-tampered	300	300	100
Frame Addition	300	300	100
Frame Removal	200	180	90
Spatial Tampering	200	170	85
Total	1000	950	95

Table 2. Theoretical comparison of the proposed video authentication algorithm with the motion trajectory based video authentication algorithm (Yan & Kankanhalli, 2003)

Category	Motion Trajectory based Video Authentication (Yan and Kankanhalli, 2003)	Proposed Video Authentication Algorithm
Basic Concept	Master Key computation based on motion trajectory	Statistical Local Information is computed from video frames
Classification	Using empirical threshold values and cosine correlation measure	Using Non-linear Support Vector Machine for classification
Advantage	Simple algorithm, It handles frame addition and frame removal attack	In addition of frame addition and frame removal attack, it handles frame alteration attack (Spatial Tampering)
Disadvantage	It cannot handle frame alteration and other attacks	Computationally expensive and a little bit slow algorithm due to the use of SVM and a video database

On the other hand, our proposed algorithm uses an intelligent technique, namely SVM classification that is able to detect both kinds of attack, spatial as well as temporal. Thus our proposed algorithm covers a wide range of tampering attacks with good classification accuracy and a minor increase in computational time.

6. CHALLENGING SCENARIOS FOR VIDEO AUTHENTICATION

In some of the surveillance systems storage and transmission costs are the important issues. In order to reduce the storage and transmission cost only those video clips which contain objects of interest are required to be sent and stored. Moreover, in most of the surveillance applications, background object changes very slowly in comparison to foreground objects. A possible efficient solution in these scenarios is that only the objects of interest (mostly foreground objects) are sent out frame by frame in real time while the background object is sent once in a long time interval. In such surveillance applications, it becomes very critical to protect the authenticity of the video: the authenticity against malicious alterations and the authenticity for the identity of the transmission source (i.e. identifying the video source). In event based surveillance systems, the video sequences are captured when there is any kind of change in the scene (existence of an event) which would be captured by the camera. If there is uniformity in the scene in such a way that there is not any change in the scene then the surveillance camera does not capture any video sequence. This kind of surveillance system is used in military system for border security purpose. Authenticity for this kind of video sequences is a challenging issue because there is no proper time sequence in video sequences, which are captured by surveillance camera. These are the scenarios, which pose considerable challenges to the researchers for authentication.

7. CONCLUSION AND FUTURE DIRECTION

Video authentication is a very challenging problem and of high importance in several applications such as in forensic investigations of digital video for law enforcement agencies, video surveillance and presenting video evidence in court of law and in critical scenarios where the integrity of any individual is challenged by video information. Most of the existing video authentication algorithms use watermarking or digital signature based algorithms. Digital signature based algorithm can be deceived, if the location where digital signature is stored is compromised and watermarking based algorithms are not acceptable in court of law because they may alter the content of video during watermark embedding and extraction. To address these issues we have proposed an efficient intelligent video authentication algorithm, which can detect multiple video tampering attacks. Our proposed algorithm computes the statistical local information of all of the binary difference frames of the given video and projects them into a non-linear SVM hyper plane to determine if the video is tampered or not. Our algorithm dynamically adopts the threshold values for the statistical local information of tampered video frames. It automatically opts the best suited threshold value for declaring the binary difference frames as tampered frames. The algorithm is validated on an extensive video database containing 1000 tampered and 1000 non-tampered video frames. The results show that the proposed algorithm yields a classification accuracy of 95%. In future we would like to expand our video database, which would cover some more critical conditions for video recording, like the videos captured in different light conditions such as in day light and night vision systems, and in a situation where the camera and objects are moving very fast, videos in critical weather conditions and the videos captured in hazardous condition, and apply the intelligent authentication algorithms for obtaining the results regarding all kinds of tampering attacks.

REFERENCES

Celik, M. V. (2002). Video authentication with self recovery. In *Proceedings of Security and Watermarking of Multimedia Contents 4* (*Vol. 4314*, pp. 531–541). IEEE. doi:10.1117/12.465311

Craver, S., Memon, N., Yeo, B., & Yeung, N. M. (1998). Resolving rightful ownerships with invisible watermarking techniques: Limitations, attacks, and implications. *IEEE Journal on Selected Areas in Communications, 16*(4), 573–586. doi:10.1109/49.668979

Cross, D., & Mobasseri, B. G. (2002). Water marking for self authentication of compressed video. In *Proceedings of the IEEE International Conference on Image Processing*. Rochester: IEEE Press.

Diffie, W., & Hellman, M. E. (1976). New directions in cryptography. *IEEE Transactions on Information Theory, 22*(6), 644–654. doi:10.1109/TIT.1976.1055638

Ditmann, J., Steinmetz, A., & Steinmetz, R. (1999). Content based digital signature for motion pictures authentication and content fragile watermarking. In *Proceedings of the IEEE International Conference on Multimedia Computing and Systems*, (vol. 2, pp. 209-213). IEEE Press.

Dittman, J., Mukharjee, A., & Steinbach, M. (2000). Media independent watermarking classification and the need for combining digital video and audio watermarking for media authentication. In *Proceedings of the International Conference on Information Technology: Coding and Computing*. IEEE Press.

Farid, H. (2006). Digital doctoring: How to tell the real from fake. *Significance, 3*(4), 162–166. doi:10.1111/j.1740-9713.2006.00197.x

Gennaro, R., & Rohatgi, P. (1997). How to sign digital stream. [Crypto.]. *Proceedings of Crypto, 1997*, 180–197.

Geradts, Z. J., & Bijhold, J. (1999). Forensic video investigation with real time digitized uncompressed video image sequences. In *Proceedings of the Investigation and Forensic Science Technologies*. IEEE.

Guerrini, F., Leonardi, R., & Migliorati, P. (2004). A new video authentication template based on bubble random sampling. In *Proceedings of the European Signal Processing Conference 2004*. IEEE.

Hauzia, A., & Noumeir, R. (2007). Methods for image authentication: A survey. *Proceedings of the Multimedia Tools and Applications, 39*, 1–46. doi:10.1007/s11042-007-0154-3

He, D., Sun, O., & Tian, Q. (2003). A semi fragile object based video authentication system. In *Proceedings of IEEE ISCAS 2003*. Bangkok, Thailand: IEEE Press.

Johns Hopkins. (2012). *Johns Hopkins APL creates system to detect digital video tampering*. Retrieved from http://www.jhu.edu/

Johnson, N. F. (1999). *An introduction to watermark recovery from images*. Fairfax, VA: George Mason University.

Kovesi, P. D. (1999). Image features from phase congruency. *Videre: Journal of Computer Vision Research, 1*(3).

Liang, C.-Y., Li, A., & Niu, X.-M. (2007). Video authentication and tamper detection based on cloud model. In *Proceedings of the Third International Conference on International Information Hiding and Multimedia Signal Processing (IIH-MSP 2007)*, (pp. 225-228). IIH-MSP.

Lin, C.-Y., & Chang, S.-F. (1999). Issues and solutions for authenticating MPEG video. In *Proceedings of the SPIE Electronic Imaging 1999*. San Jose, CA: SPIE.

Lu, C.-S., & Liao, H. Y. M. (2003). Structural digital signature for image authentication: An incidental distortion resistant scheme. *IEEE Transactions on Multimedia, 5*(2), 161–173. doi:10.1109/TMM.2003.811621

Martinian, E., Wornell, G. W., & Chen, B. (2005). Authentication with distortion criteria. *IEEE Transactions on Information Theory, 51*(7). doi:10.1109/TIT.2005.850123

Mobasseri, B. G., & Evans, A. E. (2001). Content dependent video authentication by self water marking in color space. In *Proceedings of Security and Watermarking of Multimedia Contents 3 (Vol. 4314*, pp. 35–46). IEEE. doi:10.1117/12.435437

Park, J. M., Chong, E. K. P., & Siegel, H. J. (2002). Efficient multicast packet authentication using signature amortization. In *Proceedings of the IEEE Symposium on Security and Privacy*, (pp. 227-240). IEEE Press.

Peng, H. (2002). A semi fragile water marking system for MPEG video authentication. In *Proceedings of ICASSP 2002*. Orlando, FL: ICASSP.

Peng, Y., & Hong, H. Y. (2001). Classification of video tampering methods and countermeasures using digital watermarking. []. SPIE.]. *Proceedings of the Society for Photo-Instrumentation Engineers, 4518*, 239–246.

Podilchuk, C. I., Jayant, N. S., & Farrardin, N. (1995). Three dimensional sub band coding of video. *IEEE Transactions on Image Processing, 4*(2), 125–139. doi:10.1109/83.342187

Queluz, M. P. (1998). Toward robust, content based techniques for image authentication. In *Proceedings of the IEEE Second Workshop on Multimedia Signal Processing*, (pp. 297-302). IEEE Press.

Queluz, M. P. (2001). Authentication of digital images and video: Generic models and a new contribution, signal processing. *Image Communication, 16*, 461–475.

Quisquater, J. (1997). Authentication of sequences with the SL2 hash function application to video sequences. *Journal of Computer Security, 5*(3), 213–223.

Saikia, N., & Bora, P. K. (2007). Video authentication using temporal wavelet transform. In *Proceedings of the 15th International Conference on Advanced Computing and Communications*, (pp. 648-653). ADCOM.

Singh, R., Vatsa, M., & Noore, A. (2006). Intelligent biometric information fusion using support vector machine. In *Soft Computing in Image Processing: Recent Advances* (pp. 327–350). Berlin, Germany: Springer Verlag.

Singh, R., Vatsa, M., Singh, S. K., & Upadhyay, S. (2008). Integrating SVM classification with SVD watermarking for intelligent video authentication. *Telecommunication Systems Journal, 40*(1-2), 5–15. doi:10.1007/s11235-008-9141-x

Su, P.-C., Chen, C.-C., & Chang, H. M. (2009). Towards effective content authentication for digital videos by employing feature extraction and quantization. *IEEE Transactions on Circuits and Systems for Video Technology, 19*(5), 668–677. doi:10.1109/TCSVT.2009.2017404

Sun, Q., Chang, S.-F., & Maeno, K. (2002). A new semi fragile image authentication framework combining ECC and PKI infrastructure. In *Proceedings of the ISCAS 2002*. Phoenix, AZ: ISCAS.

Sun, Q., He, D., Zhang, Z., & Tian, Q. (2003). A secure and robust approach to scalable video authentication. In *Proceedings of ICME 2003*. ICME.

Upadhyay, S., Singh, M., Vatsa, M., & Singh, R. (2007). Video authentication using relative correlation information and SVM. In Hassanien, A. E., Kacprzyk, J., & Abraham, A. (Eds.), *Computational Intelligence in Multimedia Processing: Recent Advances*. Berlin, Germany: Springer Verlag.

Vapnik, V. N. (1995). *The nature of statistical learning theory*. Berlin, Germany: Springer Verlag.

Wang, W., & Farid, H. (2007). Exposing digital forgeries in video by detecting duplication. In *Proceedings of the 9th Workshop on Multimedia & Security*. Dallas, TX: IEEE.

Wohlmacher, P. (1998). Requirements and mechanism of IT-security including aspects of multimedia security. In *Proceedings of the Multimedia and Security Workshop at ACM Multimedia 1998*. Bristol, UK: ACM Press.

Yan, W.-Y., & Kankanhalli, M. S. (2003). Motion trajectory based video authentication. In *Proceedings of ISCAS*, (vol. 3, pp. 810-813). ISCAS. Zhao, L., Qi, W., Li, S., Yang, S., & Zhang, H. (2000). Key frame extraction and shot retrieval using nearest feature line (NFL). In *Proceedings of ACM Multimedia 2000*. ACM Press.

KEY TERMS AND DEFINITIONS

Digital Signature: A digital signature is a mathematical scheme for demonstrating the authenticity of a digital message or document. A valid digital signature gives a recipient reason to believe that the message was created by a known sender, and that it was not modified in transit.

Fragile Watermarking: In fragile watermarking, authentication data is embedded in the primary multimedia source.

Intelligent Authentication Techniques: Intelligent authentication techniques use learning based techniques for authentication purpose.

Support Vector Machine: Support Vector Machine is a powerful methodology for solving problems in nonlinear classification, function estimation, and density estimation.

Video Authentication: Video authentication is a process which ascertains that the content in a given video is authentic and exactly same as when captured.

Video Database: Video database is a database of videos, which can be used for various purposes such as video authentication.

Video Surveillance: Video surveillance is the use of video cameras to transmit a signal to a specific place, on a limited set of monitors.

Video Tampering: When the content of information, being produced by a given video is maliciously modified, then it is called video tampering.

ENDNOTES

1 The Oxford English Dictionary, 2nd Edition, Oxford University, pp. 795-796, 1989.
2 The Webster's New 20th Century Dictionary.

Chapter 2
Audio and Visual Speech Recognition Recent Trends

Lee Hao Wei
Sunway University, Malaysia

Seng Kah Phooi
Sunway University, Malaysia

Ang Li-Minn
Edith Cowan University, Australia

ABSTRACT

This chapter focuses on a brief introduction on the origins of the audio-visual speech recognition process and relevant techniques often used by researchers in the field. Brief background theory regarding commonly used methods for feature extraction and classification for both audio and visual processing are discussed with highlights pertaining to Mel-Frequency Cepstral Coefficient, and contour/ geometric based lips feature extraction with corresponding tracking methods (Yingjie, Haiyan, Yingjie, & Jinyang, 2011; Liu & Cheung, 2011). Proposed solution concepts will include time derivatives of mel-frequency cepstral coefficients for audio feature extraction, Chroma-colour-based (YCbCr) Face segmentation, Feature Point extraction, Localized Active Contour tracking algorithm, and Hidden Markov Models with Vitebri algorithm incorporated. Information contained in this chapter focuses on being informative for novice speech processing candidates but insufficient mastery knowledge. Additional suggested reading materials should assist in expediting field mastery.

DOI: 10.4018/978-1-4666-3958-4.ch002

INTRODUCTION

Visual speech recognition researches recently gain popularity after audio based speech recognition research started to saturate, leading researchers to infiltrate into other possible solutions to unsolved problems. Audio-Visual speech recognition concept was introduced based on observation regarding human capability of bimodal interpretation (D & Hennecke, 1996). At normal environment, audio interpretation supersedes visual, however visual interpretation priority increases upon attempts to understand spoken word under high noise environment (Ross, Saint-Amour, Leavitt, Javitt, & Foxe, 2006). Perfecting audio-visual speech recognition techniques can assist in developing mundane application to contribute towards society welfare.

Application of audio-visual speech recognition is possible but not limited to the field of education, business and lifestyle. In terms of education, integration of audio and visual aspects allows continuous child behaviour monitor that can be utilized to design educational system meant for optimising infant attention span on pre-school education (Westwood, 2007). Similar system can be applied to child that require special attention such as the deaf/dumb and down syndrome or slow learner children. Implementation of audio-visual speech recognition can help to counter human problems regarding limited emotional patience when educating children with special needs.

Audio-visual speech recognition in field of business relates closely to customer servicing section. A well-designed system allows for efficient customer service besides monitoring customer behaviour that would improve customer satisfaction on product, service or etc. Usage of multimodal speech recognition can better project company image when utilizing speech automated interface as part of marketing tool for customer magnet.

Last but not least applications of speech recognizer in mundane lifestyle have recently been popularized with release of Apple's latest voice command system SIRI the trend is headed into automatic speech recognition (McFedries, 2012). Besides being a fashion statement, speech recognition can also be used for accessing confidential personal matters with additional plug-ins such as biometric scanner and voice recognition for authentication purposes (Vacca, 2007). However, there are still some unresolved issues regarding real-life application of speech recognition.

In the field of audio and visual speech recognition, there are still many obstacles towards a near perfect algorithm. One of the unresolved problems revolves around synchronization problem that occur across different platforms for classification purpose (Liu & Sato, 2008). The other problem would be limited vocabulary size, which refers to inability for long continuous duration of speech recognition with slangs, pauses, and exclamations taken in consideration (Chibelushi, Gandon, Mason,

Deravi, & Johnston, 1996). Future direction in speech recognition should explore on various methods and some of their current flaws when attempting to integrate them into as a whole.

This chapter aims in reviewing various algorithms direct or indirectly involved with speech synthesis. Algorithms that will be discussed include possible state-of-the-art methods and its origins as well as commonly used algorithms that provides efficient and good recognition rate. Exposure to complexity of speech recognition in audio aspects will be minimal due to field saturation. Chapter will focus more on visual speech features with suggestions to resolve some visual problems commonly encountered in visual speech recognition. This context will also discuss on several popular techniques and briefly explain on critical sections of algorithms for bimodal recognition. Based on knowledge obtained from this chapter, upper undergraduates and novice research students should be sufficiently resourceful for personal project initiation. Long term consideration for this chapter would inspire potential researchers to venture into field of audio and visual speech recognition.

BACKGROUND

The complexity of speech recognition system often overwhelms infant researchers as various techniques and algorithms from different research fields are required for a system to work. In speech recognition there are various difficulty levels for speech synthesis which can be summarized starting with the simplest isolated words being the simplest, connected words, continuous speech and spontaneous speech being the most difficult to implement (Anusuya & Katti, 2009).

- **Isolated Words:** Recognition of single word utterances with condition of momentary pauses between each word.
- **Connected Words:** Similarity closely reassembles Isolated Words with exception of lesser pauses between words.
- **Continuous Speech:** Capable of processing natural speech without slangs or punctuations.
- **Spontaneous Speech:** Highest level of speech recognition that is able to handle combination of speech and non-speech features that occur naturally between human interactions.

Initial speech cogitative takes sole consideration of audio signals which leads to poor recognition rate in environment of high noise. Introduction of visual aspects motivated by deaf handicapped personal able to perceive speech leads to further improvement of speech recognition and opens up new doors in research field. Audio and visual based speech recognition further complicates the algorithms with immense understanding required for both fields. In order to reduce overwhelming readers, the process will be split into various sub-stages for ease of cognitive.

Speech Properties

Prior to deciding on techniques and methods, initial understandings on speech properties are required as benchmark to differentiate between speech and sound. Audio frequency value for human speech is said to be concentrated between 100 Hz to 7,000 Hz. Frequency range can be reduced to 300Hz to 3,400Hz if only speech recognition is required as range is similar to telephone audio quality. Another distinguished speech feature would refer to human throat muscle limitation that limits timeframe of speech segment duration to between 0.1 seconds to 0.5 seconds (Tashev, 2009; Breen, 1992). Temporal properties slower or faster than said range can also be ignored as words spoken will be incomprehensible even to human perception.

According to both (Tashev, 2009; Campbell, 1997) if sampling frequency is not two times higher than the highest sampled frequency in signal spectrum, possibility of aliasing will increases for repeated copies of overlapping spectrum which causes information uncertainty. Recommended sampling rate around Nyquist frequency of 10 kHz was suggested to minimize aliasing effects from under-sampling (G.K.L., 2009). This allows proper audio signal capture of up to frequency of 5 kHz which captures entire telephone quality audio frequency, sufficient for audio speech recognition.

Audio Feature Extraction

Prior to audio features being extracted, if algorithm is meant for real-time application a Voice-Activity-Detection (VAD) is required to separate between background noise and speech timeframes. VADs are basically a thresholding algorithm that segments only audio signals that contains speech features for extraction. Several examples of VAD techniques includes energy thresholds (Woo, Yang, Park, & Lee, 2000), pitch detection (Chengalvarayan, 1999), spectrum analysis (Marzinzik & Kollmeier, 2002), zero-crossing rate (ITU-T Recommendation G.729-Annex B., 1996), periodicity measure (Tucker, 1992), higher order statistics in speech feature residual domain (Nemer, Goubran, & Mahmoud, 2001), or combination of different features (Tanyer & Özer, 2000). Comparison between these techniques by (Ramírez, 2007) shows that Spectrum Analysis method yields best results for speech/non-speech separation. Note that in this chapter, complexity due to real-time processing will not be considered as motive is to review on algorithms used for speech recognition.

Audio feature extraction can be defined as estimation of variables from another set of variables with the intention of downsizing total number of input features for classification purposes at later stages (Campbell, 1997). Feature extraction works by transforming observed vectors into feature vectors with intention of reducing feature vector size but preserving information containing in the full vector values resulting in meaningful comparison done in simpler calculation. Depending on technique implied often due to vast amount of feature vectors, personals who attempt selection of all available features will most likely lead to *curse of dimensionality* (Duta & Hart, 1973) from being overwhelmed with excessive feature values. Several popular methods for audio feature extraction include Mel-Frequency Cepstral Coefficient (MFCC), Linear Predictive Codes (LPC), Perceptual Linear Prediction (PLP), LPCC, PLP, etc. The paper (Goyani, Dave, & Patel, 2010) explains that despite various methods for audio feature extraction most are derived from basic methods of LPC, PLP, and MFCC.

LINEAR PREDICTIVE CODES

Linear Predictive Codes (LPC) extracts audio features by computing a parametric model based on least mean square error theory which is also known as linear prediction method thus called Linear Predictive Codes. Linear Predictive Codes (LPC) popularity is due to algorithm's capabilities to not only extract audio features but also compresses the digital signal to allow efficient data transmission especially for wireless transmission. Respective characteristics causes popularity of LPC usage for low to medium bit rate coder (Lahouti, Fazel, Safavi-Naeini, & Khandani, 2006).

The popular formant estimation technique is also one of the most powerful speech analysis techniques as LPC algorithm initially calculates signal power spectrum prior to spectrum formant analysis (Pawar, Kajave, & Mali, 2005; Nica, Caruntu, Toderean, & Buza, 2006). Passing speech signal into speech analysis filter will cause removal of redundant signals, generating residual error as output product. This means that audio signal have been quantized into smaller bitrates than original. Using only both residual error and speech parameters the original signal can be regenerated thus amount of data for transmission have been reduced. A parametric model is then plotted based on residual error using linear prediction to approximate speech signal as linear combination of its previous samples.

Based on the model multiple peaks are identified along with their corresponding frequencies which are called the formant frequencies (Yuhas & Sejnowski, 1990). The rest of the values can be found by sliding a window through audio signal and estimating formant frequencies based on parametric model of searching out spectrum peaks. The Linear Predictive Coefficients are found as it refers to every formants of an audio signal.

PERCEPTUAL LINEAR PREDICTION

Perceptual Linear Prediction (PLP) is modelled after concept of non-linear hearing (Hermansky, 1990). Similar to LPC, PLP only stores crucial signal information for processing with the exception that spectral characteristics have been altered to imitate non-linear human auditory system (see Figure 1).

Basic steps of PLP comprises of estimating three main perceptual aspects which are the critical-band analysis, the equal loudness curve, and the intensity-loudness power-law relation also known as the cubic-root (Honig, Stemmer, Hacker, Brugnara, & Fabio, 2005). Detailed steps of PLP computation is shown in Figure 2.

For windowed signal, power spectrum can be calculated using the equation:

$$P(\omega) = Re(S(\omega))^2 + Im(S(\omega))^2 \tag{1}$$

Imitation of non-linear sound perception will require frequency domain to be transformed into the non-linear Bark Scale. Equation for transformation is given as the equation:

Figure 1. Shows PLP computation process

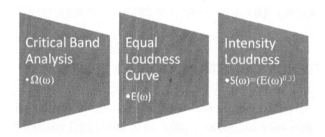

Figure 2. PLP detailed process

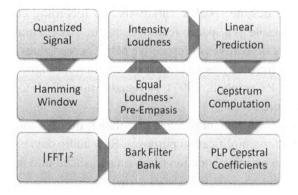

$$\Omega(\omega) = 6\ln\left[\left[\frac{\omega}{1200\pi} + \left[\left(\frac{\omega}{1200\pi}\right)^2 + 1\right]^{0.5}\right]\right] \tag{2}$$

Power Spectrum obtained from simulated critical-band masking curve is then convoluted with audio spectrum to simulate non-linear data extraction. Spectrum is then smoothed and down-sampled at estimate intervals of 1 Bark. Data is then passed through Bark filter bank, which contains frequency warping, smoothing and sampling functions. Outputs from filter bank are weighted based on equal-loudness pre-emphasis, which simulates hearing sensitivity. Based on power law values are transformed via power increment of 0.33. Results from transform are further processed using linear prediction which predicts coefficients of hypothetical signals as power spectrum. Recursion of predictor coefficients creates an equivalent to logarithm spectrum model which is then inversed Fourier Transform to obtain cepstral coefficients (Honig, Stemmer, Hacker, Brugnara, & Fabio, 2005).

Comparing between LPC and PLP, PLP's analytical methods closely resemble human non-linear speech perception. LPC's analysis takes in consideration of all range of signal frequency and equal power distribution for formant analysis which varies greatly to human perception of sound as spectral hearing resolution decreases beyond 800Hz while sound perception is more sensitive in the middle ranges of spectrum (Hermansky, 1990).

MEL-FREQUENCY CEPSTRAL COEFFICIENTS

Mel-Frequency Cepstral Coefficient (MFCC) functions similar with PLP where algorithm utilizes non-linear audio perception to imitating human listening features (Chibelushi, Deravi, & Mason, 2002). Multiple usage of MFCC can be detected among many researchers and evidence regarding functionality of MFCC is clearly mentioned in numerous papers. The characteristics of MFCC coefficients being robust and reliable despite speaker variations and recording conditions make it considerable favourable as a speech feature extractor. Recent trend in MFCC utilization includes time derivatives of respective MFCC core values with the intention of modelling audio trajectory as additional information for higher audio perception efficiency (Joseph P.Campbell, 1997). A visualization of MFCC process can be observed from Figure 3.

Mel-Frequency Cepstral Coefficients calculation process can be broken down into multiple parts for simplification purposes. Raw audio data is initially obtained usually after a voice activity detection filtration and sliced into individual overlap-

Figure 3. Mel-frequency cepstral coefficient feature extraction (Chibelushi, Deravi, & Mason, 2002)

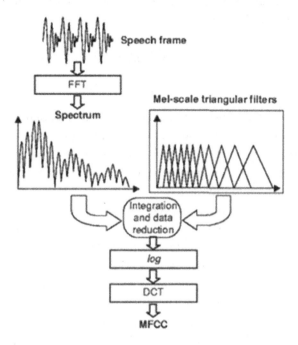

ping frames. Many audio pre-processing uses 20ms as the duration of each individual frame but commonly used frames ranges between 10 ms to 50 ms depending on researcher preference (Tashev, 2009). Once framed, signal is windowed using Hamming or Hanning to avoid signal discontinuities at edges (Zoric, 2005; Chen, 1998). Windowed signal will enhance center frame values and causes overlapping frame values obtained. Hamming window equation is given below.

$$w(n) = \begin{cases} 0.54 - 0.46\cos\left(\dfrac{2\pi n}{N-1}\right), & if\, 0 \le n \le N-1 \\ 0, \; Otherwise \end{cases} \tag{3}$$

where N total sample number, n is current sample number.

After windowing Fast Fourier Transformation is used on signal to convert time domain into frequency region and filtered with Mel-scale triangular filters producing raw feature vectors for each triangle filters with intention of dimension reduction. This Mel-scale is linear up to 1 kHz before increasing logarithmically (Leong, 2003). Log function is applied to filter output and finally vectors are transformed back into time domain using Discrete Cosine Transformation (DCT), obtaining the specified number of MFCC coefficients (Leon, 2009). The relation between frequency and mel-scale is given as following:

$$Mel\left(frequency\right) = 2595\log(1 + \frac{frequency(Hz)}{700}) \tag{4}$$

Note that MFCC coefficients are calculated for each speech frames so if a speech length of 2 seconds is taken in consideration, framing done at 20ms will yield a total of 198 overlapping frames with each frames consisting of 39 coefficients with number of coefficients of each frames dependent on researcher's preference. Overall MFCC process is shown in Figure 4.

Based on a comparison made by (Goyani, Dave, & Patel, 2010) these three basic feature extractors in regards to speech recognition performance, there does not exist significant recognition rate difference between these three technique, however it would seem that MFCC and PLP fare better than LPC perhaps due to fact that both MFCC and PLP are modelled based on non-linear human sound perception. However with reference to (Fook, Hariharan, Yaacob, & Adom, 2012) it would appears that classification using neural networks for MFCC fare at around 99.04% while LPC yields accuracy of 92.92%. Resultant of higher accuracy when utilizing MFCC algorithm suggests prime algorithm selection should be MFCC feature extraction technique.

Visual Speech Processing

Utilization of visual speech aspects recently State-of-the-Art audio only speech recognition continues to be hindered by lack of system robustness to channel environment noises which leads to utilization of visual aspects for speech recognition to

Figure 4. Mel-frequency cepstral coefficient algorithm

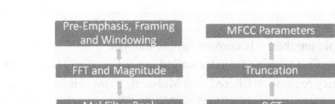

assist in solving acoustic noise problems (Juang, 1991; Talea & Yaghmaie, 2011). Reason behind audio limitation is similar to human's capability where the ear cannot interpret sound under heavy noise despite being the most powerful biological speech recognition system.

In visual speech recognition, the only Region Of Interest (ROI) would be the mouth area and therefore the pre-processing priority will be to detect, isolate and track respective region of interest. Depending on algorithm utilized, some algorithm requires identification of other facial regions prior to locating lips such as detection of eye pupils and corners, nose and nostrils before moving to mouth and lip corners (Majumder, Behera, & Subramaniam, 2011). Location of those mentioned features occasionally tend to be different due to possible facial expressions and illuminations conditions, thus making automatic feature extraction a challenging task to perform (Liew & Wang, 2009). General algorithm for visual speech recognition consists of region segmentation, tracking, feature extraction, and classification illustrated in Figure 5.

FACE DETECTION AND SEGMENTATION

Pre-processing algorithms such as Region Of Interest (ROI) segmentation are required in most speech recognition process (Liew & Wang, 2009). In speech recognition, area of interest refers to mouth region which is located within the face region. This leads to initial requirement for basics face detection algorithms being the preliminary step prior to mouth region detection. Process for this region of interest segmentation is similar to face recognition algorithm process illustrated in Figure 6 (Zhao, Chellappa, Philips, & Rosenfeld, 2003) with the exception that there is an additional step after face detection and tracking is not done at face detection phase.

Among techniques used for face detection, Viola and Jones object detection algorithm which utilizes multiple haar-like rectangular and skin-colour-based segmentation algorithms seemed to produce good detection results.

Figure 5. General visual speech algorithm

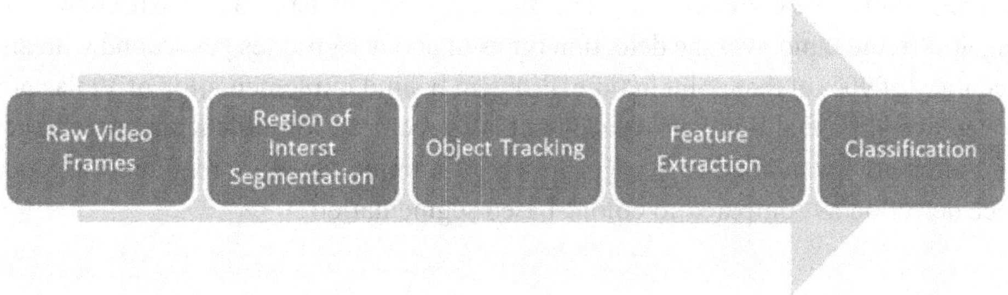

Figure 6. General image processing procedure

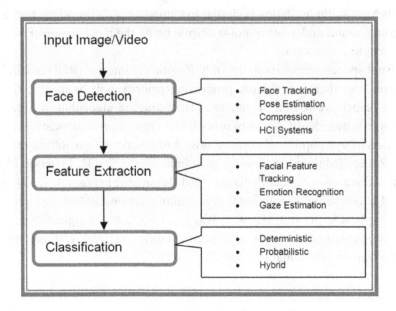

Most researchers would agree that one of the most robust face detection algorithms would be Viola and Jones face detection algorithm. This algorithm uses multiple haar basic functions to compute gradient of images for various features instead of directly compute image intensity. Using this algorithm facial feature such as face, eyes and nose can be detected (Majumder, Behera, & Subramaniam, 2011). Rapid computational of features is achieved by using integral image representation for images instead of original images. Integral of image is computed using few operations per pixel and with this Haar-like features computation can be done regardless of scale or location in constant time.

In order to ensure fast classification, a large portion of available features needs to be excluded and only focuses on critical or influential features. Technique for doing so revolves in altering Adaptive Boosting algorithm (AdaBoost) in such a way that the weak learner is constrained so that every classifier considered weak will respond only to a single feature instead of each independent feature (Liew, Leung, & Lau, 2000). The complete face detection cascade consist of 32 classifiers working at extreme rapid average detection times of about 15 frames per second with an accuracy of 90% at that point in time. Problem behind implementation of Viola and Jones would be that number of face templates required for high accuracy is large and often are not available. A huge amount of training faces are required for good face detection as compared to colour-based segmentation.

Alternative method to Viola and Jones would be skin-colour-based face segmentation. In colour based segmentation, initial step would be to choose the appropriate colour space for segmentation. Available colour spaces include Red-Green-Blue (RGB) (Barbu, 2011), Chroma Components (YCbCr), Hue-Saturation-Intensity (HSI) (Chiou & Hwang, 1997), and others. Characteristics that need to be taken in consideration when selecting appropriate colour space includes distinct colour value difference between face-lips and rate of illumination influence in colour values (Lakshmi & PatilKulakarni, 2010). Colour space YCbCr best represents the non-linear retinal interpretation of visual images with illumination difference less likely to affect colour values (Mahmoud, 2008; Rahman, Wei, & See, 2006).

The entire process is simple and procedure can be summarised as thresholding individual pixel values towards a specific colour boundary to determine if pixel belonged to human skin. Post-processing can be done to refine results such as proposed in the paper by Lakshmi & PatilKulakarni, 2010 where edge detection algorithms such as Sobel, Prewitt and Roberts is integrated with colour segmentation for clearer region separation between background and face region. This is done by removing all edge pixels from segmented image, drawing a distinct boundary between regions with gradient difference. The paper by Barbu (2011) is another interesting technique used in face segmentation. The paper basically suggests using a simple clustering method such as nearest neighbour method to cluster similar value pixels together. The disadvantage of colour-based segmentation would be requirement of ample skin samples for initial colour-map plotting and boundary definition for segmentation (Liew & Wang, 2009).

REGION OF INTEREST (ROI) SEGMENTATION (MOUTH)

Based on segmented face region, a boundary created would assist in narrowing down search area for lips region which would save some computational power. The next processing phase requires mouth region to be located for feature extraction purposes. The papers by Majumder, Behera, & Subramaniam, 2011 and WenJuan, YaLing, & MingHui, 2010 proposed using basic facial geometry concepts as novel techniques to locate position of mouth, nose and eyes. Figure 7 shows the process flow from raw image to lip feature extraction level.

Successful detection of face region is only the first step to seeking out mouth region. Next stage would be to estimation location for eyes and nose as it will assist in enhancing mouth region detection accuracy in visual speech recognition. The basic concept of eye detection lies in fact that human eye pupil hole contain reddish information from the that can be separated easily with some simple thresholding of hue region. Fact that the eye is located around the first 1/3 of the face region, search

Figure 7. Flow chart in face feature extraction

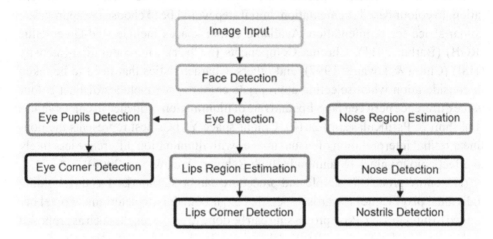

region can be limited to top half of the face with vertical height of 1/3 (Majumder, Behera, & Subramaniam, 2011). Narrowing down region of interest will assist in faster search computation for eye location. Based on eye pupils' location, other information can also be determined such as face tilt angle for other computational purposes.

Coordinates of eyes allows for nose region computation where it is usually located at the center-point of both eye pupils with 1/3 of face height after eyes region. Nostrils location can be computed by thresholding nose region in gray-scale as nostrils are relatively darker than surrounding regions (Majumder, Behera, & Subramaniam, 2011). Some morphological techniques are used to clean up the thresholded images and centroid of darker areas of the image can be classified as nostrils.

Mouth region can now be estimated utilizing information from both eyes and nose location as a guideline. Mouth detection is done by simple usage of fundamental facial geometries where mouth approximate width is the width between both eye centroid locations and vertical region starts after nose tip definable as the nostrils center-point (WenJuan, YaLing, & MingHui, 2010). Height of the mouth is esti-mated to be ¾ of total nose height but some researchers prefer to use similar height as nose, which is 1/3 of entire face region for calculation (Majumder, Behera, & Subramaniam, 2011). Reason behind doing so is to capture lips corners when people smile as well. Angle tilting of eye-pupils can be used to calculate the tilted mouth region thus allowing a more specified region of interest to be formed and detected.

Attempts to track mouth edges cause problems as uncertainty of environment illumination and occurrences of occlusion would cause sudden disappearance and appearance of lip corners. The paper in (Majumder, Behera, & Subramaniam, 2011) suggests using Shi-Tomasi's corner detection method to detect lip corners. The algorithm can be expressed as gray-level image extraction of mouth region and threshold image to provide edge information before applying Shi-Tomas's corner detection in thresholded image. Shi-Thomas's techniques would only pinpoint out edges without regard for proper location, therefore reference to lips axis center is required in order to determine if corner is located at the left or right side. This is done by determining if the corner is the positive or negative value based on deduction of edge coordinates with center axis. A positive would means the left and vice versa for right mouth corner.

Alternative method to using the Golden Ratio (Winfrey, 2009) for mouth region boundary would be based on work done in paper (Kumatani & Stiefelhagen, 2006). The algorithm requires prior training before being utilized for region segmentation using Principle Component Analysis (PCA), Discrete Cosine Transformation (DCT) and Gaussian Mixture Model (GMM). Initial training requires huge amount of mouth images all scaled into same image size and processed through DCT or PCA to obtain feature vector meant for training. Region is then located after training by computing similar size windows across every pixel of images and calculates the likelihood of window belonging to mouth region based on trained GMM. Problem with this alternative method would be the fact that a huge training data is hard to find and computing every pixel in search for only the mouth region is commutatively expensive. Obtaining mouth region allows for the next processing stage of extracting feature vectors for classification purposes.

VISUAL FEATURE EXTRACTION

Lip information extraction is the most important part in speech recognition by visual means. Extraction of lips feature methods can be classified into various categories which are but not limited to geometry based methods, motion based methods and colour or contour based (Yingjie, Haiyan, Yingjie, & Jinyang, 2011) after utilizing point-based method to placing points that creates boundary around the mouth (Liu & Cheung, 2011).

The convention methods for visual feature extraction are based on absorbing entire image data for processing. The rectangular mouth region is segmented from face image and pre-processed using dimension reduction techniques such as Principal Component Analysis and Linear Discriminant Analysis (Liew & Wang, 2009). Results from dimension reduction and immediately used as feature vectors for classification. Some recent techniques for dimension reduction utilizing these method and fuses it with various other dimension reduction techniques as well as implemented it with other non-linear methods to produce feature vectors for more effective classification. Algorithm that relates closely to said condition would be based on the paper (Yaling, Wenjuan, & Minghui, 2010) that initially performs Discrete Cosine Transform to every frame of ROI and rearranges them into a single array matrix. The coefficients obtain is then passed through Locality Sensitive Discriminant Analysis (LSDA) feature translation matrix which respects both discriminant and geometrical structure of data. Final feature values from LSDA are used for classification purposes. Alternative method would either takes closely segmented lip-region for processing or defining feature points and conduct some post-processed to obtain feature vectors.

Region-based approach allows tolerances for more robust tracking results. Some examples of region-based methods are Deformable Template (DT), Active Contour Model (ACM), Active Shape Model (ASM), and Active Appearance Model (AAM) (Liu & Cheung, 2011). The DT algorithm basically divides region into partitions of lips and non-lips using a parametric model. Poor performance of DT algorithm occurs when poor contrast between lips and skin region occurs and lip shape being irregular (Liew, Leung, & Lau, 2000). The conventional ACM algorithm first forms a closed curve around region of interest before deforming it to effectively minimizing region energy till an accurate object contour is obtained. The downside of this approach is that it is sensitive to uneven illumination and parameter initialization (Chiou & Hwang, 1997). The ASM works by defining a set of landmark points pertaining to described lip shape and are controlled in a closed loop modes derived from training data. This method is tedious as usually researchers would rather not perform additional training just for lip shape determination. Similar to ASM the AAM algorithm replaces parts of algorithm with the Eigen-analysis instead (Matthews, Cootes, Bangham, Cox, & Harvey, 2002).

Point-based technique defines a set of characteristic points created through low-level spatial cues such as lips colour, edges, with prior knowledge of the lip structure. Disadvantage of point based method would be sensitivity issues and initial positioning of feature points ambiguity. Once initial point is wrongly defined entire system would fail. In paper (Yingjie, Haiyan, Yingjie, & Jinyang, 2011), a fusion of geometry and motion feature of lips is suggested for information extraction. Method can be summarized as finding and tracking lips key points in image sequence and extract geometry as well as motion characteristics with constant comparison to database or lip model. This method requires manual placing of initial tracking points for initialization.

In a concept proposed by (Liu & Cheung, 2011), a technique for robust lip tracking algorithm using localized colour active contours and deformable models is proposed. This method combines semi-ellipse and initial evolving curve to compute for localized energies in colour space. This procedure will result in separation of original lip image into lip and non-lip region. Dynamic radius from local region selection is presented with 16-points deformable model to achieve lip tracking. The algorithm proposed is adaptive to lips motion from a sequent of frames and robust against teeth and tongue influence.

The technique extends Localized Active Contour Models (LACM) to Localized Colour Active Contour Models (LCACM) with combined semi-ellipse as initial evolving curve to extract lip contour for initial first frame. A subsequent dynamic radius selection of local region with 16-points is presented for lip tracking shown in Figure 8. An advantage of using LCACM is that complex appearance of colour objects can be segmented with localized energies upon failure of global energies.

Despite having 16-points, the crucial points are points P1, P5, P9 and P13, the four points that creates mouth boundary. The four points at each four corner of the mouth, left and right corner as well as middle top and bottom lip segments. Based on work done by (Li & Cheng, 2009) and (Eveno, Caplier, & Coulon, 2004) the four main points stated can be determined automatically. Referring to empirical studies, lip shape can be approximately surrounded by two semi-ellipses which can be initially assumed as the evolving curve in Localized Colour Active Contour Model. Using only 4 points does not yield smooth lip contour, therefore the paper suggest usage of 16 points deformable model with cubic spline interpolation connected to model the lips. The paper declared that result from obtained from simulation reveals a 95% satisfactory rate.

Another interesting concept is by (Talea & Yaghmaie, 2011) that uses colour-based algorithm for lips feature extraction mainly Red Exclusion and Colour Trans-

Figure 8. Illustration of 16 lips feature points (Liu & Cheung, 2011)

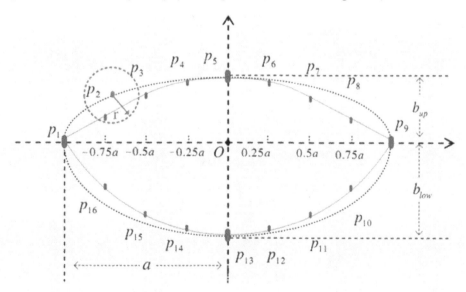

form. Red Exclusion Algorithm uses green and blue colour levels of image pixels to exclude lips from entire image. The theory behind this method is the fact that most lips are predominantly red. The paper also uses colour transform of red and green information which is similar to pseudo of hue transform. Colour Transform method will cause lip segment to emerge brighter than skin region. The next step is to convert transformed image into binary colour code based on specific threshold related to on maximum histogram value. Illustration of process output can be observed in Figure 9.

Authors suggest combined usage of both features to obtain a full lip region. Red Exclusion will help to eliminate many defects pertaining to nose shadow and deep chin for lower lip while red and green colour transform can be exploited to separate upper lip from other face components. Merging of both datasets will obtain whole mouth image. Process flowchart is shown in Figure 10.

Figure 9. Illustration of process output

Figure 10. Sample algorithm for lips segmentation

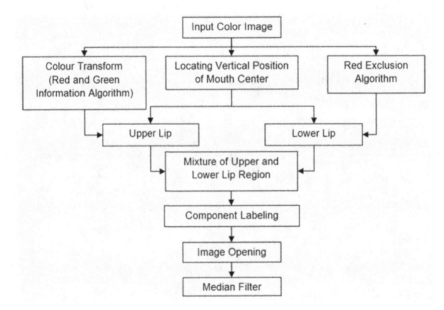

Labelling of mouth region can be done once proper region is extracted from face image. Component labelling is used to separate individual parts from each other as well as eliminate excessive and noisy parts. Region around active mouth model uses an opening operation that removes image pixels that have less than 500 pixels connected to region of interest to remove redundant pixels. Removal of sharp edges and probable region of teeth effects in order to obtaining a smooth contour is done using a median filter. Feature points are then placed surrounding segmented lip region systematically either clockwise or anti-clockwise to form a boundary around segmented region. With the points obtained, geometrical feature can be computed accordingly and analysis for speech recognition purposes. The points are then tracked between frames sequence. Marked image can be observed in Figure 11.

Further processing of feature points obtain can be done using several techniques mentioned in (Sujatha & Krishnan, 2012) where upon lip segmentation, depending on preference up to sixteen feature points which makes up lip region boundary are taken in consideration for feature processing. Normalized distance between each point towards mouth center coordinates are computed and processed as feature vectors. Discrete Cosine Transform can also be applied after obtaining normalized distance and utilized as feature vectors. Illustration for normalized distance is shown in Figure 12 where each distance is normalized and taken as a feature vector.

Figure 11. Points identified on lips using algorithm (Talea & Yaghmaie, 2011)

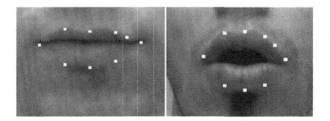

Figure 12. Distance between sixteen points to be normalized

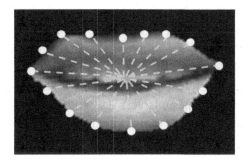

OBJECT TRACKING ALGORITHMS

Depending on algorithm utilized, sometimes lip tracking works along side with feature extraction such as the case of Snake algorithm (Lu, Wu, & Jia, 2010). Tracking of lips had been considered difficult due to various interference factors such as tongue, teeth, white-noise, and different lip shapes/colour/size between speakers (Liu & Cheung, 2011). Prior to selecting the appropriate tracking algorithm various consideration regarding tracking characteristic are required to narrow down the algorithm scope. Based on (Liew & Wang, 2009) several visual speech properties can be summarised as follows. First characteristic which needs to be taken in consideration is fact that there is no absolute fixed shape for the lips when in speech motion. Tracking algorithm must not be too reliant on lip geometrical feature as some features will be unavailable in certain parts of speech frames. The other important fact about visual speech is that combination of speech and occasion head motion concluded that lips motions are non-parametric and does not follow a specific movement patterns. Due to previous fact, tracking algorithm needs to be capable for non-linear motion tracking. Final characteristic is based on preference than facts. It is desirable for tracking algorithm to be robust and fast for possible real-time applications. In order for fast tracking speed, number of calculations and features being tracked needs to be minimized (dimension reduction). Further elaboration on term robust can be summarised as less likely to be affected with image illumination variations and constant orientation changes. A summarised set of characteristic for ideal tracking algorithm would be a fast and robust multi-shape objects non-linear tracking based algorithm.

Several tracking methods that fulfils initial requirement can be grouped into three huge categories which are Deformable Contours Tracking, Visual Learning and Feature Tracking. Deformable Contours Tracking normally predicts location based on object's Computer-Aided-Design-like model which is computational expensive. Modern methods implies Snake algorithm where object shape is bound by an internal elastic boundaries using image gradient and force vectors (Cohen, 1991). Utilizing these values the snake algorithm wraps itself around the object and changes its shape to match with object (Lu, Wu, & Jia, 2010). Alternative method to modern snake would be the B-Spline which uses both parametric and geometric model that captures object contour and continuously tracks it. This technique uses object shape space, which requires appropriate parameterization for complex deformable models (Blake & Isard, 1998).

Visual learning uses a different approach where it implies algorithm to initially learn and remember object shape and tracks it by consistently searching for it. Often other feature extraction methods are used as medium for shape learning such as

Principal Component Analysis due to its capability of capturing features of complex shapes (A & Hogg, 1994; Murase & Nayar, 1995). The tracking segment for visual learning commonly uses both Kalman Filtering and deformation parameters included in state vector. Tracking is done via searching region of next frame for learnt shape based on shape location on present frame. This method is only limited to linear or static state parameters and has little tolerance towards noise (A & Hogg, 1994).

Feature tracking method tracks the image's features directly instead of the overall object of interest. Features such as object edge, line, contour, or specially defined regions from either present frame or predefined values are stored and tracking is conducted by attempting to match stored features with values obtain from the next frame. Application to lip reading would means tracking algorithm for feature tracking will require multiple target tracking which deem particle filter technique to be of high possibility (Isard & Blake, 1998). Problem with feature tracking is that select features will require being robust towards orientation, illumination and possible noisy environment in order for proper tracking (Smith, 1999). Once proper feature is selected, based on characteristics of features particle filter tracking implies Monte Carlo method of selection of randomly distributed region surrounding location of feature in previous frame which will calculate a possibility function of feature located at each randomly selected regions (Arulampalam, Maskell, Gordon, & Clapp, 2002).

Data Classification

Pattern matching and classification of data is another branch and most of the time the final phase of speech recognition system. Pattern matching is divided into two types of models namely Stochastic Models and Template Models.

Template models in pattern matching is deterministic and observation of data that are assumed to be flawed replica of template (Campbell, 1997). Algorithm works by comparing frames to template and selecting the minimum distance between model features and observed features. Likelihood of template based models is approximated through exponential functions of utterance match scores resulting method being considered more towards intuitive method. Template Models can be dependent or independent with respect to time allowing some freedom for research to explore alternative methods. Some examples of Template Models are Dynamic Time Warping (DTW), Vector Quantization (VQ), and Nearest Neighbour (NN) (Campbell, 1997).

Stochastic Models in pattern matching is based on probability function and results are based on likelihood or conditional probability of observation when comparing to the speech model (Campbell, 1997). Stochastic models are developed to be more flexible and provide higher theoretically meaningful probabilistic likelihood score. Pattern matching problems by stochastic models are formulated as a measure of likelihood of an observation when provided the speech models.

A popular stochastic model for speech recognition is the Hidden Markov Model (HMM). Hidden Markov Models is a finite-state machine where a set of probability distribution function is associated with each state. This mathematically complicated method can only be observed through a different set of stochastic process that produces sequence of observation.

Based on comparison by numerous of research papers, it is clarified that HMM may be the best classifier for speech recognition when used in automatic speech recognition especially for continuous or long vocabulary recognition (Shivappa, Trivedi, & Rao, 2010). Usually used in conjunction with Hidden Markov Models, the Viterbi Algorithm which is a dynamic programming algorithm is used to seek out most likely sequence of hidden states (Viterbi, 2006) categorized under the likelihood calculation. The algorithm makes a number of assumptions.

- First, both the observed events and hidden events must be in a sequence. This sequence often corresponds to time.
- Second, these two sequences need to be aligned, and an instance of an observed event needs to correspond to exactly one instance of a hidden event.
- Third, computing the most likely hidden sequence up to a certain point t must depend only on the observed event at point t, and the most likely sequence at point $t - 1$.

Based on these assumptions the algorithm then backtrack progress of classifier to determine the most likely hidden state sequence corresponding to a stream of feature vectors containing either words or vocal phoneme. Besides Viterbi other likelihood methods for statistical models includes maximum likelihood estimation can also be used as a probability function to determine spoken words.

Maximum-Likelihood Estimation (MLE) utilizes a statistical model for comparison with given data set to estimate model's parameters (Du, Hu, & Jiang, 2011). Based on availability of certain values for some samples of the overall data set, MLE is capable to estimate the mean and variance of entire populace. In situation with fixed data set and statistical model provided, the MLE method calculates and chooses the data that produces a distribution with highest probability close to statistical model (Du, Hu, & Jiang, 2011). MLE provides good estimation approach for normal distribution cases. In some complicated problems the MLE are unsuitable for utilization.

Audio-Visual Speech Recognition

In an article by (Potamianos, Gravier, Garg, & Senior, 2003) it is said that integration of information obtained between audio and visual can be divided into three categories.

1. Early/Feature Integration
2. Intermediate Integration
3. Late/ Decision Integration

Early integration refers to integrating feature values extracted from audio and visual before it reaches recognizer. Fusion of values usually takes place before recognizer which is either at sensory level or feature level. Simple data concatenation and weighted data summation are among few examples of such method of fusion. Feature level fusion is said to be an intuitive fusion technique (Liew & Wang, 2009) where data tendency of problems related to dimensional mismatch would occur.

Intermediate/Hybrid integration process initiates fusion at the recognition process which often alters parameters of the recognizer directly during speech recognition process. Assuming system utilized a multi-stream Hidden Markov Model (HMM), weight interlinks may be manipulated to increase or decrease influential level of model. Manipulation of this magnitude allows for modality influence adjustment closely related to varying timeline and allows for scale ranges from state levels, phonetic levels and even word or sentence stage as well (P.Varga & Moore, 1990). Downside would be that there are tradeoffs involved with limited HMM recognition structure choices (Liew & Wang, 2009).

Decision level or late integration refers to combination of output values from individual modal namely after independent recognizer of audio and video modals resulting a single final system output. Integration of this level usually utilized a scoring-level or decision level where method for computing final optimized path for each classified path is done based on a voting system, N-Best list, and Boolean operators (Potamianos, Gravier, Garg, & Senior, 2003; Dupont & Luettin, 2000). Another example of decision level fusion can be given by Score-level fusion which most commonly associated with weighted summations, products or other classifiers based on machine learning. Advantages of late integrations allows for comparatively vast freedom towards information fusion techniques compared to intermediate fusion which allows for various time-scale fusion (see Figure 13).

In terms of fusion methods, neurologist favours feature-level or early data fusion which correspond more closely to human interpretation of speech besides the fact that feature-based methods are less sensitive to illumination, viewpoints, and face localization inaccuracy. The problem with this method is the lack of accuracy in

Figure 13. Audio-visual speech recognition process

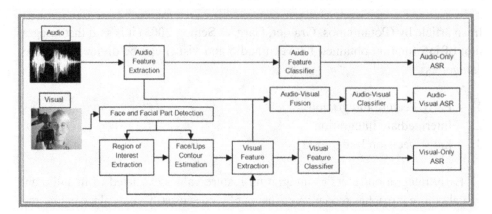

critical decision making aspects (Zhao, Chellappa, Philips, & Rosenfeld, 2003). This leads majority researchers to favour decision-level fusion instead where audio and visual speech modals are separately analysis and process before fusing them together after recognizer or individual modals.

Another crucial part in audio-visual speech recognition fusion is none other than synchronization of features vectors between audio values and video values. It is mentioned that if audio-visual synchrony drift occurs, human perception satisfaction will reduced. If audio proceeds video by 5 video frames, viewers satisfaction would reduced by 84%. In short, audio should never lead video by more than 15ms and should never lag more than 45ms (Liu & Sato, 2008).

Respective perception on audio-visual synchrony should be applied in audio-visual speech recognition as unsynchronized data between visual features and audio features will also causes downfall in speech recognition accuracy. Research in this aspect is considered advance level and difficult to tackle as there have been numerous attempts to synchronize audio-visual drifts however these methods drains too much computational power for real-time continuous speech application (Liu & Sato, 2008). Reason behind high computational requirement revolve around algorithm to search every frame for the said lips and consistently comparing lips motion to audio speech motion.

MINIMIZATION OF COSTS, TIME, AND PROCESSING POWER IN AUDIO VISUAL SPEECH PROCESSING

The problem that this chapter will attempt to solve would revolve around the three main factors of time, power and research costs. Research funds are usually limited which would require careful expenses when investing on hardware, software and information. Cost minimization can be done by attempting to research into techniques which does not requires training or algorithms that uses less computational power. Often training would require purchase of specialized databases depending on which algorithm, which is not cheap and higher computational algorithms would require more expensive machines for efficient research. Avoiding training would also help in reducing time required for certain aspects of research as training often requires long idle hours for system to train while research in minimizing complex algorithms will help in reducing computational power required for system to run, making it possible for real-time application besides minimizing on hardware requirements which as discussed, can be expensive.

Issues and Problems

Most researcher are too focused in increasing detection accuracy which leads them to design extremely complicated algorithms of multiple layer of calculations and computations for better detection rate. These leads to huge increased in computational power for a slight improvement in accuracy. Higher computational power used will indirectly causes higher cost incurrence for better specification hardware and higher electricity consumption. All these will lead to higher research costs. A balance between cost and accuracy need to be established such that possible end product will still be commercial-able to people from all walks of life. Suggestive solution to sustainability will be to minimize the dependency on high computational algorithms as well as unnecessary utilization of training corpuses.

In terms of computing power, possible solution for computational reduction will be to bring research focus towards step minimization via skipping certain steps when seeking out lips region or combining algorithms and simplifying them to reduce total number regarding repeated calculations for each region individually. A simple example will be to try and make algorithm to directly segment lips region instead of seeking out every facial region. As for training reduction solution, instead of using databases to conduct tracking, identifying and template matching for face and lips region search as well as tracking lips features; possible research area to be explored is to use known characteristics to determine all the mentioned above. An example will be to replace Viola and Jones algorithm that requires training with skin-based face detection algorithm and instead of using template matching for tracking, utilize non-linear statistical algorithms instead. An efficient and good feature tracking algorithm can help avoid requirement of reprocessing steps to determine location of features plus does not require any prior training. The above are issues regarding sustainability and the next section will discuss some non-sustainability issues.

Synchronization between Audio and Visual Features is another issue that most researchers tend to avoid. In this chapter, we will only discuss some basic concepts on this issue as the problem is still an ongoing research topic. Combination of audio and visual feature vectors would provide researchers surplus of classification features which highlights initially mentioned *curse of dimensionality*. Fact that captured data for both audio and visual are separated with different frame speeds. Majority of visual frames are captured at the rate of 30 Frames per second while audio signals are in terms of sampling rate often around 4,000 to 8,000 signals per second sliced into individual frames of overlapping 20ms. The difference in timeline for both audio and visual occasionally causes selective features from both aspects to no belong under the same instantaneous time which will cause misclassifications. In the proposed algorithm, we will introduce a simple concept to solving simple synchronization problems without going too in-depth in the topic.

Fusion Technique for feature classifications has often been a topic of debate in academia. Researchers tend to vote for decision level where features for both audio and video are previously classified and result from both concurrent sections will then be multiplied by a certain weights distribution for priority in classifying depending on environment. This technique often causes synchronization problems as classifications are done separated from each other. Human interpretation for speech would more closely assimilate towards feature level classifications where raw feature vectors from both audio and visual are taken in directly for final classification. However under high noise environment, inaccuracies of audio section will drastically causes classification algorithm to often misclassified data. We proposed to use hybrid algorithm that allows advantages from both decision and feature level to be combined for better classification. However we will not go too in-depth as well for this topic.

Proposed Audio and Visual Speech Recognition

Research field in audio-visual speech recognition is extremely huge and complicated, therefore as a beginner's guide several parameters are predefined for simplification purposes in proposed algorithm. The criterions are as follows:

- Only one speaker is present in each frame
- Visual capture for each frames are limited to the following:
  - Entire face and partial upper body section
  - Slight facial orientation with both eyes visible
  - Minimal illumination interference to visual information extraction

- Minimal acoustic noise level interfering with system
- Data for both audio and visual have been pre-segmented according to individual speech data

The proposed algorithms used to make up entire system will be based on those criterions. Components include speech activity detection, audio feature extraction, face and lips region searching, visual feature extraction, feature point tracking and statistical classification method. Previously we have mentioned that voice activity detection will not be covered as we are not looking into real-time recognition at the moment therefore the first section that we will look into is the audio signals information extraction.

Assumptions were that the audio signals have been segmented therefore we will start with extraction process of feature vectors. Suggested method for audio feature extraction is the improved Mel-Frequency Cepstral Coefficients (MFCC) based on the paper by (Hossan, Memon, & Gregory, 2010). The paper uses basic concept of conventional MFCC where we have the mel-scale equation, Discrete Cosine Transformation, Triangular Filter-Bank to obtain coefficients. Hossan, Memon and Gregory suggest of taking the coefficients a notch up by utilizing their time derivative coefficients for both velocity and acceleration. Algorithm process suggested for audio feature extraction will be briefly described. Further information regarding formulas involved can be found in the paper.

Upon obtaining audio data containing speech, the signal is sliced into overlapping frames of redefined 20ms, overlapping at 10ms using hamming windowing function.

$$w(n) = 0.54 - 0.46cos\left(\frac{2\pi n}{N-1}\right) \tag{5}$$

$$h(n) = g(n)w(n) \tag{6}$$

where $0 \leq n \leq N-1$, N = number of samples in each frame, n = sample number in series of frames, w(n) = Hamming Window function, g(n) = framed audio speech signal, h(n) = output windowed signal.

Result is converted from time-domain to frequency-domain using Discrete Fourier Transformed which gives the power spectrum. Convoluting power spectrum with triangular filter bank will provide power coefficients in each specific frequency range corresponding to each triangle. In this case we defined such that a total number of coefficients obtain are thirteen. Triangle filter-bank is illustrated as in Figure 14.

Fourier-based coefficients are then transformed back into time-domain using Discrete Cosine Transformation given

$$C_m = \sqrt[2]{\frac{2}{N}} \sum_{l=0}^{(Q-1)} \log[e(l+1).\cos[m\left(\frac{2l+1}{2}\right).\frac{\pi}{Q}] \tag{7}$$

where m=0, 1, 2... R-1, R = Number of Desired Coefficients, Q = Number of Inputs

Result from the process yields audio features in coefficients form. Suggestions by (Hossan, Memon, & Gregory, 2010) using the time derivatives or delta functions and double delta functions will create 26 more coefficients plus the existing 13 coefficients with a total of 39 audio coefficients. Time derivatives for both velocity and acceleration use the same equation and can be shown below.

$$d_t = \frac{\sum_{\theta=1}^{k} \theta(C_{i+\theta} - C_{i-\theta})}{2\sum_{\theta=1}^{k} \theta^2} \tag{8}$$

where d_t = delta coefficient at time (t), i = frame value, k = size of delta window

In Figure 15 with reference from left to right, first graph shows variation towards MFCC values due to different speech data while the next two graphs showing similar data variation of similar speech data spoken by different individuals. The first 13 coefficients are the main MFCC coefficients, second line refers to time derivatives of first line and the last line are time derivatives of the second line data. Some experimental results shows that time derivatives of original coefficients potentially separates different speech data more clearly which will help in improve classifica-

Figure 14. Illustration of triangle filter-banks

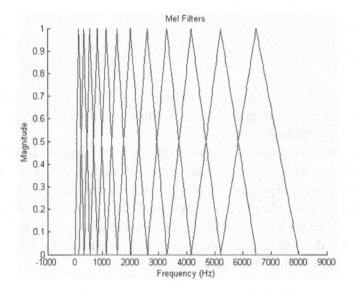

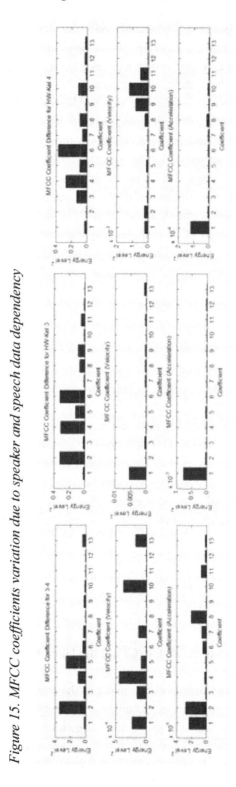

Figure 15. MFCC coefficients variation due to speaker and speech data dependency

tion accuracy. Audio features obtained are only the first section for audio-visual speech recognition. The next concurrent phase would be visual feature extraction.

Visual feature vector extraction consist of several sections mainly region of interest segmentation, image correction, feature extraction and finally tracking algorithm. In region segmentation we have face detection and lip region boundary. A robust and sustainable algorithm for face detection purposes would be referring to algorithm that has minimal calculations and training. Here we proposed using Face Detection Method based on Skin Segmentation by (Barbu, 2011). In the paper, face is segmented by thresholding image with skin-colour boundary, clustered and compared with ratio and threshold to determine validity of extracted shapes corresponds to face ratio. Based on input colour values in Red-Green-Blue (RGB), the paper recommends using chroma colour-based (YCbCr) space skin segmentation due to YCbCr colour space is less prone with varying illumination conditions. Conversion between raw red-blue-green colour values to YCbCr can be given by the following equations.

$$Cr = 0.15R - 0.3G + 0.45B + 128 \tag{9}$$

$$Cb = 0.45R - 0.35G + 0.07B + 128 \tag{10}$$

where R refers to red-colour values, G refers to green-colour values and B refers to blue-colour values.

Skin-colour based thresholding does not require any prior training which therefore can shorten research time. The skin colour threshold is obtained by plotting colour-map based on numerous skin samples from variety of people. The boundary is define and converted into equation with purpose of select boundary for separate skin from background. Colour-type suggested for usage it the YCbCr of course and thresholding based on equation below will segregate skin pixels.

$$Skin = \begin{cases} 1, if\, Cr\,(i,j) \in [150,165] \bigcap Cb\,(i,j) \\ \in [145,190] \bigcap H\,(i,j) \in [0.02,0.1] \\ 0, Otherwise \end{cases} \tag{11}$$

where i-j = pixel x-y position, H, Cb, Cr are the Hue (Y), Blue Chrome and Red Chroma pixel value.

This process is done towards every pixel in the raw image region and saved into a binary matrix of similar rows and column as initial image. Possible improvements for this method would be to resize raw image into smaller dimension and this would help save computational power with reduced accuracy. Additional assistance to separate segmented regions can include the implementation of edge detection techniques for an example, the canny edge detection algorithm. The edge information is obtain from original image and used to deduct from segmented skin image. Resultant segmented binary image uses metamorphic technique of erode followed by dilate in order to separate nearly separated regions clearly. The next part would be to determine if clustered segmented skin are possible candidates for human face (see Figure 16).

Candidacy of human face based on segmented skin is done by taking boundary of cluster and compare height-width ratio. The equation for that can be given below.

$$
\begin{aligned}
Area\left(Si\right) &\geq T_i \times \frac{Area(Fill\left(Si\right))}{Area(Box(Si))} \\
&\geq \frac{Width(Box(Si))}{Height(Box(Si))} \in [T_3, T_4]
\end{aligned}
\tag{12}
$$

Area () computes number of pixels in the area. Fill () fills up empty region in enclosed area. Box () refers to area region boundary. Height and Width refers to respective height and width of boundary. Area Threshold, T1 = 130, Solidity Threshold, T2 = 0.65, Width to Height threshold range, T3 = 0.6, T4 = 1.8

Final face determination from candidates is based on two equations.

$$
\forall i \in \left[1, K\right], I_i = face \leftrightarrow v(I_i) \geq T
\tag{13}
$$

Figure 16. From left to right, raw image, CbCr segmentation, YCbCr segmentation

$$v(I_i) = \frac{1}{N} \sum_{j=1}^{N} \frac{\sum_x \sum_y \left[I_i^e(x,y) - \mu(I_i^e)\right]\left[F_j^e(x,y) - \mu(F_j^e)\right]}{\left(\sum_x \sum_y \left[I_i^e(x,y) - \mu(I_i^e)\right]^2\right)\left(\sum_x \sum_y \left[F_j^e(x,y) - \mu(F_j^e)\right]^2\right)} \tag{14}$$

K-Face Candidates, I_i – Face Candidate Number, $v(I_i)$-image mean value, T-Chosen threshold, $\mu()$-detonates matrix mean computation, I_i^e and F_j^e refers to corresponding edge images to Image I_i (Skin Image) and F_j (Face Image),

Once a cluster has been identified as a proper human face, boundary of said cluster is taken and processed in order to obtain mouth region. Information regarding face boundary location will enable us to easily determine location of other features (Jian-Zheng, 2011). For lip region segmentation proposed method in paper (Talea & Yaghmaie, 2011) is suggested.

The method based on (Talea & Yaghmaie, 2011) technique of utilizing facial geometry to determine lip boundary location. This method originally proposed to searching for eye pupils and corner, nose region and nostrils and finally capturing the lip region. We proposed based on the Golden Ratio (Winfrey, 2009) by just seeking out the eye pupils centroids we can determine an estimated location of the mouth region (see Figure 17).

Once the face region boundary was obtained, computation to search for eye location can be done by thresholding the first 1/2 of face region as often eyes are located at the top section of face boundary. Converting only eye region search into Hue region will causes the pupils to 'glow' from higher intensity value. Thresholding to a specific hue value will segment out eye pupils for centroid computation. From the centroid face tilt angle can be calculated and based on that we determine

Figure 17. Two illustrated images on golden ratio measurement (Goldennumber.net)

lip region. Note that according to the golden ratio edge of lips is located along a vertical path from the pupil centroids and the region for lips starts 1/3 after eye boundary. For correction purposes, we can redefine face height ratio distance according to distance between eye pupils as it is supposed to be 1/3 of face height. Based on the newly defined length, lip region can be determined to be located 1/3 from eye region with width for lip region slightly wider than horizontal distance between eye centroids (see Figure 18).

Locating lip region will assist in the final phase for visual features which is the feature extraction and tracking. The method introduced by (Cheung, Liu, & You, 2012) consist of good feature extraction and tracking method. Their paper consists of two processing phases; Lip Contour Extraction and Lip Tracking. Initial stage takes segmented mouth region through an illumination equalization method. The proposed illumination equalization consists of two stage illumination correction, the horizontal and vertical illumination correction. Both of these equations are given in Box 1.

Proposed Localized Color Active Contour Model (LCACM) algorithm takes corrected images and attempts to segment the lip contours. The algorithm uses a combination of two different semi-ellipses to surround initial suspected lip region instead of just using whole ellipse. Established boundary will be used as initial evolving curve for lip contour enclosure. Using intensity variations, colour cues and lip elliptical boundary, lip corner dots can be detected and identified (see Figure 19).

Combined Semi-ellipse will be used as initial evolving curve embedded in LCACM. Obtaining the outer curve is only part of the process. The next phase will be to model lip based on segmented region. The author proposed using 16-points geometric shape of lip contours based on (Wang, Lau, & Leung, 2004) with more flexible and physically meaningful. Once all key-points are obtained, a cubic spline

Figure 18. Algorithm results showing from left to right, face boundary, eye region, eye pupil centroids, mouth region

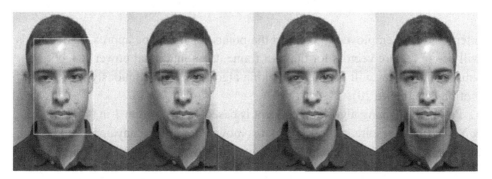

Box 1.

Horizontal Illumination,

$$\hat{L}(i,j) = \begin{cases} L(i,i) + \dfrac{(n-2j+1)\big(r(p)-l(p)\big)}{2(n-1)}, i \in [1,p] \\[2em] L(i,i) + \dfrac{(n-2j+1)\big(r(m-p)-l(m-p)\big)}{2(n-1)}, i \in (m-p,m] \\[2em] L(i,i) + \dfrac{(n-2j+1)\big(r(i)-l(i)\big)}{2(n-1)}, i \in [p,m-p] \end{cases} \quad (15)$$

Vertical Illumination,

$$\hat{L}(i,j) = \begin{cases} L(i,i) + \dfrac{(m-2i+1)\big(b(q)-t(q)\big)}{2(m-1)}, i \in [1,q] \\[2em] L(i,i) + \dfrac{(m-2i+1)\big(b(n-p)-t(n-p)\big)}{2(m-1)}, i \in (n-q,n] \\[2em] L(i,i) + \dfrac{(m-2i+1)\big(b(j)-t(j)\big)}{2(m-1)}, i \in [q,n-q] \end{cases} \quad (16)$$

i and *j refers to* x-coordinates and y-coordinates, Mean Value Local Region Size = (2p+1)×(2q+1), Image Size = m × n, L = Image Luminace before, = Image Luminance after, l(i) and r(i) = Left and Right Border mean intensity, t(j) and b(j) = border mean intensity for top and bottom.

Figure 19. From left to right, two semi-ellipse that enclose lip region, general lip shape, sixteen lip feature points (Cheung, Liu, & You, 2012)

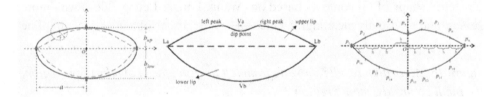

interpolation is employed to connect the points for lip shape approximation. This will be the feature vectors for the first frame. Computational power reduction for subsequent frames will be due to tracking algorithm to continuously track points' motion (see Figure 20).

Proposed tracking algorithm concept is based on Algorithm 1 in (Cheung, Liu, & You, 2012). Despite in motion pictures movement of lips may appear to be fast, but slicing a motion into individual frames shows little motion per frame which

Figure 20. Sixteen feature points being tracked in each frame

means search area for points must not vary too far from original previous frame location. Prior to processing segmented lip region, some pre-processed via noise removal and illumination equalization are required. In initial first frame we obtain all the lip parameters using convention means discussed previously. These parameters lip contour values will be extracted as feature vectors. Frame contour information and localized energy estimated location for the feature will be computed and points will be moved according to calculated motion vectors. These processes will be repeated until an acceptable level of the evolving curve surrounding majority of lip segment. Results obtain will be used for classification and for next frame computation. Process output will result in providing classification section lip curve and geometric constraints to be used as feature vectors.

Feature vectors from both audio and visual speech aspects can now be sent into a classifier for classification, however prior to classifying these features a speech model template obtaining from training said speech model for comparison purposes. There are two more aspects which we propose to conduct before sending data into classifier. The first aspect that requires some attention is the synchronism of both audio and visual features. As mentioned previously both audio and visual features are obtained at different time ratio. Seeing that video frames always lag audio frames to a factor, we proposed a concept of down sampling audio frames to match with video frequency. This concept basically averages audio feature vectors belonging to numerous 20ms audio frames that are in sequence to the extent of being in the same speed as video frames. For an example a single video frame constitutes to 0.033 seconds or 33ms while an audio frame belongs to time fraction of 20ms. However note that audio frames are overlapping frames of 10ms. Combining two frames of audio would constitute to 30ms of data which is somewhat close to visual frames of 33ms. Once both feature vectors are at the same speed, data is feed into classifier.

Other than synchronization issue, another section would refer to fusion level of both audio and visual features. We proposed using a hybrid method where weights at both prior and after classification. Proposed concept should be adaptive towards signal-to-noise ratio as increased noise levels in audio usually signify higher possibility for a misclassification. Based on ratio of noise, concept revolves at distributing normalized weights between audio features and visual features. Higher audio noise levels will cause weights to adjust accordingly and increase priority of visual features and decrease reliability on audio features for decision making. Weighted features are placed into Hidden Markov Models for both training and classification purposes. Based on literature review conducted, an article mentioned that Hidden Markov Models (HMM) is one of the best classification algorithms for speech recognition (Shivappa, Trivedi, & Rao, 2010). Reason behind such claim states that statistical method of HMM takes in consideration of countless probability for a spoken sentence and decide based on highest probability function. Complicating mathematical functions of Hidden Markov Models will not be covered as there is an overwhelming amount and by itself is a highly sufficient postgraduate research area.

FUTURE RESEARCH DIRECTION

Possible future research for audio and visual speech recognition aspects that can be venture into includes but not limited to minimizing computational power required for processing, designing algorithms that are more robust towards environmental influences. Further research can be done in attempting to minimize computational steps by deriving simplified equations from theoretical complicated functions along with data compression methods for efficient storage. Visual data requires huge storage system and high processing power, which leads to increased cost. Compression of data for processing can assist in hasting commercial ready visual and audio speech devices.

Besides reduction in complex equations, alterative research area includes designing robust algorithms towards human errors, environmental factors, and speaker dependency. Real-life implementation requires consideration of extreme conditions such as illumination and high-noise levels (image) are extreme common occurrences in reality. Besides environmental conditions, there are also speaker variables such as multiple head poses, facial feature localization, face detection, tracking and algorithm robustness to unconstrained speakers.

Artificial intelligence and classification is another huge field of venture. Proper fusion will assist in improving algorithm performance and robustness. Depending on how the weights are distributed research in seeking the optimum weight distribution will allow for higher dependency on visual features under high audio noise levels while self-adapting it to increase audio feature weight values in locations with drastic illumination conditions. Among other research areas that can be further investigated are speaker identification/verification (Chan, Goswami, Kittler, & Christmas, 2012), visual text-to-speech conversion (Tang, Fu, Tu, Hasegawa-Johnson, & Huang, 2008), speech event detection (Tan & Lindberg, 2010), video indexing and retrieval (Chen, Hero, & Savarese, 2012), speech enhancement (Sigg, Dikk, & Buhmann, 2012), and speaker localization (Fallon & Godsill, 2012). Improvement in these aspects will lead to creation of better and more humane Human-Computer Interfaces (HCI).

CONCLUSION

This chapter identified one of the many problems revolving around audio and visual speech recognition implementation. Focusing on minimizing computational power and reducing time requirement for training, proposed conceptual algorithms includes Mel-Frequency Cepstral Coefficient (MFCC) and its time derivatives, Mouth Region Segmentation based on Golden Ratio concept, Visual Feature Point Normalization, Localized Active Contour Model for Tracking, and Hidden Markov Models with its likelihood probability function. In this chapter, we also suggest numerous possible research field options for novice researchers to venture. Popular trends for current era involves improving system robustness and efficiency with some focusing more on the artificial intelligence and classification aspects. Improving robustness and efficiency will assist in development of real-time commercial production of humanoid speech recognition systems.

REFERENCES

A, B., & Hogg, D. (1994). Learning flexible models from image sequence. In *Proceedings in Euro Conference Computing Visual Journal*, (pp. 299-308). IEEE.

Anusuya, M. A., & Katti, S. K. (2009). Speech recognition by machine: A review. *International Journal of Computer Science and Information Security*, 6(3), 181–205.

Arulampalam, M. S., Maskell, S., Gordon, N., & Clapp, T. (2002). A tutorial on particle filters for online nonlinear/non-gaussian bayesian tracking. *IEEE Transactions on Signal Processing*, 50(2), 174–188. doi:10.1109/78.978374

Barbu, T. (2011). An automatic face detection system for RGB images. *International Journal of Computers, Communications & Control*, 4(1), 21–32.

Blake, A., & Isard, M. (1998). *Active contours*. London, UK: Springer-Verlag. doi:10.1007/978-1-4471-1555-7

Breen, A. (1992). Speech synthesis models: A review. *Electronics & Communication Engineering Journal*, 4(1), 19–31. doi:10.1049/ecej:19920006

Campbell, J. P. (1997). Speaker recognition: A tutorial. *Proceedings of the IEEE, 85*(9), 1437–1462. doi:10.1109/5.628714

Chan, C. H., Goswami, B., Kittler, J., & Christmas, W. (2012). Local ordinal contrast pattern histograms for spatiotemporal, lip-based speaker authentication. *IEEE Transactions on Information Forensics and Security, 7*(2), 602–612. doi:10.1109/TIFS.2011.2175920

Chen, X., Hero, A., & Savarese, S. (2012). Multimodal video indexing and retrieval using directed information. *IEEE Transactions on Multimedia, 14*(1), 3–16. doi:10.1109/TMM.2011.2167223

Chengalvarayan, R. (1999). Robust energy normalization using speech/non-speech discriminator for German connected digit recognition. [Budapest, Hungary: EUROSPEECH.]. *Proceedings of EUROSPEECH, 1999*, 61–64.

Cheung, Y.-M., Liu, X., & You, X. (2012). A local region based approach to lip tracking. *Conference on Pattern Recognition and image. Analysis, 45*(9), 3336–3347.

Chibelushi, C., Gandon, S., Mason, J., Deravi, F., & Johnston, R. (1996). Design issues for a digital audio-visual integrated database. In *Proceedings of the IEEE Colloquium on Integrated Audio-Visual Processing for Recognition, Synthesis and Communication*, (pp. 1-7). IEEE Press.

Chibelushi, C. C., Deravi, F., & Mason, J. S. (2002). A review of speech-based bimodal recognition. *IEEE Transactions on Multimedia, 4*(1), 23–37. doi:10.1109/6046.985551

Chiou, G., & Hwang, J.-N. (1997). Lipreading from color video. *IEEE Transactions on Image Processing, 6*, 1192–1195. doi:10.1109/83.605417

Cohen, L. D. (1991). On active contour models and balloons. *Computing Visual Imaging Understanding, 53*(2), 211–218. doi:10.1016/1049-9660(91)90028-N

D, G. S., & Hennecke, M. (1996). *Speechreading by humans and machines*. Berlin, Germany: Springer.

Du, J., Hu, Y., & Jiang, H. (2011). Boosted mixture learning of gaussian mixture hidden markov models based on maximum likelihoof for speech recognition. *IEEE Transactions on Audio, Speech, and Language Processing, 19*(7), 2091–2100. doi:10.1109/TASL.2011.2112352

Dupont, S., & Luettin, J. (2000). Audio-visual speech modeling for continuous speech recognition. *IEEE Transactions on Multimedia, 2*(3), 141–151. doi:10.1109/6046.865479

Duta, R., & Hart, P. (1973). *Pattern classification and scene analysis*. New York, NY: Wiley.

Eveno, N., Caplier, A., & Coulon, P.-Y. (2004). Accurate and quasi-automatic lip tracking. *IEEE Transactions on Circuits and Systems for Video Technology, 14*, 706–715. doi:10.1109/TCSVT.2004.826754

Fallon, M., & Godsill, S. (2012). Acoustic source localization and tracking of a time-varying number of speakers. *IEEE Transactions on Audio, Speech, and Language Processing, 20*(4), 1409–1415. doi:10.1109/TASL.2011.2178402

Fook, C., Hariharan, M., Yaacob, S., & Adom, A. (2012). A review: Malay speech recognition and audio visual speech recognition. In *Proceedings of the International Conference on Biomedical Engineering*, (pp. 479-484). IEEE.

G. K. L. C. (2009). Robust computer voice recognition using improved MFCC algorithm. In *Proceedings of the IEEE International Conference on New Trends in Information and Service Science*, (pp. 835-840). IEEE Press.

Goyani, M., Dave, N., & Patel, N. (2010). Preformance analysis of lip synchronization using LPC, MFCC and PLP speech parameters. In *Proceedings of the IEEE International Conference on Computational Intelligence and Communication Networks*, (pp. 582-587). IEEE Press.

Hermansky, H. (1990). Perceptual linear predictive (PLP) analysis of speech. *Acoustical Society of America Journal, 87*, 1738–1752. doi:10.1121/1.399423

Honig, S. F., Hacker, G., Brugnara, C., & Fabio. (2005). Revising perceptual linear prediction. In *Proceedings of INTERSPEECH-2005*, (pp. 2997-3000). INTERSPEECH.

Hossan, M., Memon, S., & Gregory, M. (2010). A novel approach for MFCC feature extraction. In *Proceedings of the International Conference on Signal Processing and Communication Systems*, (pp. 1-5). IEEE.

Isard, M., & Blake, A. (1998). Condensation-conditional density propagation for visual tracking. *International Journal of Computer Vision, 29*(1), 5–28. doi:10.1023/A:1008078328650

ITU-T Recommendation G.729-Annex B. (1996). *A silence compression scheme for G.729 optimized for terminals conforming to recomendation V.70*. Retrieved from http://www.itu.int

Jian-Zheng, L. (2011). Fully automatic and quickly facial feature point detection based on LK algorithm. In *Proceedings of the International Conference on Networked Computing and Advanced Information Management*, (pp. 190-194). IEEE.

Juang, B. (1991). Speech recognition in adverse environments. *Computer Speech & Language, 5*, 275–294. doi:10.1016/0885-2308(91)90011-E

Kumatani, K., & Stiefelhagen, R. (2006). Mouth region localization method based on gaussian mixture model. In *Proceedings of Advances in Machine Vision, Image Processing, and Pattern Analysis*. IEEE. doi:10.1007/11821045_12

Lahouti, F., Fazel, A., Safavi-Naeini, A., & Khandani, A. (2006). Single and double frame coding of speech LPC parameters using a lattice-based quantization scheme. *IEEE Transaction on Audio. Speech and Language Processing, 14*(5), 1624–1632. doi:10.1109/TSA.2005.858560

Lakshmi, H. C., & PatilKulakarni, S. (2010). Segmentation algorithm for multiple face detection in color images with skin tone regions using color spaces and edge detection techniques. *International Journal of Computer Theory and Engineering, 2*(4), 552–558.

Leon, C. G. (2009). Robust computer voice recognition using improved MFCC algorithm. In *Proceedings of the International Conference on New Trends in Information and Service Science*, (pp. 835-840). IEEE.

Leong, A. T. (2003). *A music identification system based on audio content similarity.* (Thesis of Bachelor of Engineering). The University of Queensland. St. Lucia, Australia.

Li, M., & Cheng, Y. (2009). Automatic lip localization under face illumination with shadow consideration. *Journal of Signal Processing, 89*(12), 2425–2434. doi:10.1016/j.sigpro.2009.05.027

Liew, A., Leung, S., & Lau, W. (2000). Lip contour extraction using a deformable model. *International Conference on Image Processing, 2*, 255-258.

Liew, A. W.-C., & Wang, S. (2009). *Visual speech recognition: Lip segmentation and mapping.* Hershey, PA: IGI Global. doi:10.4018/978-1-60566-186-5

Liu, X., & Cheung, Y.-M. (2011). A robust li tracking algorithm using localized color active contours and deformable models. In *Proceedings of the IEEE International Conference on Acoustics, Speech and Signal Processing*, (pp. 1197-1200). IEEE Press.

Liu, Y., & Sato, Y. (2008). Recovering audio-to-video synchronization by audiovisual correlation analysis. In *Proceedings of the IEEE 19th International Conference on Pattern Recognition*, (pp. 1-4). IEEE Press.

Lu, K., Wu, Y., & Jia, Y. (2010). Visual speech recognition using convolutional VEF snake and canonical correlations. In *Proceedings of the IEEE Youth Conference on Information Computing and Telecommunications*, (pp. 154-157). IEEE Press.

Mahmoud, T. M. (2008). A new fast skin color detection technique. In *Proceedings of 43rd World Academy of Science, Engineering and Technology*, (pp. 501-505). IEEE.

Majumder, A., Behera, L., & Subramaniam, V. K. (2011). Automatic and robust detection of facial features in frontal face images. In *Proceedings of the UKSim 13th International Conference on Modelling and Simulation*, (pp. 331-336). UKSim.

Marzinzik, M., & Kollmeier, B. (2002). Speech pause detection for noise spectrum estimation by tracking power envelope dynamics. *IEEE Transactions on Speech and Audio Processing, 10*(6), 341–351.

Matthews, I., Cootes, T., Bangham, J., Cox, S., & Harvey, R. (2002). Extraction of visual features for lipreading. *IEEE Transactions on Pattern Analysis and Machine Intelligence, 24*, 198–213. doi:10.1109/34.982900

McFedries, P. (2012). *iPhone 4S portable genius*. Indianapolis, IN: John Wiley & Sons, Inc.

Murase, H., & Nayar, N. (1995). Visual learning and recognition of 3-D objects from appearance. *International Journal of Computer Vision, 14*, 5–24. doi:10.1007/BF01421486

Nemer, E., Goubran, R., & Mahmoud, S. (2001). Robust voice activity detection using higher order statistics in the PLC residual domain. *IEEE Transactions on Speech and Audio Processing, 9*(3), 217–231. doi:10.1109/89.905996

Nica, A., Caruntu, A., Toderean, G., & Buza, O. (2006). Analysis and synthesis of vowels using matlab. *IEEE Conference on Automation, Quality and Testing. Robotics, 2*, 371–374.

Pawar, R., Kajave, P. P., & Mali, S. N. (2005). Speaker identification using neural networks. *Proceeding of World Academy of Science, Engineering and Technology, 7*.

Potamianos, G., Gravier, G., Garg, A., & Senior, A. W. (2003). Recent advances in the automatic recognition of audio-visual speech. *Proceedings of the IEEE, 91*(9), 1–18.

Press, O. U. (2001). *Oxford dictionary of English*. Shah Alam, Malaysia: Oxford Fajar Sdn Bhd.

Rahman, N. A., Wei, K. C., & See, J. (2006). RGB-H-CbCr skin colour model for human face detection. In *Proceedings of The MMU International Symposium on Information & Communications Technologies*. MMU.

Ramírez, J. M. (2007). Voice activity detection: Fundamentals and speech recognition systems robustness. In Grimm, M., & Kroschel, K. (Eds.), *Robust Speech Recognition and Understanding* (pp. 1–22). I-Tech Education and Publishing. doi:10.5772/4740

Ross, L. A., Saint-Amour, D., Leavitt, V. M., Javitt, D. C., & Foxe, J. J. (2006). Do you see what i am saying? Exploring visual enhancement of speech comprehension in noisy environment. *Oxford Journals Life Sciences & Medicine Cerebral Cortex, 17*(5), 1147–1153. doi:10.1093/cercor/bhl024

Shivappa, S. T., Trivedi, M. M., & Rao, B. D. (2010). Audiovisual information fusion in human-computer interfaces and intelligent environments: A survey. *Proceedings of the IEEE, 98*(10), 1–24. doi:10.1109/JPROC.2010.2057231

Sigg, C., Dikk, T., & Buhmann, J. (2012). Speech enhancement using generative dictionary learning. *IEEE Transactions on Audio. Speech and Language Processing, 20*(6), 1698–1712. doi:10.1109/TASL.2012.2187194

Sujatha, P., & Krishnan, M. R. (2012). Lip feature extraction for visual speech recognition using hidden Markov model. In *Proceedings of the International Conference on Computing, Communication and Applications*, (pp. 1-5). IEEE.

Sumby, W. H., & Pollack, I. (1954). Visual contribution to speech intellligibility in noise. *The Journal of the Acoustical Society of America, 26*, 212–215. doi:10.1121/1.1907309

Talea, H., & Yaghmaie, K. (2011a). Automatic combined lip segmentation in color images. In *Proceedings of the IEEE 3rd International Conference on Communication Software and Networks*, (pp. 109-112). IEEE Press.

Talea, H., & Yaghmaie, K. (2011b). Automatic visual speech segmentation. In *Proceedings of the IEEE 3rd International Conference on Communication Software and Networks*, (pp. 184-188). IEEE Press.

Tan, Z.-H., & Lindberg, B. (2010). Low-complexity variable frame rate analysis for speech recognition and voice activity detection. *IEEE Journal of Selected Topics in Signal Processing, 4*(5), 798–807. doi:10.1109/JSTSP.2010.2057192

Tang, H., Fu, Y., Tu, J., Hasegawa-Johnson, M., & Huang, T. (2008). Humanoid audio–visual avatar with emotive text-to-speech synthesis. *IEEE Transactions on Multimedia, 10*(6), 969–981. doi:10.1109/TMM.2008.2001355

Tanyer, S., & Özer, H. (2000). Voice activity detection in nonstationary noise. *IEEE Transactions on Speech and Audio Processing, 8*(4), 478–482. doi:10.1109/89.848229

Tashev, I. (2009). *Sound capture and processing practical approaches.* Chippenham, UK: John Wiley and Sons Ltd. doi:10.1002/9780470994443

Tsuhan Chen, R. R. (1998). Audio-visual integration in multimodal communication. *IEEE Proceedings, 86*(5), 837-852.

Tucker, R. (1992). Voice activity detection using a periodicity measure. *Proceedings of the Institution of Electrical Engineers, 139*(4), 377–380.

Vacca, J. (2007). *Biometric technologies and verification systems.* Burlington, VT: Elsevier.

Varga, P., & Moore, R. (1990). Hidden Markov model decomposition of speech and noise. In *Proceedings in International Conference in Acoustic, Speech and Signal Processing,* (pp. 845-848). IEEE.

Viterbi, A. (2006). A personal history of the viterbi algorithm. *IEEE Signal Processing Magazine, 23*(4), 120–142. doi:10.1109/MSP.2006.1657823

Wang, S., Lau, W., & Leung, S. (2004). Automatic lip contour extraction from color. *Pattern Recognition, 37*(12), 2375–2387.

WenJuan. Y., YaLing, L., & MingIIui, D. (2010). A real-time lip localization and tracking for lip reading. In *Proceedings of the 3rd International Conference on Advanced Computer Theory and Engineering,* (pp. 363-366). IEEE.

Westwood, P. (2007). *Commonsense methods for children with special educational needs* (5th ed.). New York, NY: Routledge.

Winfrey, O. (2009, August 14). *Measuring facial perfection - The golden ratio.* Retrieved April 10, 2012, from http://www.oprah.com/oprahshow/Measuring-Facial-Perfection-The-Golden-Ratio

Woo, K., Yang, T., Park, K., & Lee, C. (2000). Robust voice activity detection algorithm for estimating noise spectrum. *Electronics Letters, 36*(2), 180–181. doi:10.1049/el:20000192

Yaling, L., Wenjuan, Y., & Minghui, D. (2010). Feature extraction based on LSDA for lipreading. In *Proceedings of the International Conference on Multimedia Technology*, (pp. 1-4). IEEE.

Yingjie, M., Haiyan, Z., Yingjie, H., & Jinyang, L. (2011). Lip information extraction based on the fusion of geometry and motion features. In *Proceedings of the 8th International Conference on Fuzzy Systems and Knowledge Discovery*, (pp. 2186-2190). Shanghai, China: IEEE.

Yuhas, B. P., Jr. M. H., & Sejnowski, T. J. (1990). Neural network models of sensory integration for improved vowel recognition. *IEEE Proceedings, 78*(10), 1658-1668.

Z., Z., P., M., & S., H. T. (2009). *Emotion recognition based on multimodal information, affective information processing*. London, UK: Springer Verlag.

Zhao, W., Chellappa, R., Philips, P., & Rosenfeld, A. (2003). Face recognition: A literature survey. *ACM Computing Surveys, 35*(4), 399–458. doi:10.1145/954339.954342

Zoric, G. (2005). *Automated lip synchronization by speech signal analysis*. (Master Thesis). University of Zagreb. Zagreb, Croatia.

ADDITIONAL READING

Anusuya, M. A., & Katti, S. K. (2009). Speech recognition by machine: A review. *International Journal of Computer Science and Information Security, 6*(3), 181–205.

Arulampalam, M. S., Maskell, S., Gordon, N., & Clapp, T. (2002). A tutorial on particle filters for online nonlinear/non-gaussian bayesian tracking. *IEEE Transactions on Signal Processing, 50*(2), 174–188. doi:10.1109/78.978374

Barbu, T. (2011). An automatic face detection system for RGB images. *International Journal of Computers, Communications & Control, 4*(1), 21–32.

Blake, A., & Isard, M. (1998). *Active contours*. London, UK: Springer-Verlag. doi:10.1007/978-1-4471-1555-7

Breen, A. (1992). Speech synthesis models: A review. *Electronics & Communication Engineering Journal, 4*(1), 19–31. doi:10.1049/ecej:19920006

Campbell, J. P. (1997). Speaker recognition: A tutorial. *Proceedings of the IEEE, 85*(9), 1437–1462. doi:10.1109/5.628714

Chen, X., Hero, A., & Savarese, S. (2012). Multimodal video indexing and retrieval using directed information. *IEEE Transactions on Multimedia, 14*(1), 3–16. doi:10.1109/TMM.2011.2167223

Cheung, Y.-M., Liu, X., & You, X. (2012). A local region based approach to lip tracking. *Conference on Pattern Recognition and image. Analysis, 45*(9), 3336–3347.

Chibelushi, C. C., Deravi, F., & Mason, J. S. (2002). A review of speech-based bimodal recognition. *IEEE Transactions on Multimedia, 4*(1), 23–37. doi:10.1109/6046.985551

Cohen, L. D. (1991). On active contour models and balloons. *Computing Visual Imaging Understanding, 53*(2), 211–218. doi:10.1016/1049-9660(91)90028-N

D, G. S., & Hennecke, M. (1996). *Speechreading by humans and machines.* Berlin, Germany: Springer.

Du, J., Hu, Y., & Jiang, H. (2011). Boosted mixture learning of gaussian mixture hidden markov models based on maximum likelihoof for speech recognition. *IEEE Transactions on Audio, Speech, and Language Processing, 19*(7), 2091–2100. doi:10.1109/TASL.2011.2112352

Duta, R., & Hart, P. (1973). *Pattern classification and scene analysis.* New York, NY: Wiley.

Gómez-Mendoza, J.-B., Preto, F., & Redarce, T. (2011, May/June). Automatic lip-contour extraction and mouth-structure segmentation in images. *Scientific Image Processing.*

Hazen, T. (2006). Visual model structures and synchrony constraints for audio-visual speech recognition. *IEEE Transactions on Audio, Speech, and Language Processing, 14*(3), 1558–7916. doi:10.1109/TSA.2005.857572

Hermansky, H. (1990). Perceptual linear predictive (PLP) analysis of speech. *Acoustical Society of America Journal, 87*, 1738–1752. doi:10.1121/1.399423

Honig, S. F., Hacker, G., Brugnara, C., & Fabio. (2005). Revising perceptual linear prediction. In *Proceedings of the INTERSPEECH-2005*, (pp. 2997-3000). INTERSPEECH.

Liew, A. W.-C., & Wang, S. (2009). *Visual speech recognition: Lip segmentation and mapping.* Hershey, PA: IGI Global. doi:10.4018/978-1-60566-186-5

Potamianos, G., Gravier, G., Garg, A., & Senior, A. W. (2003). Recent advances in the automatic recognition of audio-visual speech. *Proceedings of the IEEE, 91*(9), 1–18.

Rabiner, L. R. (1989). A tutorial on hidden markov model and selected applications in speech recognition. *Proceedings of the IEEE, 77*(2), 257–286. doi:10.1109/5.18626

Ramírez, J. M. (2007). Voice activity detection: Fundamentals and speech recognition systems robustness. In Grimm, M., & Kroschel, K. (Eds.), *Robust Speech Recognition and Understanding* (pp. 1–22). I-Tech Education and Publishing. doi:10.5772/4740

Shivappa, S. T., Trivedi, M. M., & Rao, B. D. (2010). Audiovisual information fusion in human-computer interfaces and intelligent environments: A survey. *Proceedings of the IEEE, 98*(10), 1–24. doi:10.1109/JPROC.2010.2057231

Viterbi, A. (2006). A personal history of the viterbi algorithm. *IEEE Signal Processing Magazine, 23*(4), 120–142. doi:10.1109/MSP.2006.1657823

Zhao, W., Chellappa, R., Philips, P., & Rosenfeld, A. (2003). Face recognition: A literature survey. *ACM Computing Surveys, 35*(4), 399–458. doi:10.1145/954339.954342

Chapter 3
A Survey of Human Activity Interpretation in Image and Video Sequence

Xin Xu
Wuhan University of Science and Technology, China

Dongfang Chen
Wuhan University of Science and Technology, China

Li Chen
Wuhan University of Science and Technology, China

Xiaoming Liu
Wuhan University of Science and Technology, China

Xiaolong Zhang
Wuhan University of Science and Technology, China

Xiaowei Fu
Wuhan University of Science and Technology, China

ABSTRACT

In the past, a large amount of intensive research has been dedicated to the interpretation of human activity in image and video sequence. This popularity is largely due to the emergence of the wide applications of video cameras in surveillance. In image and video sequence analysis, human activity detection and recognition is critically important. By detecting and understanding the human activity, we can fulfill many surveillance related applications including city centre monitoring, consumer behavior analysis, etc. Generally speaking, human activity interpretation in image and video sequence depends on the following stages: human motion detection and human motion interpretation.

DOI: 10.4018/978-1-4666-3958-4.ch003

In this chapter, the authors provide a comprehensive review of the recent advance of all these stages. Various methods for each issue are discussed to examine the state of the art. Finally, some research challenges, possible applications, and future directions are discussed.

INTRODUCTION

After the tragic event on September 11 and the subsequent terrorist attacks around the world, the interpretation of image and video sequence has attracted much more attention. It can witness a wide range of uses in different visual surveillance related applications. By analyzing human activity in image and video sequence, especially the abnormal human motion patterns, we can predict and recognize the happening of crime and antisocial behavior in real time, such as drunkenness, fights, vandalism, breaking into shop windows, and etc.

Human activity interpretation aims to draw a description of human action and interactions through the analysis of their motion patterns (Kautz, 1987). From technique viewpoint, the interpretation of human activity in image and video sequence may be considered as a classification problem towards time varying data. It can be divided into two level procedures: the lower level extracts human motion feature from image and video sequence; while the higher level detects and interprets the temporal human motion pattern. Visual information is at first extracted from image and video sequence, and then represented in relevant features, which can be used to match with the features extracted from a group of labeled reference sequences representing typical human activity.

Generally speaking, the interpretation of human activity should consider three kinds of features including character of single object, global feature of multiple objects, and relation between object and background.

The investigation of single object's specific feature for activity interpretation has an early start. This kind of features, such as position, velocity, veins, shape, and color, can be extracted during the detecting and tracking procedure, and used to predict the corresponding information in the next time step. Then this information is used to compare with the obtained object's information to check whether an activity have taken place. However, it should be noted that the occurrence of an activity may not only change the feature of single object, but also influence the global feature of multiple objects. In a public transportation application, for example, traffic accident may be caused by break down or rear-end collision of multiple vehicles. As a result, the global feature of multiple objects should be considered. The basic principle of global feature analysis aims to detect activity using the information of multiple objects, such as average speed, region occupancy, and relative positional variations. In addition, human activity can not be analyzed without considering the influence from environment. Most of current methods for activity recognition imply the assumption of specific situation, which may contain large amount of prior knowledge. This assumption can reduce the computational complexity of environment analysis and improve the performance; however it may inevitably degrade the popularity of the technique at the same time. Thus background analysis should be taken into consideration during the recognition of human activity, and can be used to extract the relation with foreground objects.

Figure 1 illustrates the general framework for human activity interpretation. Cameras are used to capture image and video sequences. In order to improve the robustness of visual surveillance in different applications, these cameras may be of different modality including thermal infrared camera, visible color camera, etc. Using the image processing techniques, background can be extracted from the image and video sequence, which can be used to obtain aforementioned three kinds of features. After then, the image interpreting stage includes two main procedures: human detection and segmentation, and human activity interpretation. Our emphasis in this paper is to discuss the recent advance of the techniques in the image interpreting stage. Thus we focus on the two main procedures in this stage, and endeavor to provide summary of progress achieved in the research direction.

Beyond human activity interpretation, other similar fields may include behavior understanding, motion interpretation, event detection, goal recognition, or intent prediction. As pointed out in (L. Liao, 2006), although these terms may emphasize

Figure 1. General framework for human activity interpretation

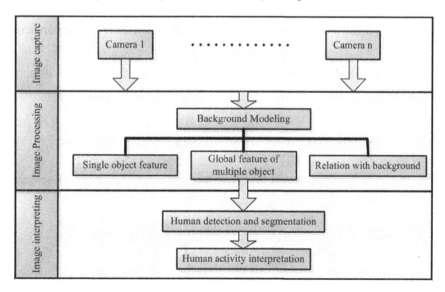

different aspects of human activity, their essential goals are the same. Therefore, in this paper, we use the term activity recognition and do not distinguish the minor differences among the different terms mentioned above.

The remainder of this chapter is organized as follows. Section 2 introduces the approved research project on human activity interpretation, and reviews its recent advance. Section 3 discusses detecting and tracking of human beings, Section 4 details the recognition and interpretation of human activity. The conclusion and future planned works are given in Section 5.

RESEARCH PROJECTS FOR HUMAN ACTIVITY INTERPRETATION

Most of the previous research projects for human activity interpretation aimed to provide easy ways for visual surveillance through processing, analysis and understanding image and video sequence using computer vision and image processing techniques. In recent years, several efforts have been made to make a description of image and video sequence based visual surveillance system (Amer, 2005; Kumar, 2008; Wang, Hu, and Tan, 2003). As stated in (Kumar, 2008), an automatic surveillance system contains a set of cameras, image and video processing unit, image and video storage unit, and visual control unit. These units are interconnected through network or other kind of device. In the framework, image and video processing unit plays an important role, which contains several procedures including human detection and segmentation, human tracking, and human activity interpretation.

From the perspective of system architecture, the development of these research projects for human activity interpretation can be divided into four stages (Kumar, 2008). Figure 2 illustrates the past approved surveillance systems for human activity

Figure 2. Past visual surveillance related research projects for human activity interpretation

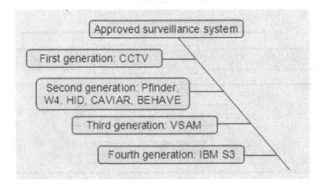

interpretation. The first generation surveillance systems embodied a number of cameras connected to a set of monitors using automatic control switches. For example, Nwagboso integrated a number of Closed Circuit Television (CCTV) system with Charge Couple Diode (CCD) Cameras technologies into existing traffic control systems. This integration can assist recognizing the events in traffic network and finally provide better traffic control, incident management and traffic law enforcement (Nwagboso, 1998). However, due to the lack of analyzing human activity in image and video sequence, the first generation surveillance systems were used in terms of a forensic tool after the events taken place, but not in terms of a facility for real-time surveillance.

Accordingly, the second generation surveillance systems were proposed, which integrated computer vision technology with CCTV systems, to automatically detect alarming events proactively rather than record them passively. The basic principle of these systems aimed at providing robust detection, tracking, and classification algorithm for activity interpretation. For example, The MIT Media Laboratory developed a real time system called Pfinder to track human and recognize their activities (Wren, 1997). Pfinder has been used in many real world applications including American Sign Language recognition, interaction video games, and distributed virtual reality. In Pfinder, the human head and hands were represented using a color and shape based multiclass statistical model to provide a wide two-dimensional viewing range. In order to solve the problem of single person tracking in complex scenes, image analysis architecture was utilized after tracking and initialization of two-dimensional images. After then, in order to monitor multiple human beings and isolated people in different postures, the University of Maryland undertook the real-time visual surveillance system W4, which can detect and track multiple people as well as monitor their activities in an outdoor environment (Haritaoglu, 2000). W4 took use of appearance models to determine human identity (who); and constructed dynamic models of people's movements to recognize human activities (what), and detect the location (where) and time (when) of these activities. This system used single camera and gray scale sensor, thus it can recognize the interaction in night-time or other low lighting conditions. The biometric feature of human can also be used for visual surveillance related applications. A typical example can be the Human Identification at a Distance (HID) project sponsored by DARPA in 2000. The basic idea of HID aims to make use of automated biometric identification technologies to detect, recognize and identify humans at significant standoff distances (Toole, 2005). The use of biometric technologies in HID can enable fast and accurate human identification at great distances, thus it was used to provide useful early warning support for force protection and homeland defense to deal with terrorist, criminal, and other human-based threats.

In spite of the above surveillance systems in America, European countries have also supported several visual surveillance related research projects. For example, the European Union sponsored the University of Reading to develop the VIEWS system for automatic monitoring of road and airport ground traffic (Tan, 1998). The three main modules in this system were Movement Detection, Vehicle Localization and Discrimination, and Vehicle Tracking. The Movement Detection module analyzed input images from a CCD camera to find Regions Of Interest (ROI) which contained road vehicles. Then Vehicle Localization and Discrimination module processed data in these ROI to determine 3D pose and category of the detected vehicles, which were used as the input of Vehicle Tracking module to automatically track each vehicle. During 2002 and 2005, the Information Society Technology (IST) funded a multi-institution project on Context Aware Vision using Image-Based Active Recognition (CAVIAR) undertaken by England, France and Portugal (List, 2005; Ribeiro, 2005; Tweed, 2005). CAVIAR aimed to provide rich description for local image through hierarchal visual process as well as using information of task, scene, function, and object contextual knowledge. This project aimed at solving two kinds of problem. The first one was city centre surveillance. Despite video cameras had been installed in city center, the lack of semi-automatic analysis of video stream led to missing real time alarm towards nighttime crime and antisocial behavior including drunk-enness, fights, vandalism, breaking and entering shop windows, etc. The other one was customers' commercial behavior analysis. Automatic analysis of customer behavior could enable marketers to evaluate their interested information such as shop layouts, changing display and promotional effect. The UK's Engineering and Physical Science Research Council funded the BEHAVE: Computed-assisted prescreening of video streams for unusual activities project undertaken by the University of Edinburgh (Andrade, 2005; Blunsden, 2006). The goal of this program was to filter out uninteresting normal activities and not occurring activities from video stream. Two image analysis processes were proposed in BEHAVE. The first one was to detect, understand, and discriminate between similar interactions, where the dynamic Hidden Markov Model was used to track individuals. And the other one was to analysis crowd scene. Due to the inconformity of tracking individuals in this scene, global probabilistic models were adopted to analysis image data obtained from short-time tracking.

In order to achieve wide area surveillance, third generation surveillance systems were designed using distributed, heterogeneous and synergistic cameras. This kind of systems was mainly used for wide range region monitoring, such as public transport and military on battlefield. For example, during 1997 and 1999, the Defense Advanced Research Projection Agency (DARPA) funded a multi-institution project on Video Surveillance and Monitoring (VSAM) undertaken by the Robotics Institute at Carnegie Mellon University (CMU) and the Sarnoff Corporation (Collins, 2000).

VSAM used cooperative multi-sensor to track human and vehicle persistently in a cluttered environment. Human and vehicle data was at first parsed from raw video sequence, after then their geolocations were calculated and inserted into dynamic scene visualization. The main goal of this project was to monitor the condition in battle field through automatically collecting and disseminating real-time information, hoping that the situational awareness of commanders and staff can be improved. The Center for Biometrics and Security Research (CBSR) at Institute of Automation, Chinese Academy of Sciences developed an intelligent visual surveillance system, which can ensure public safety and enhance protection from terrorist attacks (Fang, 2004; Liu, 2004; Wang, Tan, Ning, et al., 2004). The main function of this system included recognition of anomaly and abnormal behavior from objects, detection of deposited or missed objects, tracking of multiple objects at night time, and displaying overall traffic situation in panoramic monitoring screen through fusion of information from multiple cameras.

Recently, fourth generation surveillance systems were investigated to provide real time event alerts and long term statistical patterns from large scale distributed video cameras through standard IP-network infrastructure. This kind of systems migrated monitoring to digital IP-based network and further to wireless interconnection network. For example, IBM Corporation developed a middleware named Smart Surveillance System (S3) for surveillance systems to provide video based activities analysis capabilities (Tian, 2008). S3 can not only automatic monitor a scene, but also perform surveillance data management, event based retrieval, web based real time events alarm, and long term activity pattern statistics. There are two main components in S3. The first one was Smart Surveillance Engine (SSE), which provided the front end video analysis capabilities; and the other one was Middleware for Large Scale Surveillance (MILS), which enabled data management and retrieval functions. These two components can be used along with the IBM DB2 and IBM WebSphere Application Server to realize a series of functions, including local and web based real time surveillance and event notification, web based surveillance event retrieval, and web based surveillance event statistics.

HUMAN DETECTION AND TRACKING IN IMAGE AND VIDEO SEQUENCE

As stated previously, human activity interpretation contains two level procedures: human motion detection and tracking, and human motion recognition and understanding. Almost every image and video sequence based surveillance system for human activity interpretation starts with human motion detection and tracking. The basic principle of this task is based on the detection and segmentation of the

ROI corresponding to static or moving human beings, which provides a basis for subsequent processing such as human tracking and human behavior recognition. An illustration of this task is shown in Figure 3.

Human Detection and Segmentation

Human detection and segmentation in image and video sequence aims to detect regions corresponding to static or moving human. These regions can then used to provide a basis for later processing such as human tracking and activity interpretation. Because human detection and segmentation is related to object segmentation, thus we do not limit the scope of our topic and widen the discussion to include the detection of different foreground objects. Most of current methods were based on frame differencing or change detection. Figure 4 illustrates the typical approaches for human detection and segmentation.

Background Subtraction

Background subtraction is a simple but popular method for object detection in image and video sequences, and has been investigated since the late 1970s (Jain, 1979). It can detect moving regions in scenery with static background by taking the difference between the current image and the reference background image in a pixel-by-pixel or region-by-region mode. Most of them followed the original pixel-by-pixel mode.

Figure 3. Human detection and tracking in image and video sequence

Figure 4. Typical approaches for human motion detection

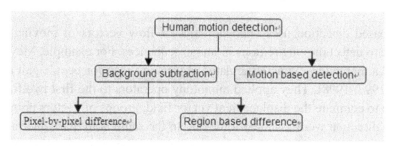

Early approaches assumed that the color or grayscale value of a pixel over time in a static scene could be modeled by a single Gaussian distribution (Wren, 1997). Later, the single Gaussian distribution assumption was loosened to a mixture of Gaussians to account for the multimodality of the background caused by shadows, repetitive object motion such as moving leaves (Friedman, 1997; Stauffer, 2000). A problem with mixture of Gaussians mode lies in the setting of the number of Gaussians according to different applications. In order to address this problem, El Gammal et al. proposed a nonparametric estimation method for background modeling (Elgammal, 2002). Since the utilized kernel density estimation was a data-driven process, multiple modes in the background were handled. A similar approach was also proposed by Mittal and Paragios (Mittal, 2004).

Besides the pixel-by-pixel difference method, there are a few region based methods for background subtraction. Toyama et al. proposed a three levels algorithm for background maintenance: the pixel level, region level and frame level. Region and frame-level information was used to verify pixel level inference(Toyama, 1999). Jing et al. (Jing, 2003) and Monnet et al. (Monnet, 2003) proposed a method to explicitly model the dynamic, textured background via an Autoregressive Moving Average model, which was incrementally learned and then used to segment foreground objects. Different from other methods, Ko et al represented the signature of each pixel using a distribution of pixel intensities in a neighborhood (Ko, 2008). The distribution signature is relatively insensitive to small movements of the textured background and at the same time they are more robust than individual pixel statistics in detecting foreground objects. Benedek et al. proposed a new model for foreground and shadow detection in image sequences (Benedek, 2008). The foreground model is based on spatial statics of the neighboring pixel values, which improves the detection of background or shadow-colored object parts. A Markov Random Field (MRF) model is used to enhance the foreground and background separation. The model can work without any restrictions or assumptions on image quality, objects' shape and speed.

Motion-Based Detection

Motion based detection uses characteristics of flow vectors of moving objects over time to detect moving regions in image sequences. For example, Meyer et al. proposed a method to extract articulated objects in video for people gait analysis (Meyer, 1997, 1998). They applied monotony operators to the first two frames of the video to compute the displacement vector field, groups of vectors pointed into the same direction were assumed to belong to the same body part, and then each body part was extracted and tracked by its contour. To extract the 3D motion and position of the body part, they matched the 2D contour extracted from the image sequence and the contour of the projection of 3D block onto the image plane. They could obtain the trajectories of the different body parts (the head, the trunk, the legs, and the arms) by estimating these positions. Optical-flow based methods can be used to detect independently moving objects or object parts. However, they are computation intensively and are sensitive to noise.

Besides the above methods, there are several other approaches for object detection. Jabri et al. proposed a method to detect and locate people in video using adaptive fusion of color and edge information (Jabri, 2000). Foreground confidence maps were built from color channels and edge magnitude with mean and standard deviation values, and used to represent the results of background subtraction. The foreground was extracted from the confidence map with threshold of the final integrated confidence map. Zhao et al. investigated individual human segmentation from foreground in crowded situations from a static camera in a Bayesian framework (Zhao, et al., 2008; Zhao & Nevatia, 2003, 2004). The foreground blobs were extracted by a change detection method. They used human shape information to build the model. Four ellipsoids corresponding to head, torso and two legs are used to build the human shape. The segmentation was formulated into a Bayesian framework, several factors such as human shape, human height, camera model, human head candidates are integrated into the framework, and finally the problem was computed with a Markov chain Monte Carlo approach. Later, they extended their work to more detail segmentation and body posture estimation. Sheikh et al. used a joint domain-range representation of image pixels utilized the correlation information of spatially proximal pixels, and built both background and foreground models simultaneously (Sheikh, 2005). The final background and foreground segmentation was achieved in a MAP-MRF framework.

Human Tracking

After segmentation, tracking is generally the next step for visual surveillance systems. Tracking human beings typically involves matching human in consecutive frames using features such as points, lines or regions. In the view of the features to tracking and following the classification used in (Wang, Hu, and Tan, 2003), we divide the tracking methods into four major categories: region based tracking, contour based tracking, feature based tracking and model based tracking. Certainly, the classification is not absolute, some methods may belong to different categories (Yilmaz, 2006). The typical approaches for human tracking are shown in Figure 5.

Region-Based Tracking

Region based tracking algorithms track objects according to features extracted from image regions corresponding to the moving objects. These methods are generally used with background subtraction to detect moving regions (Karmann, 1990). Wren et al. presented a system named Pfinder to track human body in indoor environment with static background (Wren, 1997). The background scene was modeled as a texture surface with a mean color value and a distribution about that mean for each pixel. The background model was updated recursively for new visible pixels. People were modeled as a combination of some blobs which representing various body parts such as head, torso and the four limbs. Each blob was described in statistics of a spatial (x,y) and color (Y,U,V) Gaussian distributions over the pixels. The background scene was modeled with Gaussian distribution of pixel color values. A pixel was assigned to body part blobs or background with a log likelihood measure. A moving human can be successfully tracked by tracking each small blob in their method. Hager et al. proposed a framework for object tracking which can deal with the problem of geometric distortion due to pose changing, illumination changing and partial oc- clusion (Hager, 1998). In their method, all points in the target region are assumed to move coherently, which enable them to develop a low-order parametric model for the image motion. The motion tracking problem was solved by minimizing the sum-of-squared differences between two regions. Based on the same framework, illumination change was integrated naturally without increasing the complexity

Figure 5. Typical approaches for human tracking

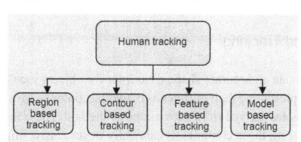

of computation. The partial occlusion problem was solved in the same framework with robust optimization problem and Iteratively Reweighted Least Squares (IRLS) technique was applied. The method was tested on human face tracking with good results. McKenna et al. proposed an adaptive background subtraction combining color and gradient information to deal with shadows and unreliable color information for people tracking (McKenna, 2000). The background model combined pixel RGB and chromaticity values with image gradients, and was adaptively updated. Variances of these features were used to delineate foreground from background. The combined RGB and gradient could eliminate some types of shadows. The tracking was performed at three levels of abstraction: region, people and groups. Regions could be deleted, merged or split during the tracking process considering their tracking consistency, position distance. The foreground model was represented with color histogram and color distributions. The tracking system has been successfully run using several different camera and frame-grabber setups. Lipton et al. presented a tracking system from a real-time video stream. In the method, moving targets are detected with temporal differencing (Lipton, 1998). After obtaining the absolute difference between the current frame and the previous frame was obtained, a threshold was used to detect motion regions. The moving regions were classified using maximum likelihood estimation with temporal consistency constraint into three categories: human, vehicle or background clutter. After classification, targets were tracked by a combination of appearance-based correlation matching and motion detection. The method has been successfully applied to human and vehicular tracking. Ahn et al. proposed an integrated computer vision system to track multiple persons and extract their silhouette with a pan-tilt stereo camera (Ahn, 2009). The system consists of three modules: detection, tracking and silhouette extraction. Detection was performed by camera ego-motion compensation and disparity segmentation. Tracking was achieved with histogram based mean shift method and graph-cut was used for silhouette extraction.

Region based tracking method are robust to small disturbances and work well in scenes with only a few objects. However, they cannot reliably handle occlusion between humans and they have difficulties when dealing shadows, perhaps one way to deal with the shadow was to exploit the fact that shadow usually changes the Luminance but not chroma.

Contour-Based Tracking

Contour can provide an accurate shape descriptor for objects such as hands, head, and human by representing their outlines as bounding contours. Most contour based tracking methods are derived from active contour method. These methods perform tracking by updating these contours dynamically in successive frames (Paragios,

2000; Peterfreund, 1999; Rathi, 2007). Peterfreund proposed a nonrigid object tracking method using Kalman-filter based active contour model (Peterfreund, 1999). The model used image gradient and optical flow measurements along the contour as system measurements. Velocity measurements which are not consistent with previous motion estimation and the corresponding edge-based potential field measurements were rejected, which improved the robustness to image clutter and to occlusions. Two tracking methods were proposed, a Batch-Mode model using estimates of image velocity at the contour position as input, and a Real-Time mode using optical-flow measurement and measurements of image-gradient as input. The batch-mode method could derive better tracking results under high clutter background while the real-time mode method could achieve higher speed. Paragios et al. proposed a variational framework to detect and tracking multiple moving objects in video (Paragios, 2000). Motion detection was determined using a probabilistic edge detector that is based on the analysis of the interframe difference function, which was approximated as a mixture model of two components, the static background, and the moving objects. The tracking boundaries were initialized using an edge detector applied to the original frame. The detection and tracking problem were solved in a common framework employing the geodesic active contour objective function. The function was minimized using a gradient descent method and the level set was used to representing the evolving curve. They reduced the computation cost by a new numerical method exploiting advantages from both the Narrow Band and Fast Marching algorithms. They tested the method on car tracking in highway sequence and football player sequences and good results were obtained. Relied on the one direction propagation evolution and only edge information was exploited, their method has several limitations, such as could not deal with cluttered moving background, could not deal with fast moving objects, and could not deal with occlusion. Rathi et al. proposed a particle filtering algorithm for geometric active contours to track moving and deforming objects (Rathi, 2007). They incorporated a prior system model into the observation model. A particle filter was used to estimate the conditional probability distribution of global rigid motion and the contour. Their method could deal with partial occlusions and could robustly track the target even in the absence of a learnt model. Based on geometric active contour algorithm, their method allowed for changes in topology of tracking target. Their method has been tested on car sequences and people sequences.

Compared with region based tracking algorithm, contour based algorithm is more efficient. Another advantage is that when the contour is represented with level set, the topology changes of region split or merge can be handled well. A disadvantage of contour based tracking method is that they require an accurate initialization, which is difficult for complex articulated objects.

Feature-Based Tracking

Feature based tracking methods use features such as distinguishable points or lines on the object to realize the tracking task. It includes feature extraction and feature matching. Features including point, edge, color and texture features. Kalman and particle filtering have been well developed in the computation vision community for tracking.

Nummiaro et al. proposed an integration of color distributions into particle filtering (Nummiaro, 2003). Color distribution is invariant to rotation and scale, is robust to partial occlusion and has low-cost to calculate. Their color distribution of pixels was weighted by distances from the region center, which decrease the weight of pixels far from the region center. Distribution distance was measured based on Bhattacharyya coefficient. The target model was updated with a forgetting process. Their method was compared with mean shift algorithm and Kalman tracker. Perez et al. proposed a sequential Monte Carlo tracking technique using color histogram information (Pérez, 2002). The state (consists of position and scale of the object) transfer was modeled in a second-order auto-regressive dynamics. Hue-Saturation-Value (HSV) color space was chosen to model the color histogram, and the distance between distributions was derived from the Bhattacharyya similarity coefficient between histograms. Their framework has been extended in several ways, such as multi-part color model, background modeling, and multiple objects tracking. An automatic initialization based on skin was also proposed for people tracking applications. Their method could robustly track fast moving regions and could deal with temporary occlusion problem.

Model-Based Tracking

Model based tracking algorithms perform tracking by matching object models to image data. The geometric structure of human body can be represented as stick figure, 2D contour or 3D volumetric models. So model based tracking can be classified accordingly.

The stick figure representation includes structure information of the human skeleton with a combination of line segments linked by joints, with line representing the head, torso and four limbs (Iwasawa, 1997; Karaulova, 2000). The stick figure model can be obtained in various ways, such as using a medial axis transformation and a distance transformation (Iwasawa, 1997). Karaulova et al. proposed a hierarchical stick figure model of human dynamics for view independent tracking of the human body with Hidden Markov Models in image sequences (Karaulova, 2000).

2D contour representation of human body is related to human body structure projections in image planes, and human body parts are generally represented as 2D ribbons or blobs. Chang et al. developed a ribbon-based vision system to analyze the motion information of walking people (Chang, 1996). They use eight joint angles on the human body (on shoulders, elbows, hips, and knees). Arms and legs are positioned with a ribbon finding procedure after segmentation. The principal axes of each ribbon (arm or leg) are calculated with Hotelling transform. Angles between limb and body are extracted from the principal axes and are used for motion analyses.

A disadvantage of 2D model is that it is affected by the viewing angle, thus several researchers have used 3D volumetric models to overcome this disadvantage. Rohr introduced a model based approach for the recognition of pedestrians, in which the human body is presented by a 3D model consisting of cylinders (Rohr, 1994). The human body is represented by 14 cylinders with elliptic cross sections which are connected by joints. The origin of the coordinate system of the whole body is at the center of the torso. The straight line contour model is matched with gray-value edges. Data from medical motion studies are used to model the movement of walking and Kalman filter is used to estimate model parameters. Sigal et al. proposed a 3D human tracking method using a graphical model (Sigal, 2004). Human body is modeled as a collection of loosely-connected limbs. Human pose and motion estimation is solved with non-parametric belief propagation using a variation of particle filtering. Limb and head detectors permit automatic initialization and are incorporated into the inference process during tracking. Brubaker et al. proposed a physical-based model for 3D person tracking (Brubaker, 2010). The model captures important physical properties of bipedal locomotion such as balance and ground contact based on a biomechanical characterization of lower-body dynamics. Tracking is performed by simulating the model with a particle filter, producing physically plausible estimates of human motion for the torso and lower body. The tracker can handle occlusion, varying gait styles and produce realistic 3D reconstructions. Caillette et al. introduced a 3D human body tracker based on Monte-Carlo Bayesian framework (Caillette, 2008). The human body model is based on a kinematic tree consisting of 14 segments. The parameter space is automatically partitioned into Gaussian clusters each representing an elementary motion, and the transitions between clusters use the predictions of a variable length Markov model. The efficient evaluation scheme is based on volumetric reconstruction and blob fitting. Their method was tested on tracking long video sequences exhibiting rapid and diverse movements.

The advantage of 3D model method is that it is robust to occlusion and contains more information for further analysis. A disadvantage of 3D model method is it often makes unrealistic assumptions regarding possible motions and kinematic constraints, and requires intensive computation.

HUMAN ACTIVITY INTERPRETATION

After detecting and tracking of moving human beings in image and video sequences, features can be extracted and used for the interpretation of human activities. Activity interpretation aims to analyze and recognize human motion patterns. Activity interpretation may be considered as a classification problem of time varying data. There are two key issues should be addressed during the recognition of human motion. The first one is how to obtain primitive features and motion patterns from training sets; the other one is how to enable the training and matching methods effectively to cope with the minor deviation in both temporal and spatial scales both for primitive and complex motion patterns. An illustration of this task is shown in Figure 6.

Currently, the investigation of human activity interpretation mainly focused on the movement of head, gesture, and gait. From technique viewpoint, the interpretation of human motion patterns is mainly based on image processing and artificial intelligence. As stated in (Aggarwal, 1999), these techniques can be divided into two kinds of approaches: template matching and state space.

Template Matching

Template matching method aimed to extract motion features from the given image sequence, and transferred into certain motion pattern. These motion patterns were compared with a group of labeled reference sequences representing typical human activities. This method has an early start. For example, Niyogi used this method for human gait analysis (Niyogi, 1994). The XT-slice, which was used to detect motion pattern, was generated by connecting the lowest line in each image. A person walking frontoparallel to image plane in XYT volume was represented as a characteristic pattern. Due to the over time variations of contours of the walkers, snakes were used to find the bounding contours. Individual gait can be recognized by the similarity comparison of these spatiotemporal snakes with detected motion pattern. After then, Oren improved Niyogi's method. He proposed trainable object detection architecture

Figure 6. Human activity interpretation in image and video sequence

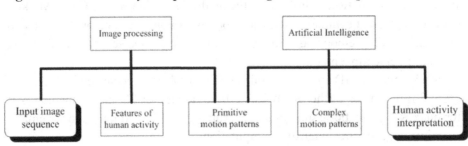

to recognize pedestrian in static images with cluttered scene (Oren, 1997). Different from Niyogi's method, this architecture did not rely on any priori model or motion template, but defined the shape of an object as a series of regions and relationships between them using the wavelet template. These wavelet templates were compared with the image frames, in order to search for the matching action. This template matching system had a pedestrian detection rate of 52.7% on frontal and rear views, with a false positive rate of 1 for every 5000. Ben-Arie described human behavior as temporal sequence of pose vectors that represent the motion of major body parts (Ben-Arie, 2002). They constructed a database for major body parts, in which all the activity templates were stored in multidimensional hash tables in the form of pose entries. Voting Approach and multidimensional indexing were used in the recognition stage to improve the efficiency and stability of matching. This method was used to recognize eight different human activities, including jumping, kneeling, picking up an object, putting down an object, running, sitting down, standing up, and walking. Result indicated that the recognition of these activities can be invariant to viewpoint variations to the extent of 30 degrees in viewing angle.

As stated previously, the interpretation of human activity can be treated as a classification problem of time varying data. Dynamic Time Warping (DTW) therefore can be used to form template for matching human motion pattern. For example, Takahashi proposed a method to recognize dexterous manipulation actions, such as hand motion (Takahashi, 1994). The model was represented using spatio-temporal vector fields and a spotting algorithm with segmentation-free and frame-by-frame characteristic. They presented a multiview motion model according to several standard sequence patterns obtained from different views. This method was used to recognize six actions during reading, such as place a book, open a book, turn to the next page, turn to the previous page, close a book, and take a book. Results show that this method got a good performance in recognizing these actions even if the viewing direction of the input image deviated from those of standard sequence patterns. Bobick and Wilson define a gesture as a series of states in the measurement and configuration space, which can be proved to be repeatable and variable from training sets of the sample trajectories (Bobick and Wilson, 1995). These states were positioned and shaped according to a prototype of the gesture; therefore, the ensemble of examples was tightly constrained along with a great deal of variability. They computed a prototype trajectory for an ensemble trajectory, through which they defined the configuration state. Then the gesture can be recognized from an unsegmented, continuous stream of sensor data. The configuration-state representation had been computed the motion trajectory taken from three devices: the two-dimensional movements of a mouse input device, the hand movement obtained from a magnetic spatial position and orientation sensor, and changing eigenvector projection coefficients measured by an image sequence.

Above methods interpret human activity through detecting and recognizing specific parts of actor. However, it may encounter difficulty with repetitive motion. In order to improve the robustness, low-level features of human motion are adopted. For example, Polana and Nelson presented a method to recognize walking or other repetitive motion, and developed a real-time system to recognize and classify these activities in gray-level image sequence (Polana, 1994). The segmentation and tracking of motion was at first computed in optical flow field between successive frames, and then the optical flow frame was decomposed along the X and Y coordinate in space grid. Each scale change of the grid was accumulated to form a high dimensional vector template for recognition. Bobick and Davis proposed a view based method to represent and recognize action (A. Bobick, and Davis, J., 1996). They used a static image called Motion-History Image (MHI), where intensity is a function of recent motion sequence. The MHI was used to represent the activity, and stored as temporal template to match against the instances of actions. A real time system was developed based on this method and applied to room monitoring and an interactive game. Result indicated that this system can recognize 180° views of the actions including sitting, arm waving, and crouching. After then, they introduced Motion Energy Images (MEI) to incorporate MHI to represent and recognize human activity (Bobick and Davis, 2001). Image sequence was at first processed by background subtraction and binarization. The MEI can be accumulated over time by these binary motion images which contained the motion field, and enhanced to be MHI. Each activity was composed of MEI and MHI in different views, from which the square based motion features can be abstracted for template matching. They examined this method in a set of 18 aerobic exercises, and got a good classification result. Lu developed a system to automatically track multiple hockey players and simultaneously recognize their actions (Lu, et al., 2009). This system used Hue–Saturation–Value (HSV) color histogram and the Histogram of Oriented Gradients (HOG) descriptor to represent the color and shape information of the image of hockey players respectively. Switching Probabilistic Principal Component Analysis (SPPCA) template updater was used to predict and update the template when the shapes of players changed. The parameters of SPPCA template updater can be trained off-line through a set of labeled examples. As a result, the position and size of the player can be efficiently tracked by the combination of SPPCA template updater and Boosted Particle Filter (BPF). And the action description can be generated using a Sparse Multinomial Logistic Regression (SMLR) classifier which classified the HOG descriptors into action categories.

Template matching approach establishes an internal list of human motion pattern, which can be used as template to match with an ongoing activity. The matching can be computational simple, and is quite proper for real time visual surveillance. However, template matching approach also presents several drawbacks. The significant one is that, in view of the way of generating template, new motion pattern cannot be discovered (Zhao and Nevatia, 2004). In addition, template-matching method is sensitive to the variation of motion duration and noise.

State Space

For human activity interpretation, most efforts have been concentrated on using state space approaches (Farmer, 1991). State space approach defined each static posture as a single state, which was then correlated with each other using statistical model. Thus the motion sequence can be treated as an ergodic process through different states. For each motion sequence, the joint probability was calculated to find the maximum value for classification. This method can overcome the problem of motion duration variation, because each state was accessed several times. However, state space approach pose two major difficulties. The first one is the establishment of intrinsic nonlinear models, which takes complex iterative computation; the other one lies in the model adaptability to different applications.

Pattern Recognition Methods

Early efforts for human activity interpretation are based on pattern recognition techniques. Typical methods include Petri Net (Castel, 1996), declarative models (Rota, 2000), finite state machine (Ayers, 1998), probabilistic syntactic approach (Ivanov, 2000), etc. Lu and Ferrier proposed a two-threshold, multidimensional segmentation algorithm to automatically divide complex behavior into a series of simple linear dynamic models (Lu and Ferrier, 2004). No prior assumption needed to be made about the number of models or about the interval of task cycle. Each model can represent motion in a compact form using parameters of a damped harmonic dynamic model. Thus, event classification can be performed through cluster analysis with the model parameters as input. They used this method to analyze a karate sequence, which got a good performance in motion segmentation and event classification.

Neural Network is another popular used pattern recognition technique, and has been used to interpret human activity. Neural Network is able to match time varying data. For example, Rosenblum proposed a radial basis function network architecture to learn the relationship between motion pattern of facial feature and human emotions (Rosenblum, 1994). The learning of relationship was divided into three levels. At the high level the emotions were identified; at the mid level detected motion of facial features; at the low level recovered motion directions. They used individual emotion network to recognize the smile and surprise emotions through training by viewing a set of sequenced one emotion for many subjects. The results show that the success rates of retention, extrapolation, and rejection ability were respectively about 88%, 73%, and 79%. Guo proposed a stick figure model to represent human body structure, and used a BP neural network to classify motions of the stick figure (Guo, 1994). Human activity can be recorded as a series of stick figure parameters, which can be used as the input of a motion pattern analyzer. The recognition of human motion pattern can be divided into two stages. In the first stage, model-based method was used to track human behavior, which was to find the stick figure model in each frame. In the second stage, BP neural network was used to classify human motion into three categories: walking, running and other motions. The time sequence of stick figure model parameters was then transformed into Fourier domain by DFT, and the first four Fourier components were selected as the input of the neural network.

An extension of Neural Network, Space-Time Delay Neural Network (STDNN), was proposed by Lin to process the space-time dynamic information in activity recognition (Lin, 1999). STDNN is a unified structure fused with the low-level spatio-temporal feature extraction and high-level spatio-temporal recognition, which inherited the spatio-temporal shift-invariant recognition ability from the Time Delay Neural Network (TDNN) and Space Displacement Neural Network (SDNN). Different from Multilayer Perceptron (MLP), TDNN, and SDNN, STDNN was composed by vector-type nodes and matrix-type links, thus it can accurately represented in a neural network. This method was then used in two set of experiments. The first one was to test STDNN's spatiotemporal shift-invariant ability through the Moving Arabic Numerals (MAN), and results show good generalization ability. The other one was the lipreading of Chinese isolated words, in which the lip motions based on the inputs of real image sequences can be recognized.

Graphical Model

Most of the current efforts for state space based human activity interpretation used graphical models, which can serve as an efficient way to do probability inference representing as factorization in computation. Graphical model is a powerful tool for modeling dependencies among random variables, and can be divided into two categories: Directed Acyclic Graph (DAG) and Undirected Graphical Models (UGM). The typical approaches are shown in Figure 7.

Hidden Markov Model

One of the most typical directed acyclic graphs is Hidden Markov Model (HMM). HMM, a kind of statistical model, was broadly used in speech recognition in early year, then it was successfully applied in the interpretation of human activity. For

Figure 7. State-space approach for human activity interpretation

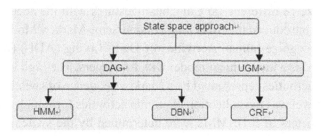

example, Yamato proposed a bottom-up approach to recognize human behavior using the low-level features including motion, color, and texture from two dimensional 25*25 pixel blocks (Yamato, 1992). The temporal pattern for each activity was used to train HMM respectively. Then optimization of the HMM model was fulfilled by the Baum-Welch algorithm. And the result of forward calculation can be used for recognition in the given image sequence. Babu presented a method to classify human independent action in compressed MPEG video (Babu, 2001). The features for classification were extracted from motion vectors in partial decoding of the MPEG video including three categories: Projected l-D feature, 2-D polar feature, and 2-D Cartesian feature. These motion vectors were used as the input of HMM to classify 7 different actions: walk, run, jump, bend up, bend down, twist right, and twist left. Starner and Pentland applied HMM in another application: American Sign Language (ASL). They presented an extensible system to recognize sentence level ASL (Starner, 1995). The tracking procedure obtained information in terms of only a coarse description of hand shape, orientation, and trajectory, not in terms of an explicitly modeling of fingers. Then this information was used as input of HMM for recognition of the signed words.

In order to model the dependence on the parameter of HMM explicitly, extension of the standard HMM should be investigated. Wilson and Bobick proposed a framework to model parameterized movements which can simultaneously extract the parameter of interest movement and recognize them (Wilson, 1998). This framework added a global parametric variation in the output probabilities of the states of the HMM to extend the standard HMM method for gesture recognition. And Expectation-Maximization (EM) method was used to train this parametric HMM. This framework was successfully used to recognize two different set of actions: a size gesture and a point gesture. Besides the extension in parameter, the extension in the coupling of several HMMs with temporal causal was also studied. Brand proposed an algorithm for coupling two HMMs with temporal causal (Brand, 1997). This algorithm inducted conditional probabilities between component HMMs and a joint HMM to establish their projection relationships. They used this algorithm for recognizing the gestures in Tai Chi Chuan. Results indicated Coupled HMMs were able to recognize 18 different Tai Chi Chuan gestures with the accuracies as high as 94%. Duong introduced the Switching Hidden Semi-Markov Model (S-HSMM) to study and recognize human Activities of Daily Living (ADL) (Duong, 2005, 2009). S-HSMM is a hierarchical model with two layers. The high level contained a set of atomic activities represented by a Markov sequence of switching variables; while the low level was the collection of atomic activities form high-level and their duration, parameters of S-HSMMs were determined by the switching variable at the high level. Captured atomic activities were at first modeled in the low level, and then form high-level activities in the house.

Recently, HMM was incorporated with other machine learning method to improve the effectiveness of recognition. Ahmad used Principal Component Analysis (PCA) to reduce the feature space of body shape image, then human activity can be effectively represented by multidimensional discrete HMM (Ahmad, 2006, 2008). In this method, the optical flow velocity feature was used for modeling human actions in different view directions, which was extracted from RGB color components and human body shape feature. This method was tested in the Korea University gesture database, and got a robust and accurate result. Tran and Davis interpreted human activity using FOL rules and Markov Logic Networks (Tran, 2008). Based on these techniques, the common sense domain knowledge can be represented. Detected events were at first used to generate ground logical rules in the knowledge base, which was then added into the Markov network to update the network parameters or structures. The marginal probability of any event can be determined through the probabilistic inference on this network. This system was successfully used in parking lot to recognize the interactions between human and vehicles.

HMM can be served as an efficient solution for human activity interpretation, and widely used until recently. However, it also presents several drawbacks. The significant one lies in the probabilistic dependency of HMMs. Each human activity needs large number of training samples for interpretation. During the recognition procedure, an ongoing activity needs to match with an internal list of activity pattern. As a result, it is difficult to interpret new human activity because of the lack of the internal list based training sample.

Dynamic Bayesian Network

Bayesian is another example of Directed Acyclic Graph, and has been applied in interpreting human activity for many years. For instance, Buxton and Gong developed a visual surveillance system, in which they used Bayesian belief networks to model dynamic dependencies between parameters involved in visual interpretation (Buxton, 1995). Conceptual knowledge of both the scene and the visual task were used to provide constraints, and they controlled the system using dynamic attention and selective processing. This method was used in a traffic surveillance application to fulfill the task including behavioral evaluation, motion segmentation, and tracking. Results show that such an approach had a good performance to recognize simple tasks like overtaking and give-way behavior involving just two vehicles, and it was capable of segmenting very close moving objects under incomplete visual evidence. Madbahushi and Aggarwal used a Bayesian framework to automatically recognize human behavior (Madbahushi, 1999). A static CCD camera captured images at 2 frames per second from both the frontal and lateral view. The movement of head was tracked through the comparison of consecutive frames in monocular grayscale image sequences, and then the difference in the co-ordinates of the head over successive frames was computed to design the system. The action with least differences value was identified to be closest to the sample activity model. In order to evaluate the system, 77 sequences including 38 training sets and 39 testing ones were selected for experiment, which were taken of a person walking, standing, sitting, bending down, getting up, falling, squatting, rising and bending sideways. And 31 motions from the 39 testing sequence were accurately recognized.

There are also investigations on the fusion of Bayesian Network with HMM. Robertson and Reid developed a video sequence based system for activity recognition (Robertson, 2006). The input and output of HMM was the feature in terms of distributions over action types, not in terms of low level visual features. Position and velocity information were selected as features for searching in a training set. The results of searches were then fused with Bayesian Network to find the Maximum Likelihood (ML) spatio-temporal action at each instant, and then modeled human action sequence using HMM. High level activities can be recognized through calculation the probabilities of current action in HMM. They successfully used this method to recognize human actions in tennis game. Oliver developed a real-time visual surveillance system to recognize the type of interaction between people, such as following another person, altering one's path to meet another, and so forth (Oliver, 2000). The modeling of interaction used a Bayesian approach to recognize both prior knowledge and evidence from data. And they compared HMM and CHMM for recognition of behaviors and interactions. Result indicated that the CHMM model performed better in efficiency and accuracy. Manfredotti recently proposed a novel method to improve the multi-target tracking task for surveillance purpose, which was based on Relational Dynamic Bayesian Networks (RDBN) to represent the interactions between moving objects (Manfredotti, 2009). In this RDBN-based model, relationships were treated as variables with changing values. As a result, the evolution of objects relationships can be tracked during tracking them in the domain. Then he detailed a transition model that used First-Order Logic relations and a two-phase Particle Filter algorithm to track the relations.

CRF

A typical example of Undirected Graphical Models is Conditional Random Fields (CRF), which have been emerged into behavior understanding in the last few years. Vail compared Conditional Random Fields (CRFs) to Hidden Markov Models (HMMs) (Vail, 2007a). CRFs, compared with HMMs, can easily incorporate domain knowledge because of three key factors. First, sophisticated features typically incorporated information from more than a single time step, which violated the independence assumptions in HMM. Then, link state features in model were far from easy to interprete, due to its way to factorize probabilities. And finally, the difference can be found between HMM and CRF models for activity recognition. They tested these two models both in the hourglass and the unconstrained tag domains. In all of the experimental results, conditional random fields scored higher or on par with hidden Markov models in terms of classification accuracy. Chieu applied Conditional Random Fields (CRF) to solve the two activity recognition tasks proposed at the Physiological Data Modeling Contest (PDMC) (Chieu, 2006). The Linear Chain CRF (L-CRF), compared with other participants at the PDMC, can get the best recognition result. And the Generalized Expectation Maximization was used to train the partially labeled sequences to further improve the discrimination. In addition, they proposed a Mixture CRF (M-CRF) to make use of the user data which allowed inference either with or without this information. Result of the TV task indicated that M-CRF outperformed L-CRF even when the user was assumed to be unknown during testing.

In order to take into consideration of the correlation and context of high-level user, hierarchical CRF was proposed. Liao developed a system to recognize human behavior and label their places, which was modeled by a hierarchical CRF (Liao, et al., 2007). High-level user's context was taken into consideration when detecting significant places, thus it can interpret user's data in detail including transportation activities as well as activities performed at particular places. This system performed inference using loopy belief propagation, and its parameter was determined by pseudo-likelihood. In addition, Fast Fourier Transforms was computed within belief propagation to efficiently reason about aggregations. They collected GPS data traced from four different persons, approximately six days of data per person, for experiment. And the result indicated the robustness of this system. Hu and Yang presented a probabilistic and goal-correlation based two-level framework to deal with concurrent and interleaving goals from observed activity sequences (Hu, 2008). At the low level, Skip-Chain Conditional Random Fields (SCCRF) was used to estimate whether a newly goal exist in the given observed activity. While at the high level, relational graph was adopted to represent the correlation between different goals. They used three datasets in a cross validation setting to compare this algorithm with two other methods, including an interleaving but not concurrent goal recognizer SCCRF and Factorial Conditional Random Field (FCRF). And their algorithm outperformed these baseline algorithms.

Due to the need of selecting the most relevant features from incomplete information or low-level noise sensor data, some measures were used to incorporate with CRF. Vail adopted l1 regularization for the feature selection in CRF to incorporate many non-independent features of the sensor data and the most relevant features (Vail, 2007b). They tested this method in the robot tag domain using data from both real and simulated robots. CRF was trained with either no regularization, l1 regularization, or l2 regularization. Result demonstrated that l1 regularization can produced comparable recognition rates to other algorithms while at the same time eliminating more than 90% features in the model. Truyen proposed a semi-supervised method to train the CRFs and the Maximum Entropy Markov Model (MEMMs) aiming at incomplete information from low level noise sensor data (Truyen, 2008). The EM algorithm was used as an alternative to maximise the log-likelihood with respect to the incomplete data, its expectation (E-step) and maximisation (M-step) at step j was respectively to calculate the quantity and maximised the concave lower bound of the log-likelihood with respect to w. Thus, this method can reduce the labeling effort, and was more adaptable and accurate. They applied this method in the video surveillance domain, and compared the performance with the equivalent Partially Hidden Markov Models (PHMMs). Results indicated the proposed method outperformed PHMMs. Yin proposed a Spatio-Temporal Event Detection (STED) algorithm based on Dynamic Conditional Random Field (DCRF) model (Yin, 2009). The DCRF model incorporated temporal constraints among contiguous spatial fields to extend CRFs. Different from DBNs and MRFs, DCRFs relaxed independent spatial-temporal relationship among events in a unified probabilistic framework, and thus it can deal with partial sensor data and interaction between contiguous events. In order to realize real time surveillance, an approximate inference method was used to efficiently estimate the occurrences of events from the historical observed data. Three different algorithms were compared on both real data and synthetic data, including a MRF model, a DBN model in which Markov chain Monte Carlo was used for structure learning, and a 2D-CRF model. Experimental results indicated STED method can accurately detect events from large-scale sensor networks in real time.

FUTURE RESEARCH DIRECTIONS

Robust interpretation of human activity depends on rapid human detection, reliable human tracking, and accurate activity interpretation (Amer, 2005; Wang, Hu, and Tan, 2003). Due to the complexity of background information, it is not easy to clearly detect human with his body interaction. Besides background information, other factors may also influence the effect of object recognition, such as clarity of camera, distance of object, and posture of human (Kumar, 2008). Even after a correct detection and tracking, activity interpretation is still difficult due to the lack of specific background information, which may contain large amount of prior knowledge.

Although a large amount of work has been done in human behavior recognition, there are still many open issues needed to be investigated in future, especially in the following areas. Due to the fact that large amount of prior knowledge is contained in surrounding scene and task context, a same behavior may have different meanings when the surrounding scene and task context changed. However, most existing investigation for human behavior recognition still rely on the assumption of specific circumstance and motion patterns (Ji, 2010; Wang and Mori, 2009), which at the same time degrades the popularity of recognition technique. It remains an open issue to understand human behavior in complex unconstrained scenes (Ji, 2010). In other words, recognition of behavior patterns constructed by self-organizing and self-learning from unknown scenes is a future research direction. Features based on local patches may be suitable for scene recognition or object recognition. However, it is uncertain whether or not they contain sufficient information about the ongoing action (Wang and Mori, 2009). Thus, representation of human behavior used features extracted from various visual cues is another interesting topic for future research.

ACKNOWLEDGMENT

This work was supported in part by the Young Scientists Foundation of Wuhan University of Science and Technology (2012xz013), the Project (2008TD04) from Science Foundation of Wuhan University of Science and Technology, the Program of Wuhan Subject Chief Scientist (201150530152), the Open Foundation (2010D11) of State Key Laboratory of Bioelectronics, Southeast University, and the Project (2009CDA034) from Hubei Provincial Natural Science Foundation, P. R. China, the project from Wuhan Chen Guang Project (201150431095), the Program for Outstanding Young Science and Technology Innovation Teams in Higher Education Institutions of Hubei Province (T201202), as well as National Natural Science Foundation of China (60975031, 61100055, 61201423, 61273303, 61273225).

REFERENCES

Aggarwal, J. K., & Cai, Q. (1999). Human motion analysis: A review. *Computer Vision and Image Understanding*, *73*, 428–440. doi:10.1006/cviu.1998.0744

Ahmad, M., & Lee, S. W. (2006). Human action recognition using multi-view image sequences features. In *Proceedings of the 7th International Conference on Automatic Face and Gesture Recognition*. IEEE.

Ahmad, M., & Lee, S. W. (2008). Human action recognition using shape and CLG-motion flow from multi-view image sequences. *Pattern Recognition, 41*(7), 2237–2252. doi:10.1016/j.patcog.2007.12.008

Ahn, J. H. (2009). Human tracking and silhouette extraction for human - Robot interaction systems. *Pattern Analysis & Applications, 12*, 167–177. doi:10.1007/s10044-008-0112-3

Amer, A., & Regazzoni, C. (2005). Introduction to the special issue on video object processing for surveillance applications. *Real-Time Imaging, 11*, 167–171. doi:10.1016/j.rti.2005.06.001

Andrade, E., Blunsden, S., & Fisher, R. (2005). Simulation of crowd problems for computer vision. In *Proceedings of the First International Workshop on Crowd Simulation*. IEEE.

Ayers, D., & Shah, M. (1998). Monitoring human behavior in an office environment. In *Proceedings of the Inteprretation of Visual Motion*, (pp. 65-72). IEEE.

Babu, R. V. (2001). Compressed domain action classification using HMM. *Pattern Recognition Letters, 23*(10), 1203–1213. doi:10.1016/S0167-8655(02)00067-3

Ben-Arie, J. (2002). Human activity recognition using multidimensional indexing. *IEEE Transactions on Pattern Analysis and Machine Intelligence, 24*, 1091–1104. doi:10.1109/TPAMI.2002.1023805

Benedek, C., & Sziranyi, T. (2008). Bayesian foreground and shadow detection in uncertain frame rate surveillance videos. *IEEE Transactions on Image Processing, 17*, 608–621. doi:10.1109/TIP.2008.916989

Blunsden, S., Fisher, R., & Andrade, E. (2006). *Recognition of coordinated multi agent activities: The individual vs the group*. Technical Report No. EDI-INF-RR-0830. Edinburgh, UK: The University of Edinburgh.

Bobick, A., & Davis, J. (1996). Real-time recognition of activity using temporal templates. In *Proceedings of IEEE Workshop on Applications of Computer Vision*. IEEE Press.

Bobick, A., & Davis, J. (2001). The recognition of human movement using temporal templates. *IEEE Transactions on Pattern Analysis and Machine Intelligence, 23*(3), 257–267. doi:10.1109/34.910878

Bobick, A. F., & Wilson, A. D. (1995). A state-based technique for the summarization and recognition of gesture. In *Proceedings of International Conference on Computer Vision*. IEEE.

Brand, M., et al. (1997). *Coupled hidden markov models for complex action recognition*. Paper presented at the IEEE Computer Society Conference on Computer Vision and Pattern Recognition. New York, NY.

Brubaker, M. (2010). Physics-based person tracking using the anthropomorphic walker. *International Journal of Computer Vision, 87*, 140–155. doi:10.1007/s11263-009-0274-5

Buxton, H., & Gong, S. (1995). Visual surveillance in a dynamic and uncertain world. *Artificial Intelligence, 78*(1-2), 431–459. doi:10.1016/0004-3702(95)00041-0

Caillette, F. (2008). Real-time 3-D human body tracking using learnt models of behaviour. *Computer Vision and Image Understanding, 109*, 112–125. doi:10.1016/j.cviu.2007.05.005

Castel, C., et al. (1996). *What is going on? A high level interpretation of sequences of images*. Paper presented at the the European Conference on Computer Vision. London, UK.

Chang, I. C., & Lin, H. C. (1996). Ribbon-based motion analysis of human body movements. In *Proceedings of the 13th International Conference on Pattern Recognition*. IEEE.

Chieu, H., et al. (2006). Activity recognition from physiological data using conditional random fields. In *Proceedings of the Singapore-MIT Alliance Computer Science Program*. MIT.

Collins, R. T., et al. (2000). *A system for video surveillance and monitoring: VSAM final report*. Technical Report No. CMU-RI-TR-00-12. Pittsburgh, PA: Carnegie Mellon University.

Duong, T. V., et al. (2005). *Activity recognition and abnormality detection with the switching hidden semi-Markov model*. Paper presented at the IEEE Computer Society Conference on Computer Vision and Pattern Recognition. New York, NY.

Duong, T. V. (2009). Efficient duration and hierarchical modeling for human activity recognition. *Artificial Intelligence, 173*(7-8), 830–856. doi:10.1016/j.artint.2008.12.005

Elgammal, A. (2002). Background and foreground modeling using nonparametric kernel density estimation for visual surveillance. *Proceedings of the IEEE, 90,* 1151–1163. doi:10.1109/JPROC.2002.801448

Fang, Y., Wang, Y., & Tan, T. (2004). Improving face detection through fusion of contour and region information. *Chinese Journal of Computer, 27,* 482–491.

Farmer, J., Casdagli, M., Eubank, S., & Gibson, J. (1991). State-space reconstruction in the presence of noise. *Physica D. Nonlinear Phenomena, 51*(1-3), 52–98. doi:10.1016/0167-2789(91)90222-U

Friedman, N., & Russell, S. (1997). *Image segmentation in video sequences: A probabilistic approach.* Paper presented at the Thirteenth Conference on Uncertainty in Artificial Intelligence. New York, NY.

Guo, Y., et al. (1994). *Understanding human motion patterns.* Paper presented at the IEEE International Conference on Pattern Recognition. New York, NY.

Hager, G. D., & Belhumeur, P. N. (1998). Efficient region tracking with parametric models of geometry and illumination. *IEEE Transactions on Pattern Analysis and Machine Intelligence, 20,* 1025–1039. doi:10.1109/34.722606

Haritaoglu, I., Harwood, D., & Davis, L. S. (2000). W4: Real-time surveillance of people and their activities. *IEEE Transactions on Pattern Analysis and Machine Intelligence, 22,* 809–830. doi:10.1109/34.868683

Hu, D. H., & Yang, Q. (2008). CIGAR: Concurrent and interleaving goal and activity recognition. In *Proceedings of the National Conference on Artificial Intelligence.* IEEE.

Ivanov, Y. A., & Bobick, A. F. (2000). Recognition of visual activities and interactions by stochastic parsing. *IEEE Transactions on Pattern Analysis and Machine Intelligence, 22*(8), 852–872. doi:10.1109/34.868686

Iwasawa, S., et al. (1997). Real-time estimation of human body posture from monocular thermal images. In *Proceedings of the IEEE Computer Society Conference on Computer Vision and Pattern Recognition.* IEEE.

Jabri, S., et al. (2000). Detection and location of people in video images using adaptive fusion of color and edge information. In *Proceedings of the 15th International Conference on Pattern Recognition.* IEEE.

Jain, R., & Nagel, H. (1979). On the analysis of accumulative difference pictures from image sequences of real world scenes. *IEEE Transactions on Pattern Analysis and Machine Intelligence, 1*, 206–214. doi:10.1109/TPAMI.1979.4766907

Ji, X., & Liu, H. (2010). Advances in view-invariant human motion analysis: A review. *IEEE Transactions on Systems, Man, and Cybernetics, 40*, 13–24. doi:10.1109/TSMCC.2009.2027608

Jing, Z., & Sclaroff, S. (2003). Segmenting foreground objects from a dynamic textured background via a robust Kalman filter. In *Proceedings of the IEEE International Conference on Computer Vision*. IEEE Press.

Karaulova, I., et al. (2000). *A hierarchical model of dynamics for tracking people with a single video camera*. Paper presented at the European Conference on Computer Vision. London, UK.

Karmann, K., & Brandt, A. V. (1990). Moving object recognition using an adaptive background memory. *Time-Varying Image Processing and Moving Object Recognition, 2*, 289–296.

Kautz, H. (1987). *A formal theory of plan recognition*. (Unpublished Ph.D. Dissertation). University of Rochester. Rochester, NY.

Ko, T., et al. (2008). *Background subtraction on distributions*. Paper presented at the European Conference on Computer Vision. London, UK.

Kumar, P., Mittal, A., & Kumar, P. (2008). Study of robust and intelligent surveillance in visible and multi-modal framework. *Informatica, 32*, 63–77.

Liao, L. (2006). *Location-based activity recognition*. (Unpublished Ph.D. Dissertation). University of Washington. Seattle, WA.

Liao, L. (2007). Hierarchical conditional random fields for GPS-based activity recognition. *Springer Tracts in Advanced Robotics, 28*, 487–506. doi:10.1007/978-3-540-48113-3_41

Lin, C. T. (1999). A space-time delay neural network for motion recognition and its application to lipreading. *International Journal of Neural Systems, 9*, 311–334. doi:10.1142/S0129065799000319

Lipton, A. J., et al. (1998). Moving target classification and tracking from real-time video. In *Proceedings of the Fourth IEEE Workshop on Applications of Computer Vision*. IEEE.

List, T., Bins, J., Fisher, R. B., et al. (2005). Two approaches to a plug-and-play vision architecture - CAVIAR and psyclone. In *Proceedings of AAAI Workshop on Modular Construction of Human-Like Intelligence*. AAAI.

Liu, H., Wang, Y., & Tan, T. (2004). Multi-modal data fusion for person authentication using improved ENN. *Chinese Journal of Automation, 30*, 78–85.

Lu, C., & Ferrier, N. J. (2004). Repetitive motion analysis: Segmentation and event classification. *IEEE Transactions on Pattern Analysis and Machine Intelligence, 26*, 258–263. doi:10.1109/TPAMI.2004.1262196

Lu, W. L. (2009). Tracking and recognizing actions of multiple hockey players using the boosted particle filter. *Image and Vision Computing, 27*(1-2), 189–205. doi:10.1016/j.imavis.2008.02.008

Madbahushi, A., & Aggwaral, J. (1999). A bayesian approach to human activity recognition. In *Proceedings of 2nd IEEE Intenational Workshop on Visual Surveillance*. IEEE.

Manfredotti, C. (2009). Modeling and Inference with relational dynamic Bayesian networks. *Lecture Notes in Computer Science, 5549*, 287–290. doi:10.1007/978-3-642-01818-3_44

McKenna, S. (2000). Tracking groups of people. *Computer Vision and Image Understanding, 80*, 42–56. doi:10.1006/cviu.2000.0870

Meyer, D., et al. (1997). Model based extraction of articulated objects in image sequences for gait analysis. In *Proceedings of International Conference on Image Processing*. IEEE.

Meyer, D., et al. (1998). *Gait classification with HMMs for trajectories of body parts extracted by mixture densities.* Paper presented at the The British Machine Vision Conference. London, UK.

Mittal, A., & Paragios, N. (2004). Motion-based background subtraction using adaptive kernel density estimation. In *Proceedings of the 2004 IEEE Computer Society Conference on Computer Vision and Pattern Recognition*. IEEE Press.

Monnet, A., et al. (2003). Background modeling and subtraction of dynamic scenes. In *Proceedings of the IEEE International Conference on Computer Vision*. IEEE Press.

Niyogi, S., & Adelson, E. (1994). *Analyzing and recognizing walking figures in XYT.* Paper presented at the IEEE Computer Society Conference on Computer Vision and Pattern Recognition. New York, NY.

Nummiaro, K. (2003). An adaptive color-based particle filter. *Image and Vision Computing, 21*, 99–110. doi:10.1016/S0262-8856(02)00129-4

Nwagboso, C. (1998). *User focused surveillance systems integration for intelligent transport systems*. Boston, MA: Kluwer Academic Publishers.

Oliver, N. M. (2000). A bayesian computer vision system for modeling human interactions. *IEEE Transactions on Pattern Analysis and Machine Intelligence, 22*, 831–843. doi:10.1109/34.868684

Oren, M., et al. (1997). *Pedestrian detection using wavelet templates*. Paper presented at the IEEE Computer Society Conference on Computer Vision and Pattern Recognition. New York, NY.

Paragios, N., & Deriche, R. (2000). Geodesic active contours and level sets for the detection and tracking of moving objects. *IEEE Transactions on Pattern Analysis and Machine Intelligence, 22*, 266–280. doi:10.1109/34.841758

Pérez, P., et al. (2002). *Color-based probabilistic tracking*. Paper presented at the European Conference on Computer Vision. London, UK.

Peterfreund, N. (1999). Robust tracking of position and velocity with Kalman snakes. *IEEE Transactions on Pattern Analysis and Machine Intelligence, 21*, 564–569. doi:10.1109/34.771328

Polana, R., & Nelson, R. (1994). Low level recognition of human motion. In *Proceedings of IEEE Workshop on Nonrigid and Articulate Motion*. IEEE Press.

Rathi, Y. (2007). Tracking deforming objects using particle filtering for geometric active contours. *IEEE Transactions on Pattern Analysis and Machine Intelligence, 29*, 1470–1475. doi:10.1109/TPAMI.2007.1081

Ribeiro, P., & Santos-Victor, J. (2005). Human activities recognition from video: Modeling, feature selection and classification architecture. In *Proceedings of Workshop on Human Activity Recognition and Modeling*. IEEE.

Robertson, N., & Reid, I. (2006). A general method for human activity recognition in video. *Computer Vision and Image Understanding, 104*(2-3), 232–248. doi:10.1016/j.cviu.2006.07.006

Rohr, K. (1994). Towards model-based recognition of human movements in image sequences. *CVGIP: Image Understanding, 59*(1), 94–115. doi:10.1006/ciun.1994.1006

Rosenblum, M., et al. (1994). Human emotion recognition from motion using a radial basis function network architecture. In *Proceedings Motion of Non-Rigid and Articulated Obgects Workshop*. IEEE.

Rota, N., & Thonnat, M. (2000). *Activity recognition from video sequences using declarative models*. Paper presented at the European Conference on Artificial Intelligence. London, UK.

Sheikh, Y., & Shah, M. (2005). Bayesian modeling of dynamic scenes for object detection. *IEEE Transactions on Pattern Analysis and Machine Intelligence, 27*, 1778–1792. doi:10.1109/TPAMI.2005.213

Sigal, L., et al. (2004). Tracking loose-limbed people. In *Proceedings of the 2004 IEEE Computer Society Conference on Computer Vision and Pattern Recognition*. IEEE Press.

Starner, T., & Pentland, A. (1995). *Real-time american sign language recognition from video using hidden markov models*. Paper presented at the IEEE International Conference on Computer Vision. New York, NY.

Stauffer, C., & Grimson, W. (2000). Learning patterns of activity using real-time tracking. *IEEE Transactions on Pattern Analysis and Machine Intelligence, 22*, 747–757. doi:10.1109/34.868677

Takahashi, K., et al. (1994). Recognition of dexterous manipulations from time-varying images. In *Proceedings of the 1994 IEEE Workshop on Motion of Non-Rigid and Articulated Obgects Workshop*. Austin, TX: IEEE Press.

Tan, T. N., Sullivan, G. D., & Baker, K. D. (1998). Model-based localization and recognition of road vehicles. *International Journal of Computer Vision, 27*, 5–25. doi:10.1023/A:1007924428535

Tian, Y. L., & Brown, L. (2008). IBM smart surveillance system (S3): Event based video surveillance system with an open and extensible framework. *Machine Vision and Applications, 19*, 315–327. doi:10.1007/s00138-008-0153-z

Toole, A. J., Harms, J., & Snow, S. L. (2005). A video database of moving faces and people. *IEEE Transactions on Pattern Analysis and Machine Intelligence, 27*, 812–816. doi:10.1109/TPAMI.2005.90

Toyama, K., et al. (1999). Wallflower: Principles and practice of background maintenance. In *Proceedings of the Seventh IEEE International Conference on Computer Vision*. IEEE Press.

Tran, S. D., & Davis, L. S. (2008). *Event modeling and recognition using Markov logic networks*. Paper presented at the European Conference on Conputer Vision. London, UK.

Truyen, T. T. (2008). *Learning discriminative sequence models from partially labelled data for activity recognition* (pp. 903–912). Lecture Notes in Computer Science Berlin, Germany: Springer. doi:10.1007/978-3-540-89197-0_84

Tweed, D., Fang, W., Fisher, R., et al. (2005). Exploring techniques for behavior recognition via the CAVIAR modular vision framework. In *Proceedings of Workshop on Human Activity Recognition and Modeling*. IEEE.

Vail, D. L., et al. (2007a). Conditional random fields for activity recognition. In *Proceedings of the International Conference on Autonomous Agents*. IEEE.

Vail, D. L., et al. (2007b). *Feature selection in conditional random fields for activity recognition*. Paper presented at the IEEE International Conference on Intelligent Robots and Systems. New York, NY.

Wang, L., Hu, W., & Tan, T. (2003). Recent developments in human motion analysis. *Pattern Recognition, 36*, 585–601. doi:10.1016/S0031-3203(02)00100-0

Wang, L., Tan, T., & Ning, H. (2004). Fusion of static and dynamic body biometrics for gait recognition. *IEEE Transactions on Circuits and Systems for Video Technology, 14*, 149–158. doi:10.1109/TCSVT.2003.821972

Wang, Y., & Mori, G. (2009). Human action recognition by semi-latent topic models. *IEEE Transactions on Pattern Analysis and Machine Intelligence, 31*, 1762–1774. doi:10.1109/TPAMI.2009.43

Wilson, A. D., & Bobick, A. F. (1998). *Recognition and interpretation of parametric gesture*. Paper presented at the IEEE International Conference on Computer Vision. New York, NY.

Wren, C. R., Azarbayejani, A., Darrell, T., & Pentland, A. P. (1997). Pfinder: Real-time tracking of the human body. *IEEE Transactions on Pattern Analysis and Machine Intelligence, 19*, 780–785. doi:10.1109/34.598236

Yamato, J., et al. (1992). *Recognizing human action in time-sequential images using hidden markov model*. Paper presented at the IEEE Computer Society Conference on Computer Vision and Pattern Recognition. New York, NY.

Yilmaz, A. (2006). Object tracking: A survey. *ACM Computing Surveys, 38*(4). doi:10.1145/1177352.1177355

Yin, J., et al. (2009). *Spatio-temporal event detection using dynamic conditional random fields*. Paper presented at the the International Joint Conferences on Artificial Intelligence. New York, NY.

Zhao, T. (2008). Segmentation and tracking of multiple humans in crowded environments. *IEEE Transactions on Pattern Analysis and Machine Intelligence, 30,* 1198–1211. doi:10.1109/TPAMI.2007.70770

Zhao, T., & Nevatia, R. (2003). Bayesian human segmentation in crowded situations. In *Proceedings of the IEEE Computer Society Conference on Computer Vision and Pattern Recognition*. IEEE Press.

Zhao, T., & Nevatia, R. (2004). Tracking multiple humans in complex situations. *IEEE Transactions on Pattern Analysis and Machine Intelligence, 26*(9), 1208–1221. doi:10.1109/TPAMI.2004.73

ADDITIONAL READING

Belhumeur, P. N., Hespanha, J. P., & Kriegman, D. J. (1997). Eigenfaces vs. Fisher faces: Recognition using class specific linear projection. *IEEE Transactions on Pattern Analysis and Machine Intelligence, 19,* 711–720. doi:10.1109/34.598228

Ben-Arie, J. (2002). Human activity recognition using multidimensional indexing. *IEEE Transactions on Pattern Analysis and Machine Intelligence, 24,* 1091–1104. doi:10.1109/TPAMI.2002.1023805

Benedek, C., & Sziranyi, T. (2008). Bayesian foreground and shadow detection in uncertain frame rate surveillance videos. *IEEE Transactions on Image Processing, 17,* 608–621. doi:10.1109/TIP.2008.916989

Bobick, A., & Davis, J. (2001). The recognition of human movement using temporal templates. *IEEE Transactions on Pattern Analysis and Machine Intelligence, 23*(3), 257–267. doi:10.1109/34.910878

Brubaker, M. (2010). Physics-based person tracking using the anthropomorphic walker. *International Journal of Computer Vision, 87,* 140–155. doi:10.1007/s11263-009-0274-5

Collins, R. T., Lipton, A. J., & Kanade, T. (2000). Introduction to the special section on video surveillance. *IEEE Transactions on Pattern Analysis and Machine Intelligence, 22,* 745–746. doi:10.1109/TPAMI.2000.868676

Duong, T. V. (2009). Efficient duration and hierarchical modeling for human activity recognition. *Artificial Intelligence, 173*(7-8), 830–856. doi:10.1016/j.artint.2008.12.005

Hager, G. D., & Belhumeur, P. N. (1998). Efficient region tracking with parametric models of geometry and illumination. *IEEE Transactions on Pattern Analysis and Machine Intelligence, 20*, 1025–1039. doi:10.1109/34.722606

Haritaoglu, I., Harwood, D., & Davis, L. S. (2000). W4: Real-time surveillance of people and their activities. *IEEE Transactions on Pattern Analysis and Machine Intelligence, 22*, 809–830. doi:10.1109/34.868683

Hu, W., Tan, T., Wang, L., & Maybank, S. (2004). A survey on visual surveillance of object motion and behaviors. *IEEE Transactions on Systems, Man, and Cybernetics, 34*, 334–350. doi:10.1109/TSMCC.2004.829274

Ivanov, Y. A., & Bobick, A. F. (2000). Recognition of visual activities and interactions by stochastic parsing. *IEEE Transactions on Pattern Analysis and Machine Intelligence, 22*(8), 852–872. doi:10.1109/34.868686

Jain, R., & Nagel, H. (1979). On the analysis of accumulative difference pictures from image sequences of real world scenes. *IEEE Transactions on Pattern Analysis and Machine Intelligence, 1*, 206–214. doi:10.1109/TPAMI.1979.4766907

Ji, X., & Liu, H. (2010). Advances in view-invariant human motion analysis: A review. *IEEE Transactions on Systems, Man, and Cybernetics, 40*, 13–24. doi:10.1109/TSMCC.2009.2027608

Ke, Y., et al. (2005). *Efficient visual event detection using volumetric features.* Paper presented at the IEEE International Conference on Computer Vision. New York, NY.

Lu, C., & Ferrier, N. J. (2004). Repetitive motion analysis: Segmentation and event classification. *IEEE Transactions on Pattern Analysis and Machine Intelligence, 26*, 258–263. doi:10.1109/TPAMI.2004.1262196

Maybank, S., & Tan, T. (2000). Introduction to special section on visual surveillance. *International Journal of Computer Vision, 37*, 173–173. doi:10.1023/A:1008151520284

Oliver, N. M. (2000). A bayesian computer vision system for modeling human interactions. *IEEE Transactions on Pattern Analysis and Machine Intelligence, 22*, 831–843. doi:10.1109/34.868684

Paragios, N., & Deriche, R. (2000). Geodesic active contours and level sets for the detection and tracking of moving objects. *IEEE Transactions on Pattern Analysis and Machine Intelligence, 22*, 266–280. doi:10.1109/34.841758

Peterfreund, N. (1999). Robust tracking of position and velocity with Kalman snakes. *IEEE Transactions on Pattern Analysis and Machine Intelligence, 21*, 564–569. doi:10.1109/34.771328

Rathi, Y. (2007). Tracking deforming objects using particle filtering for geometric active contours. *IEEE Transactions on Pattern Analysis and Machine Intelligence, 29*, 1470–1475. doi:10.1109/TPAMI.2007.1081

Sarkar, S., Phillips, P. J., Liu, Z., Vega, I. R., & Bowyer, K. W. (2005). The humanID gait challenge problem: Data sets, performance, and analysis. *IEEE Transactions on Pattern Analysis and Machine Intelligence, 27*, 1–16. doi:10.1109/TPAMI.2005.39

Sheikh, Y., & Shah, M. (2005a). Bayesian modeling of dynamic scenes for object detection. *IEEE Transactions on Pattern Analysis and Machine Intelligence, 27*, 1778–1792. doi:10.1109/TPAMI.2005.213

Sheikh, Y., & Shah, M. (2005b). *Exploring the space of an action for human action.* Paper presented at the IEEE International Conference on Computer Vision. New York, NY.

Stauffer, C., & Grimson, W. (2000). Learning patterns of activity using real-time tracking. *IEEE Transactions on Pattern Analysis and Machine Intelligence, 22*, 747–757. doi:10.1109/34.868677

Tan, T. N., Sullivan, G. D., & Baker, K. D. (1998). Model-based localization and recognition of road vehicles. *International Journal of Computer Vision, 27*, 5–25. doi:10.1023/A:1007924428535

Toole, A. J., Harms, J., & Snow, S. L. (2005). A video database of moving faces and people. *IEEE Transactions on Pattern Analysis and Machine Intelligence, 27*, 812–816. doi:10.1109/TPAMI.2005.90

Wang, L., Hu, W., & Tan, T. (2003). Recent developments in human motion analysis. *Pattern Recognition, 36*, 585–601. doi:10.1016/S0031-3203(02)00100-0

Wang, Y., & Mori, G. (2009). Human action recognition by semi-latent topic models. *IEEE Transactions on Pattern Analysis and Machine Intelligence, 31*, 1762–1774. doi:10.1109/TPAMI.2009.43

Wilson, A. D., & Bobick, A. F. (1998). *Recognition and interpretation of parametric gesture.* Paper presented at the IEEE International Conference on Computer Vision. New York, NY.

Wren, C. R., Azarbayejani, A., Darrell, T., & Pentland, A. P. (1997). Pfinder: Real-time tracking of the human body. *IEEE Transactions on Pattern Analysis and Machine Intelligence, 19*, 780–785. doi:10.1109/34.598236

Yilmaz, A. (2006). Object tracking: A survey. *ACM Computing Surveys, 38*(4). doi:10.1145/1177352.1177355

Yilmaz, A., & Shah, M. (2005). *Recognizing human actions in videos acquired by uncalibrated moving cameras.* Paper presented at the IEEE International Conference on Computer Vision. New York, NY.

Yin, J., et al. (2009). *Spatio-temporal event detection using dynamic conditional random fields.* Paper presented at the the International Joint Conferences on Artificial Intelligence. New York, NY.

Zhao, T. (2008). Segmentation and tracking of multiple humans in crowded environments. *IEEE Transactions on Pattern Analysis and Machine Intelligence, 30*, 1198–1211. doi:10.1109/TPAMI.2007.70770

Zhao, T., & Nevatia, R. (2004). Tracking multiple humans in complex situations. *IEEE Transactions on Pattern Analysis and Machine Intelligence, 26*(9), 1208–1221. doi:10.1109/TPAMI.2004.73

Chapter 4
Review of Sparsity Known and Blind Sparsity Greedy Algorithms for Compressed Sensing

Chun-Yan Zeng
South China University of Technology, China

Ming-Hui Du
South China University of Technology, China

Li-Hong Ma
South China University of Technology, China

Jing Tian
Wuhan University of Science and Technology, China

ABSTRACT

Sparsity level is crucial to Compressive Sensing (CS) reconstruction, but in practice it is often unknown. Recently, several blind sparsity greedy algorithms have emerged to recover signals by exploiting the underlying signal characteristics. Sparsity Adaptive Matching Pursuit (SAMP) estimates the sparsity level and the true support set stage by stage, while Backtracking-Based Adaptive OMP (BAOMP) selects atoms by thresholds related to the maximal residual projection. This chapter reviews typical sparsity known greedy algorithms including OMP, StOMP, and CoSaMP, as well as those emerging blind sparsity greedy algorithms. Furthermore, the algorithms are analysed in structured diagrammatic representation and compared by exact reconstruction probabilities for Gaussian and binary signals distributed sparsely.

DOI: 10.4018/978-1-4666-3958-4.ch004

1. INTRODUCTION

In Compressive Sensing (CS) theory, a signal $x \in R^N$ is k-sparse if x has $k(k << N)$ nonzero entries or coefficients under a linear transform. Such a signal can be recovered from linear projections:

$$y = \Phi x \tag{1}$$

where $y \in R^M$ is the observation vector and Φ is often known as a dictionary or a measurement matrix with each column vector E_i regarded as an atom. If $k<<M$ and Φ satisfies the following Restricted Isometry Property (RIP), x can be faithfully recovered from $O(k \log N)$ measurements (Donoho, 2006):

$$(1 - \delta_k) \|x\|_2^2 \leq \|\Phi x\|_2^2 \leq (1 + \delta_k) \|x\|_2^2 \tag{2}$$

where $\delta_k \in (0,1)$ is the isometry constant, the smallest number satisfying Equation (2). When $\delta_k << 1$, the projection operator very nearly maintains the l_2 distance between each pair of $k/2$-sparse signals (Needell & Tropp, 2009).

Two common CS reconstruction strategies are l_1-norm minimization and l_0-norm minimization based. The former strategies, such as Basis Pursuit (BP), solve a convex minimization problem using Linear Programming (LP). They have some striking theoretical properties e.g. rigorous proof of exact reconstruction under seemingly quite general circumstances. Unfortunately they are sensitive to noise and often suffer from fairly heavy computationally burdens. The latter strategies approximate signals with iterative greedy pursuit (Tropp & Wright, 2010), including steps of best atom-finding, signal estimation and residual updating in each iteration. Matching Pursuit (MP) (Mallat & Zhang, 1993) and Orthogonal Matching Pursuit algorithms (OMP) (Tropp & Gilbert, 2007) reconstructed signals by matching residuals with the most correlated column of sensing matrix, though sometimes the solutions were misdirected by noisy atoms. In order to speed up the matching, Stagewise Orthogonal Matching Pursuit (StOMP) (Donoho, Drori, Tsaig, & Starck, 2006) used hard thresholding to find the atoms of significant coefficient instead of the largest one in each iteration. To prune the wrong chosen atoms, backtracking was important, as well as a known sparse level k. Subspace Pursuit algorithm (SP) (Varadarajan, Khudanpur, & Tran, 2011) and compressed sensing matching pursuit (CoSaMP) (Needell & Tropp, 2009) were all backtracking restorations focused on signals with a known k, adding and removing either k or $2k$ atoms in each search. Another backtracking method was Iterative Hard Thresholding algorithm (IHT) (Blumensath

& Davies, 2009), its non-linear operator set all but the largest *k* elements to zero. However, a known *k* is usually impractical in applications. For blind sparse reconstruction, Sparsity Adaptive Matching Pursuit (SAMP) (Do, Gan, Nguyen, & Tran, 2008), Backtracking-Based Adaptive OMP (BAOMP) (Huang & Makur, 2011), and Adaptive Sparsity Matching Pursuit (ASMP) (Wu & Wang, 2012) refined the chosen atoms and extracted the information of sparsity automatically. SAMP approached the true sparsity stage by stage using a fixed step size, while ASMP approached it using hard thresholding by analyzing the distribution of the signal proxy. BAOMP proposed a threshold based method which selected and discarded atoms by setting parameters and inferring thresholds of atom-accepted and atom-deleted.

This chapter briefly describes two kinds of greedy algorithms—sparsity known and blind sparsity methods. For the former, the following 3 algorithms are described: 1) OMP, which provided the basic frame, 2) StOMP, which introduced batched atoms selection, 3) CoSaMP, which successfully suggested the first feasible backtracking. For the latter, we introduce SAMP and BAOMP. ASMP is omited because it is similar with SAMP. At last, we compare their reconstruction performances on Gaussian and binary sparsity signals.

2. SPARSITY KNOWN GREEDY ALGORITHMS

2.1. OMP

Orthogonal Matching Pursuit (OMP) is one of the most classical greedy pursuit algorithms. Its main idea is iteratively projecting the observation residual onto all atoms, and the atom with largest amplitude coefficient is referred as optimal matching atom. All chosen atoms are orthogonalized and the residual r_n is obtained by subtracting the contribution of chosen atoms from observation vector i.e. $r_n = y - \Phi_\Lambda x_n$. Since the full backward orthogonality of the residual, OMP gives the optimal approximation x_n with respect to the selected subset of the dictionary. The current residual minimizes the energy $||y - \Phi_\Lambda x_n||_2$, so we can use Least Square (LS) to compute signal estimation x_n. The procedure of OMP is shown in Figure 1.

Since we expect the columns of the dictionary Φ to be approximately orthonormal, the energy of each set of *k* components of $\Phi^T \Phi x$ approximates the energy of the corresponding *k* components of x. So $\Phi^T \Phi x$ can serve as a proxy for the signal x and we adopt the matched filter $u = \Phi^T r_n$ to search the optimal atom. The coordinate of largest component of u is added to the candidate support set Λ_n to update the signal estimation x_n and residual r_n.

Figure 1. Scheme of OMP

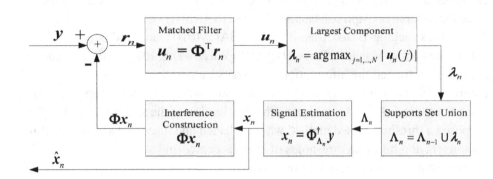

There are three common techniques to solve LS problem: QR factorization, Cholesky factorization and conjugate gradient. Solving the inverse problem using conjugate gradient method is the only viable option to solve OMP for very large problems. There are several natural stopping criteria: 1) halt after extracting exactly k nonzero elements, 2) halt when no atom explains a significant amount of energy in the residual, 3) halt when mean squared error of residual is below a threshold, 4) halt when the change in the mean squared error falls below a threshold.

Recently a new analysis for OMP shows that if the RIP is satisfied at sparsity level $O(k)$, then OMP can stably recover a k sparse signal in norm-2 under measurement noise. It implies that in order to uniformly recover a k sparse signal, only $O(k \ln N)$ random projections are needed (Zhang, 2011).

2.2. StOMP

In OMP a single atom is selected in each iteration. In order to speed up convergence, another selection strategy is thresholding to have numerous atoms selected in each iteration. For a given threshold τ, we select atoms to create index set

$$\Omega = \{ j : | u_n(j) | > \tau \} \tag{3}$$

where τ can be a constant or depend on other quantities. Stagewise orthogonal matching pursuit (StOMP) is one of the first approaches that use thresholding ideas. In StOMP, the thresholding τ is depending on the current residual

$$\tau = t \, || r_n ||_2 / \sqrt{M} \tag{4}$$

where the threshold parameter t takes values in the range $2 \leq t \leq 3$ and $\sigma_n = \parallel r_n \parallel_2 / \sqrt{M}$ is a formal noise level.

Now we will analyse how to confirm the threshold $\tau = t\sigma_n$. Firstly we process the noiseless undetermined problems as a noisy well-determined problem. If the dictionary Φ is a random matrix taken from the Uniform Spherical Ensemble (USE), and if M and N are both large, then the vector $z = \Phi^T y - x$ has a histogram which is nearly Gaussian with standard deviation

$$\delta \approx \parallel x \parallel_2 / \sqrt{M} \tag{5}$$

Empirically, the vector $z' = \Phi^T r_n - x$ has also a Gaussian behavior. Then, we view the matched filter vector $u_n = \Phi^T r_n$ as consisting of a small number of 'truly nonzero' entries, combined with a large number of 'Gaussian noise' entries. The problem of estimating original signal has converted to the problem of separating 'signal' from 'noise'. Note that x is unknown in practice, we use the RIP of Φ which nearly maintains l_2 distance between x and y to approximate δ by

$$\delta \approx \parallel y \parallel_2 / \sqrt{M} \tag{6}$$

Accordingly, the standard deviation of vector $z' = \Phi^T r_n - x$ is

$$\delta' \approx \parallel r_n \parallel_2 / \sqrt{M} \tag{7}$$

So we set formal noise level $\sigma_n = \parallel r_n \parallel_2 / \sqrt{M}$ and extract the large components in the target signal by hard thresholding.

Figure 2 gives the diagrammatic representation of StOMP. It can be seen that StOMP recruits a set of atoms using hard thresholding in the frame of OMP. Correspondingly, StOMP runs much faster than OMP. However the selection strategy in StOMP is developed explicitly for problems where Φ is generated from a USE. When applied to more general matrices Φ, Uniform Spherical Ensemble for this method are therefore not available. And the selection of the parameter t required in the method is critical for its performance, but there do not seem to be any intuitive guidelines available for this other than the suggestion $2 \leq t \leq 3$ given by its authors. Furthermore, the algorithm may get stuck when all inner products $u_n(j)$ fall below the threshold.

Figure 2. Scheme of StOMP

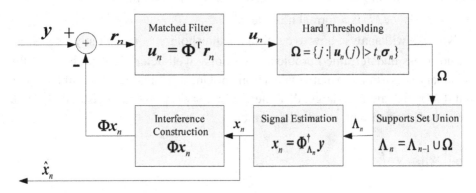

2.3. CoSaMP

Compressed Sensing Matching Pursuit (CoSaMP) is also based on OMP, but it has two obvious superiorities: backtracking and strong guarantees. CoSaMP not only selects new atoms, but also includes an atoms pruning step. This atoms updating strategy can obsolete mis-matched atoms in previous iterations. Furthermore, CoSaMP gives the upper bound of approximation error and iteration invariant for each iteration where the approximation error is highly relevant to the unrecoverable energy.

CoSaMP supposes the dictionary has restricted isometry constant $\delta_{4k} \leq 0.1$, thus as before, $u_n = \Phi^T r_n$ serves as a good proxy for the signal. Then *2k* largest components of the proxy are located and united with current supports set. The target signal is estimated using LS. Only *k* largest components of an estimated signal are reserved while other small components are pruned. Finally the residual is updated. The diagrammatic representation of CoSaMP appears as Figure 3.

Figure 3. Scheme of CoSaMP

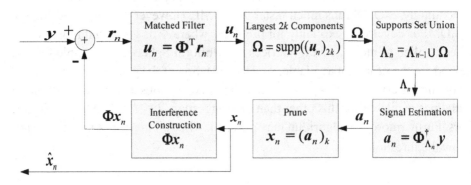

We note that CoSaMP requires the sparsity level k as part of its input. Two sparsity estimate approaches are suggested. $k \approx M / 2 \log N$ is often reasonable from phase transition analysis. Another approach is to run CoSaMP using a range of sparsity levels and select the best approximation obtained.

For the efficient use in practice, LS in signal estimation step must be analyzed carefully. In the assumption $\delta_{4k} \leq 0.1$, the matrix Φ^{T} is very well-conditioned. This suggests the use of iterative methods such as Richardson' iteration or conjugate gradient apply the pseudoinverse $\Phi^{\dagger}_{\Lambda_n} = \left(\Phi^{\mathrm{T}}_{\Lambda_n} \Phi_{\Lambda_n} \right)^{-1} \Phi^{\mathrm{T}}_{\Lambda_n}$ very quickly.

CoSaMP takes noise into account and gives the sampling model $y = \Phi x + e$, where $e \in C^M$ is arbitrary. For this sampling model, CoSaMP guarantees the significant progress during each iteration where the approximation error is large relative to the unrecoverable energy.

Theorem 1: (Iteration Invariant) For each iteration $n \geq 0$, the signal approximation x_n is k-sparse and

$$|| x - x_{n+1} ||_2 \leq 0.5 || x - x_n ||_2 + 10 v \tag{8}$$

where v is unrecoverable energy. So the fixed number of iterations is required to reduce the error to an optimal amount. The following Theorem 2 summarizes the fundamentally optimal recovery guarantees and rigorous computational costs of CoSaMP.

Theorem 2: (Recovery by CoSaMP) Suppose that Φ is an $M \times N$ sampling matrix with restricted isometry constant $\delta_{2k} \leq c$. Let $y = \Phi x + e$ be a vector of samples of an arbitrary signal, contaminated with arbitrary noise. For a given precision parameter η, the algorithm CoSaMP produces a k-sparse approximation a that satisfies

$$|| x - a ||_2 \leq C \cdot \max\{\eta, || x - x_{k/2} ||_1 / \sqrt{k} + || e ||_2\} \tag{9}$$

where $x_{k/2}$ is a best $(k/2)$-sparse approximation to x. The running time is $O(\ell \cdot \log(|| x ||_2 / \eta))$, where ℓ bounds the cost of a matrix-vector multiply with Φ or Φ^{T}. Working storage is $O(N)$.

3. BLIND SPARSITY GREEDY ALGORITHMS

3.1. SAMP

In practical CS, the sparsity k is often not available. For example, most natural image signals are compressible under an appropriate transform and the sparsity k of these signals could not be well-defined. In this case we might want to estimate the sparsity k for CoSaMP. However it would either eliminate the ability of exact recovery if we underestimate k or significantly degrade both accuracy and robustness of the algorithms if we overestimate it (Do, Gan, Nguyen, & Tran, 2008). So Sparsity Adaptive Matching Pursuit (SAMP) takes a divide and conquer principle to estimate the sparsity stage by stage. In fact, SAMP provides a generalized greedy reconstruction framework in which OMP and SP can be viewed as its special cases. In brief, SAMP divides all iterations into several stages, each of which has the same sparsity k. In each stage, SAMP approximates the estimated signal like SP. When the residual stops monotone decreasing, the process turns to next stage and the sparsity increases by a fixed step s. The concrete process is shown in Figure 4.

From Figure 4, we can analyze the relationships between SAMP, OMP and SP. When the step $s = 1$, SAMP can be roughly regarded as the OMP associated with backtracking feature that can remove bad coordinates during iterations. In this case, SAMP is more accurate than OMP although it requires a few more iterations to achieve that accuracy. In addition, when $s = k$, SAMP becomes exactly SP if the RIP condition of measurement matrix is satisfied. In this case, it only needs one

Figure 4. Schematic representation of SAMP

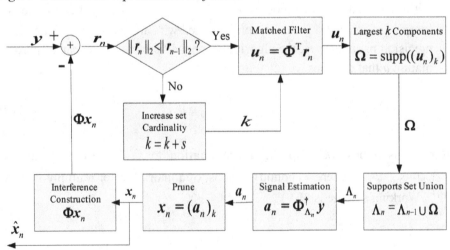

stage to find the *k* sparse approximation of the signal. Based on the proof frame of SP, SAMP gives the following exact recovery guarantee for free-noise sparse signals.

Theorem 3: (Exact Recovery by SAMP) Assume $x \in R^N$ is a *k* sparse signal and the corresponding measurement $y = \Phi x$. Let $k_s = s\lceil k / s \rceil$. If the sensing matrix Φ satisfies the RIP with parameter: $\delta_{3k_s} < 0.06$, SAMP guarantees exact recovery of *x* from *y* via a finite number of iterations.

For noisy sparse and compressible signals, Theorem 4 and Theorem 5 give the error upper bounds respectively.

Theorem 4: (Stability for sparse signals by SAMP) With the same assumption and notation of Theorem 3 and assume the measurement vector is contaminated with noise: $y = \Phi x + e$. Let energy of noise be σ^2. If the sensing matrix satisfies the RIP with parameter: $\delta_{3k_s} < 0.06$, the signal approximation $\hat{x}$ of SAMP algorithm satisfies:

$$|| x - \hat{x} ||_2 \leq c_{k_s} \sigma \tag{10}$$

where $c_{k_s} = (1 + \delta_{3k_s}) / (\delta_{3k_s}(1 - \delta_{3k_s}))$

Theorem 5: (Stability for compressible signals by SAMP) Assume when the algorithm stops, the number of coordinates in the finalist is k_{stp}. With the same assumption of Theorem 4, if the sensing matrix satisfies the RIP with parameter: $\delta_{6k_{stp}} < 0.03$, the signal approximation $\hat{x}$ of SAMP algorithm satisfies:

$$|| x - \hat{x} ||_2 \leq c_{2k_{stp}}$$
$$(\sigma + \sqrt{(1 + \delta_{6k_{stp}}) / k_{stp}} \, || x - x_{k_{stp}} ||_1) \tag{11}$$

3.2. BAOMP

Backtracking-Based Adaptive OMP (BAOMP) is another blind sparsity signal reconstruction method. Similar to OMP and StOMP, it follows a stage by stage estimation of sparsity level k and the true support set. Furthermore, like CoSaMP and SP methods, it uses a two-step selection technique to carefully choose the atoms. In preliminary selection step, a set of atoms are selected by thresholding. Then in final selection step, the previous chosen atoms' reliability is detected and the unreliable atoms are removed. However, unlike SAMP expanding the support set by a fixed step, BAOMP adaptively estimates the sparsity level according to the underlying signal. The capacity of support set of BAOMP is decided by the two adaptive thresholds. The atom-adding threshold is relative to the current maximal correlation while the atom-deleting threshold is controlled by current maximal element of estimated signal. As a result, in the first several iterations, the numbers of added and deleted atoms may be larger, but after most corrected atoms have been chosen, the chosen atoms will become much smaller, hence it is possible to speed up the convergence. The process of BAOMP is shown in Figure 5.

We note that the preset atom-adding constant μ_1 and preset atom-deleting constant μ_2 are fixed. Due to these fixed factors, a problem we encountered is that the residual might rebound in later iterations. An effective method to restrain rebound is increasing μ_1 in the later iterations. Another drawback of BAOMP is that the values of μ_1 and μ_2 are critical for reconstruction performance, but the ranges $0.4 \leq \mu_1 \leq 0.8$ and $0.4 \leq \mu_2 \leq 0.8$ given in (Huang & Makur, 2011) are empirical values. At last, BAOMP has no provable performance guarantees. However, BAOMP maintains the low complexity of OMP-type methods and experiments demonstrate it has a superior performance than several other OMP-type methods.

4. EXPERIMENTS

In this section, we compare the reconstruction probabilities of typical sparsity known greedy algorithms (OMP, StOMP, and CoSaMP) with blind sparsity greedy

Figure 5. Scheme of BAOMP

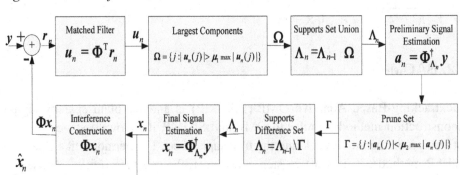

algorithms (SAMP and BAOMP). Sparselab is employed for OMP and StOMP. The stopping criterions are $n = k$ for OMP, $n = 10$ for StOMP, and $\| x - \hat{x} \|_2 \leq 10^{-5}$ for CoSaMP, SAMP and BAOMP. The sparsity increasing step in SAMP is $s=5$. Parameters in BAOMP are $\mu_1 = 0.4$ and $\mu_2 = 0.6$. The test signals are Gaussian and binary sparse signals with $N = 500$, $k = 20$. The Gaussian sparse signal is compressible in nature and the binary sparse signal represents a particularly challenging case for OMP-type reconstruction strategies (Tropp & Gilbert, 2007). An $M \times N$ Gaussian measurement is used, all kinds of simulations are performed 1000 times independently.

Two performance measurements are:

1. Fraction of measurements is defined as:

$$\alpha = M / N \tag{12}$$

2. Reconstruction $\hat{x}$ is regarded as exact recovery (ER) if $\| x - \hat{x} \|_2 < 10^{-4}$. Define ER probability (ERP) as a ratio of the number of ER signals N_r over the total number of signals N (Tropp & Gilbert, 2007):

$$p = \frac{N_r}{N} \tag{13}$$

For Gaussian sparsity signals we set fraction range of measurement $\alpha \in [0.1, 0.2]$. And for challenging binary sparsity signals, fraction range of measurement is $\alpha \in [0.15, 0.3]$. The ERP vs. fraction of measurement for Gaussian and binary sparsity signals are shown in Figure 6 and Figure 7.

Generally speaking, for Gaussian sparse signals, performances of blind sparsity greedy algorithms exceed that of sparsity known greedy algorithms. When $\alpha = 0.2$, both SAMP and BAOMP can reconstruct original signals exactly, but other algorithms fail to ER. When $\alpha < 0.18$, CoSaMP is even inferior to OMP. StOMP has pessimal performance, although it runs fastest in all the above algorithms.

For binary sparse signals, two blind sparsity greedy algorithms still have superior performance. And CoSaMP has comparable performance with SAMP. When $\alpha = 0.27$, BAOMP, CoSaMP and SAMP achieve accurate reconstruction, but $p = 81.2\%$ for StOMP and $p = 54\%$ for OMP.

Figure 6. ERP vs. fraction of measurements for Gaussian sparse signal

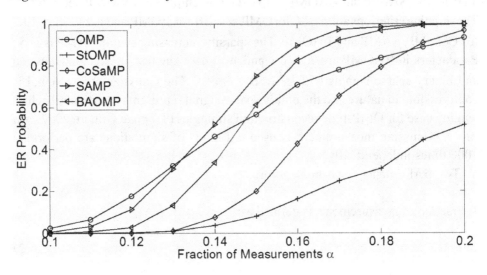

Figure 7. ERP vs. fraction of measurements for binary sparse signal

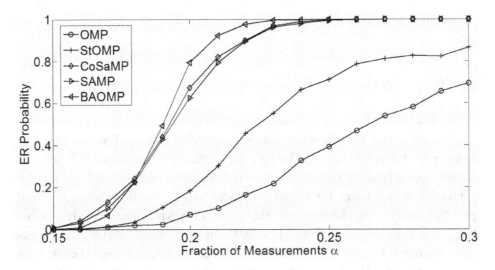

Our experiments indicate without crucial information k, blind sparsity greedy algorithms can also obtain excellent performances by exploiting the underlying signals. And backtracking is a simple but effective strategy for the reconstruction performance.

REFERENCES

Blumensath, T., & Davies, M. E. (2009). Iterative hard thresholding for compressed sensing. *Applied and Computational Harmonic Analysis, 27*(3), 265–274. doi:10.1016/j.acha.2009.04.002

Do, T. T., Gan, L., Nguyen, N., & Tran, T. D. (2008). Sparsity adaptive matching pursuit algorithm for practical compressed sensing. In *Proceedings of the 2008 42nd Asilomar Conference on Signals, Systems and Computers*, (pp. 581–587). Asilomar.

Donoho, D., Drori, I., Tsaig, Y., & Starck, J. (2006). *Sparse solution of underdetermined linear equations by stagewise orthogonal matching pursuit*. Palo Alto, CA: Stanford University.

Donoho, D. L. (2006). Compressed sensing. *IEEE Transactions on Information Theory, 52*(4), 1289–1306. doi:10.1109/TIT.2006.871582

Huang, H., & Makur, A. (2011). Backtracking-based matching pursuit method for sparse signal reconstruction. *IEEE Signal Processing Letters, 18*(7), 391–394. doi:10.1109/LSP.2011.2147313

Mallat, S. G., & Zhang, Z. (19993). Matching pursuits with time-frequency dictionaries. *IEEE Transactions on Signal Processing, 41*(12), 3397–3415. doi:10.1109/78.258082

Needell, D., & Tropp, J. A. (2009). CoSaMP: Iterative signal recovery from incomplete and inaccurate samples. *Applied and Computational Harmonic Analysis, 26*(3), 301–321. doi:10.1016/j.acha.2008.07.002

Tropp, J. A., & Gilbert, A. C. (2007). Signal recovery from random measurements via orthogonal matching pursuit. *IEEE Transactions on Information Theory, 53*(12), 4655–4666. doi:10.1109/TIT.2007.909108

Tropp, J. A., & Wright, S. J. (2010). Computational methods for sparse solution of linear inverse problems. *Proceedings of the IEEE, 98*(6), 948–958. doi:10.1109/JPROC.2010.2044010

Varadarajan, B., Khudanpur, S., & Tran, T. D. (2011). Stepwise optimal subspace pursuit for improving sparse recovery. *IEEE Signal Processing Letters, 18*(1), 27–30. doi:10.1109/LSP.2010.2090143

Wu, H., & Wang, S. (2012). Adaptive sparsity matching pursuit algorithm for sparse reconstruction. *IEEE Signal Processing Letters*, *19*(8), 471–474. doi:10.1109/LSP.2012.2188793

Zhang, T. (2011). Sparse recovery with orthogonal matching pursuit under RIP. *IEEE Transactions on Information Theory*, *57*(9), 6215–6221. doi:10.1109/TIT.2011.2162263

Chapter 5
Adaptive Edge–Preserving Smoothing and Detail Enhancement for H.263 and H.264 Video

Ji-Hye Kim
Sogang University, Korea

Ji Won Lee
Sogang University, Korea

Rae-Hong Park
Sogang University, Korea

Min-Ho Park
PIXTREE, Korea

Jae-Seob Shin
PIXTREE, Korea

ABSTRACT

For removing undesirable artifacts in video coding, a large number of filtering methods have been proposed as post-processing and in-loop processing. This chapter proposes a pre-processing method of motion-adaptive edge-preserving smoothing and detail enhancement for H.263 and H.264 video, in which temporal and spatial edges are used to define Region Of Interest (ROI). In the proposed pre-processing method, trilateral filtering with three types of weights (domain, range, and temporal weights) is used for smoothing non-ROI region while preserving temporal/spatial edges. In the proposed pre-processing method, the temporal weight preserves

DOI: 10.4018/978-1-4666-3958-4.ch005

temporal edges within ROIs and smoothes details within non-ROI. The proposed pre-processing method can make video coding more efficient under the restricted bit-rate condition. The parameter values for weight functions of a trilateral filter are selected depending on the classification of motion and edginess, and proper filtering is performed with adaptive parameter values. Experimental results with a number of H.263 and H.264 test sequences show the effectiveness of the proposed method in terms of the visual quality, the peak signal-to-noise ratio, and the mean opinion score.

INTRODUCTION

In recent years, rapid increase in the number of cellular customers has led to significant development of mobile network system. Expansion of high data-rate communication in multimedia and data services requires a wide range of bandwidth up to $50-100$ Mbps. Applications combined with streaming multimedia services such as real-time conversational voice services, point to point interactive multimedia services including interactive real-time voice, video, and other media (video telephony and white boarding), and video conferencing over wireless have been increasingly becoming a significant part of services in mobile vender market (Etoh & Yoshimura, 2005). In particular, video coding technology is an important part of video streaming services for data transmission and storage.

To ensure video quality on these multimedia services, based on streaming with the encoder such as H.263, H.264, and moving picture experts group-4 (MPEG-4), an effective video enhancement algorithm is required for high-quality images/videos under the low bit-rate and restricted bandwidth. To achieve high quality, it is important to reduce various artifacts such as block artifacts, ringing artifacts, and false-color artifacts. In particular, a video coding algorithm with block-based transform, quantization, and motion prediction produces very annoying block artifacts with low bit-rate and high Quantization Parameter (QP) values (Kim & Jeong, 2007). These artifacts are amplified in multimedia services under the embedded mobile environment such as music video, which contains a large amount of motion and illumination variation between successive frames. Many image/video enhancement approaches have been developed to reduce the artifacts.

Most of deblocking algorithms are post-processing algorithms (Kim et al., 1999; Su et al., 1999; Yu et al., 2004; List et al., 2003). For example, overlapped block motion compensation (Su & Mersereau, 2000) and a post-processing algorithm which applies a smoothing filter according to the amount of detected block artifact (Yu & Zhang, 2004) were proposed. A deblocking algorithm was proposed by adaptively selecting a filter in boundaries (List, Joch, Lainema, Bjontegaard, &

Karczewicz, 2003). The post-processing algorithm should be implemented in every decoder device such as mobile phone, thus it is not practical due to high cost and poor efficiency with regard to a large number of decoders. On the other hand, the pre-processing algorithms that are applied to encoder have been rarely studied and they require modifying encoder or parameter values. For example, re-allocation according to Region Of Interest (ROI) for efficient coding was proposed (Chai, Ngan, & Bouzerdoum, 2000).

This chapter proposes a pre-processing algorithm that can be used to improve the performance of video codec, especially focusing on reducing block artifacts without modifying encoder and any information on the encoder. Also to reduce ringing artifacts, many approaches have been proposed such as post-preprocessing based on the visible ringing measure (Oguz, Hu, & Nguyen, 1998) and the method combining deblocking and deringing (Wan, Mrak, Ramzan, & Izquierdo, 2007). Compared with modification or replacement of existing de-blocking filter or post-processing methods, the proposed algorithm has two features to enhance the quality of video. First, the proposed method is independent of codec. Most post-processing algorithms for reducing coding artifacts are dependent on the codec operation and their performances depend on parameter selection of codec. However, our algorithm is dependent only on the characteristics of the input video sequence which is to be compressed by codec and implemented without any modification of codec. Also, according to experimental results, the proposed algorithm with trilateral filtering is more suitable for multimedia streaming service which contains a lot of motion such as music video contents than other existing spatial or temporal filters.

Our previous work (Kim, Lee, Park, & Park, 2010) related to enhancement of compressed sequence is briefly discussed. Our previous work includes the processes of motion map generation, high-boost filtering for reducing coding artifacts and temporal noise, and enhancing edges according to the edge map. In this chapter, motion information is directly used as temporal weight in trilateral filtering without computing the motion map. Because of trilateral filtering which uses temporal weight for pre-processing, amount of smoothing is determined for better enhancement of motion region. Also, a high-boost filter, used for enhancing high-frequency components such as edges (Kim, Lee, Park, & Park, 2010), often degrades the quality of sequences because it excessively enhances high-frequency components. By enhancing high-frequency components, the number of bits used for the bitstream will be increased; causing degradation of the compression efficiency even though a high-boost filter gives sharp and clean edges. Also, ringing artifacts are detected in the sequence around enhanced edges by high-boost filtering. In this chapter, trilateral filtering with temporal weight gives better performance with few artifacts in compressing videos that constrains lots of moving pixels. Compared with the previous work, the proposed pre-processing method in this chapter shows better performance in terms of the objective and subjective image quality.

This chapter is organized as follows: in the second section, streaming service and related video coding technology are described. In the next section, the proposed pre-processing algorithm that performs adaptive edge-preserving smoothing and detail enhancement in video codec such as H.263 and H.264 are presented. In the fourth section, experimental results and comparison of the proposed algorithm with previous work are shown. The chapter is concluded in the final section.

BACKGROUND

We review the characteristics of conventional codec and then describe the deblocking filters that enhance the quality of decoded images.

Overview of H.263 and H.264

Common video coding algorithms use two types of redundancies: temporal and spatial redundancies. By reducing these redundancies, streaming data can be compressed into less amount of data and video coding methods have been proposed to reduce the redundancy with little degradation of image quality. For temporal redundancy reduction, most coding algorithms use the similarity between subsequent frames and detect motion vectors in each frame. However, compression based on reducing temporal redundancy suffers from visible artifacts. To reduce the spatial redundancy, for example, the discrete cosine transform (DCT) is used. For low bit-rate compression, the prediction error image is divided into non-overlapping macroblocks and each macroblock is coded by the DCT, in which high-frequency components are forced to zero by quantization, which produces block artifacts around block boundaries.

H.263 (Rijkse, 1996) is one of the most efficient video coding standards at very low bit-rate transmission in multimedia streaming service, especially in videoconference. H.263 was recommended by international telecommunication union-telecommunication sector (ITU-T) based on H.261. H.263 compression is performed based on motion-compensation and the DCT of the prediction error. The motion-compensated prediction error is transformed by the DCT and DCT coefficients are quantized and encoded into bitstream. Meanwhile, H.264 (Wiegand et al., 2003) was developed by joint team of ITU and International Standardization Organization (ISO) / International Electrotechnical Commission (IEC). It is also known as MPEG-4 part 10 and Advance Video Coding (AVC). H.264 gives better performance than H.263 and MPEG-4. At much lower bit-rate, H.264 gives better picture quality and higher compression efficiency than previous standards (such as

H.263 or MPEG-4). In comparison with previous standards, H.264 maintains the same basic framework, but for more efficient performance, it includes some modifications. For example, in comparison with H.263, H.264 supports various block sizes, 1/4-pel motion estimation, multiple reference frame selection, and multiple bi-directional mode selection in motion estimation and compensation steps. In transformation step, H.263 uses integer-based transform instead of the DCT. In entropy coding, H.264 adopts universal variable length coding, context adaptive variable length codes, and context adaptive binary arithmetic coding.

As mentioned above, block-based video coding suffers from many kinds of coding artifacts. Block artifacts are noticeable in uniform area and degrades image quality more because the Human Vision System (HVS) is very sensitive to brightness of details

H.263 and H.263+ support the deblocking filter (Zitova & Flusser, 2003) as the optional mode and most of these deblocking filters are post-filters that usually reduce block artifacts in decoder. In H.264/AVC video coding processing, the deblocking filter is used for reducing block artifacts. For example, an adaptive deblocking filter is applied for reducing block artifacts. H.264 standard includes the in-loop deblocking filter within the motion compensation prediction loop and the post-processing filter. Therefore, the deblocking filter in H.264 is not only reducing block artifacts but also improving performance in the prediction step. Even if the deblocking block is very effective in reducing coding artifacts, the in-loop filter requires high computational complexity, especially, with about 30% increase in the computation time in decoder side.

Unlike the deblocking filter used in coding standard, the proposed pre-processing algorithm is performed in front of coding process. This filter operates independently of a coding scheme so that reducing artifacts is performed without modifying the coding algorithm. In this chapter, a pre-processing algorithm for edge-preserving smoothing and detail enhancement is implemented in the context of H.263 and H.264.

BILATERAL FILTERING

A bilateral filter is a nonlinear filter that smoothes an image while preserving edges (Tomasi & Manduchi, 1998). It uses Gaussian functions in defining domain and range weights. Domain and range weights are used to compute the weighted average of intensities of neighboring pixels depending on the spatial proximity and intensity similarity, respectively, with respect to the center pixel of the window. The total weight of a bilateral filter is obtained by multiplying two weight functions, and the image enhanced by a bilateral filter $f_b(i, j)$ is defined as

$$f_b(i,j) = \frac{\sum\limits_{(m,n)\in N} W_d\big((i,j),(m,n);\sigma_d\big) W_r\big((i,j),(m,n);\sigma_r\big) f_o'(m,n)}{\sum\limits_{(m,n)\in N} W_d\big((i,j),(m,n);\sigma_d\big) W_r\big((i,j),(m,n);\sigma_r\big)} \qquad (1)$$

where $f_o'(m,n)$ is the intensity value at (m,n) of the down-sampled video f_o' and N represents the set of neighboring pixels in the window whose center pixel is at (i,j). Both weight functions are Gaussian functions. First, the domain weight is determined by the spatial proximity between two pixels (i,j) and (m,n), which is defined as

$$W_d\big((i,j),(m,n);\sigma_d\big) = \frac{1}{\sqrt{2\pi}\sigma_d} \exp\left\{-\Big(|i-m|^2 + |j-n|^2\Big)\Big/2\sigma_d^2\right\} \qquad (2)$$

where σ_d is a scale parameter of the domain filter.

The range weight is determined by the difference of intensities between two pixels, which is defined as

$$W_r\big((i,j),(m,n);\sigma_r\big) = \frac{1}{\sqrt{2\pi}\sigma_r} \exp\left\{-\big(f_o'(i,j) - f_o'(m,n)\big)^2\Big/2\sigma_r^2\right\} \qquad (3)$$

where σ_r is a scale parameter of the range filter.

PROPOSED PRE-PROCESSING ALGORITHM USING TRILATERAL FILTERING

Overview of the Proposed Pre-Processing Algorithm

Figure 1 shows the block diagram of the proposed pre-processing algorithm and coding process. First, using bicubic interpolation (Zitova & Flusser, 2003) we down-sample the original input video (f_o) to the target size, for example, Common Intermediate Format (CIF) or Quarter CIF (QCIF), which is the common size for multimedia service in mobile environment. Then, the down-sampled video (f_o') goes through the proposed pre-processing algorithm. Finally, output of pre-processing (f_b) is used as input of codec and producing codec output image (f_{dec}). In this chapter, we use trilateral filtering for pre-processing, in which temporal weighting is added to the existing bilateral filter (Tomasi & Manduchi, 1998).

Trilateral Filtering using Temporal Weight

The human eye is sensitive to object motion (Duchowski & Vertegaal, 2000), especially, in mobile environment with small-size display device and low bit-rate video coding. In this chapter, we consider region of large motion as Region Of Interest (ROI), whereas region of small motion as non-ROI. This chapter proposes a motion-adaptive pre-processing algorithm that considers the object motion by using a trilateral filter, which has a temporal weight in addition to two weights (domain and range weights) of bilateral filtering [17–20]. Similar to bilateral filtering process, trilateral filtering process is defined as shown in Box 1.

We add a temporal weight by considering the amount of motion to the existing bilateral filter. Previous work (Kim, Lee, Park, & Park, 2010) proposed two Gaussian weights (domain and range weights) in the bilateral filtering; and motion adaptive bilateral filter (Kim, Lee, Park, & Park, 2010) just considers temporal distance in the temporal domain as constraint for scale parameter selection of domain and range weights. In this chapter, we use a temporal weight for trilateral filtering, in which the Sum of Square Differences (SSD) of intensities between neighborhoods of corresponding regions of two adjacent frames is used. For more details, a window used for temporal weight is shown in Figure 2, where corresponding pixels among the windows in the previous and current frames are used for computing the SSD or SAD. Like the domain and range weights, the temporal weight is determined by the weighted SSD of intensities between two collocated pixels in windows of two adjacent frames, which is defined as shown in Box 2.

With temporal weight w_t, we can smooth non-ROI region while preserve temporal edges in ROI region for effectively reducing coding artifacts. Temporal edges represent boundaries of moving objects and should be preserved, especially

Figure 1. Block diagram of the proposed pre-processing algorithm

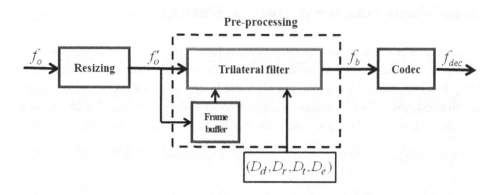

Box 1.

$$f_t(i,j;t) = \frac{\displaystyle\sum_{(m,n)\in N} w_d\left((i,j;t),(m,n;t);\sigma_d\right) w_r\left((i,j;t),(m,n;t);\sigma_r\right) W_t\left((i,j;t),(m,n;t);\sigma_t\right) f_O'(m,n;t)}{\displaystyle\sum_{(m,n)\in N} w_d\left((i,j;t),(m,n;t);\sigma_d\right) w_r\left((i,j;t),(m,n;t);\sigma_r\right) W_t\left((i,j;t),(m,n;t);\sigma_t\right)}$$

(4)

where σ_r, σ_d, and σ_t are scale parameters of the range, domain and temporal weighting function at time t, respectively. Range and domain weights (w_r and w_d) are the same as used in a bilateral filter, and the temporal weight w_t is added for temporal filtering. Also, τ represents time index of frame.

in sequence with lots of motions. The proposed method preserves temporal edges by setting small σ_t to the region of large motion, whereas large σ_t to the region of small motion. It also increases coding efficiency by reallocating more bits to preserve temporal edges in the regions of large motion while less bits to smooth the non-ROI regions of small motion. By adaptively smoothing non-ROIs and preserving details in ROIs, the proposed pre-processing method helps codec to allocate more bits to the regions of large motion, ROIs, whereas less bits to the region of small motion. According to the characteristics of the DCT used in codec, codec usually allocates more bits to the region that contains large difference with neighboring pixels. Large difference values appear around edges and details. We classify edge region and homogeneous region according to the amount of edges. Therefore, if sequence contains lots of edges, more bits are allocated, however, the compression efficiency will be decreased. On the other hand, it is possible to compress with a small number of bits in the homogeneous region that has similar intensity values over neighboring pixels. The human eye focuses on ROI, thus smoothing in non-ROI region is unnoticed. Therefore, when the non-ROI is smoothed, a small number of bits are allocated. The proposed method does not directly control bit allocation in codec but it helps the codec to efficiently allocate more bits to the region of large motion by smoothing the region of small motion.

Linear Weight Function in Trilateral Filtering

A bilateral filter has domain and range weight functions. In real-time applications, to improve the computational efficiency a linear weight function is used (Choi, Lee, Park, & Kim, 2006). In comparison with the Gaussian function, a linear weight function reduces the computation time down to 30% on the average. For example, a one-dimensional (1-D) weight function is defined as a linearly decreasing function:

$$W(d;D) = \begin{cases} 1 - \dfrac{|d|}{D}, & |d| < D \\ 0, & \text{otherwise} \end{cases}$$

(7)

Figure 2. Window of a trilateral filter

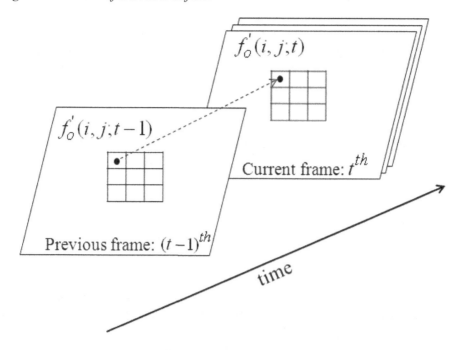

where the width of the function with nonzero values is $2D-1$, with D assumed to be a positive integer. Figure 3 shows the 1-D weight function defined by equation (7).

Also, the range weight function is defined as a 1-D weight function:

$$W_r\left((i,j),(m,n);D_r\right) = W\left(f_o'(i,j) - f_o'(m,n);D_r\right) \tag{8}$$

Box 2.

$$W_t\left((i,j;t),(m,n;t);\sigma_t\right) = \frac{1}{\sqrt{2\pi}\sigma_t}\exp\left\{-\left(\sum_{\tau \in T}\omega\left((i,j),(m,n);\sigma_e\right)\left(f_o'(m,n;t) - f_o'(m,n;\tau)\right)^2\right)^2 \Big/ 2\sigma_t^2\right\} \tag{5}$$

where T denotes the time set that includes times $t-1$, t, and $t+1$ used for computation of the temporal weight. τ represents the time index of the frame and is an element of time set T. In experiments, Ψ represents the set of neighboring pixels in the window whose center pixel is at (i,j). In equation (5), $\omega((i,j),(m,n);\sigma_e)$ denotes Gaussian weighted geometric distance in the spatial domain, which is defined as

$$\omega((i,j),(m,n);\sigma_e) = \frac{1}{\sqrt{2\pi}\sigma_e}\exp\left\{-\left(|i-m|^2 + |j-n|^2\right)\Big/2\sigma_e^2\right\} \tag{6}$$

where σ_e is a scale parameter of the domain weight function of the temporal filter (Bennett & McMillan, 2005) and the subscript e denotes temporal edge. By selecting appropriate parameter σ_t and σ_e, we can effectively preserve temporal edges.

Figure 3. 1-D weight function

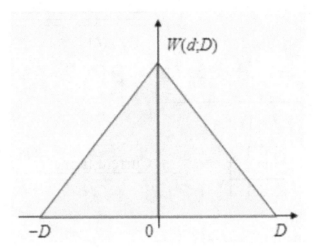

where D_r is similar to the scale parameter σ_r used in the Gaussian weight function of the conventional bilateral filter, and the width is equal to $2D_r-1$, where D_r is a positive integer.

As mentioned above, the domain filter can be represented as a two-dimensional (2-D) separable weight function (Pham & Vliet, 2005):

$$W_d\left((i,j),(m,n);D_d\right) = W(i-m;D_x)W(j-n;D_y). \tag{9}$$

In experiments, $D_d = D_x = D_y$ is assumed.

The performance of a bilateral filter is controlled by two parameters. Figure 4 shows the encoder input image pre-processed by a bilateral filter with different sets of domain and range parameter values (D_d and D_r). As D_r and D_d increase, encoder input images are smoothed more as shown in Figure 4(i) in comparison with Figure 4(a).

Figure 5 shows the decoder output images pre-processed by a bilateral filter with different sets of domain and range parameter values. As D_r and D_d increase, images are smoothed and ringing artifacts are reduced, especially in edge regions, as shown in Figure 5(i) in comparison with Figure 5(a). On the other hand, as D_r and D_d decrease, edges are preserved and blocking artifacts are reduced. In other words, in decoder output images, with small values of a bilateral filter parameter set, undesirable artifacts such as block artifacts, ringing artifacts, and false-color artifacts are shown in a decoder image. According to the HVS, artifacts in flat region are more perceptive (Duchowski & Vertegaal, 2000). Therefore, a stronger smoothing filter should be applied to flat regions than to edge regions. For instance, we can see the distortion in white flat area on the calendar in Figure 5(a). On the other hand,

Figure 4. Encoder input images pre-processed by a bilateral filter with different sets of domain and range parameter values (176×144, "mobile," 12th frame)

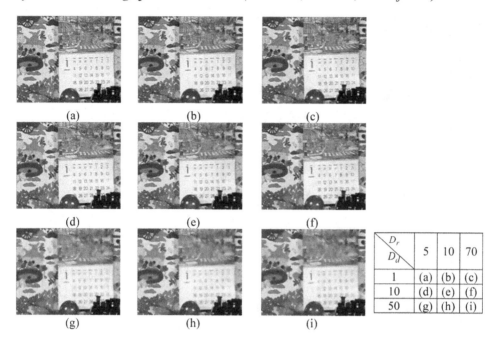

D_r D_d	5	10	70
1	(a)	(b)	(c)
10	(d)	(e)	(f)
50	(g)	(h)	(i)

large parameter values of a bilateral filter give smooth details and even coarse features. For example, numbers and picture on the calendar in Figure 5(i) are blurred and numbers are hard to read. With qualitative comparison with Figures 5(a)–5(i), we can get an optimum parameter set (D_d, D_r) in edge and homogeneous regions.

In this chapter, we add a temporal weight function:

$$
\begin{aligned}
&W_t\left((i,j;t),(i,j;\tau);D_t\right) \\
&= W\left(f_o'(i,j;t) - f_o'(i,j;\tau);D_t\right)
\end{aligned}
\tag{10}
$$

where D_t is a positive integer for the temporal weight function, with the width of the linear weight function equal to $2D_t-1$. In equation (10), τ denotes the frame number, $t-1 \leq \tau \leq t+1$ which is used for computing the temporal weight.

Parameter Selection for the Motion-Adaptive Trilateral Filter

In this chapter, we select parameter values for three weights in trilateral filtering by considering the statistical characteristics of input sequences. Especially, we consider an amount of motion and edginess as important characteristics of the sequence.

Figure 5. Decoder output images pre-processed by a bilateral filter with different sets of domain and range parameter values (176×144, "mobile," 12th frame, QP= 28)

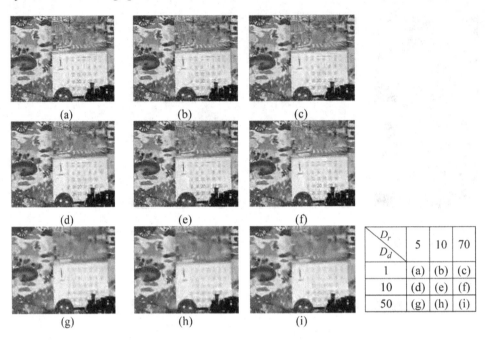

D_d \ D_r	5	10	70
1	(a)	(b)	(c)
10	(d)	(e)	(f)
50	(g)	(h)	(i)

Table 1 shows how we classify input sequences into four different groups with specific characteristics of sequences. We first divide an image into two regions: moving region and stationary region according to the amount of motion. Then, we further classify each region into two types depending on the amount of edginess: edge and homogeneous regions. According to two criteria, sequences are classified into four groups and different parameter sets are used according to the sequence group. Video sequences of Group A have ROI with lots of motion and background with lots of sharp edges, whereas video sequences of Group B have ROI with lots of motion and complex background with homogeneous regions. Video sequences of Group C have little motion and background with lots of sharp edges, whereas video sequences of Group D have little motion and background with homogeneous region. Then, in each video group, parameter values are determined by considering the characteristics of each group.

EXPERIMENTAL RESULTS AND DISCUSSIONS

Performance comparison of H.263 and H.264 video are given in term of the visual quality, object measures, and subjective measures.

Table 1. Sequence grouping and characteristics of each group

Sequence	Moving region (ROI)		Stationary region (background)		Remarks
	Edge region	Homogeneous region	Edge region	Homogeneous region	
Group A					
Bridge-close	○	✕	○	✕	ROI with lots of motion, background with lots of sharp edges
Coastguard					
Mobile					

Performance Comparisons in Terms of the Visual Quality

Computer simulations are conducted to show the effectiveness of the proposed pre-processing with various test video sequences (Sullivan, 2001). We use H.263 video codec with four QP values: 20, 24, 28, and 30 (Wu, Pan, Lim, Wu, Li, Lin, Rahardja, & Ko, 2005). Figures 6 and 7 show the comparison of the decoder output images with and without pre-processing for H.263. Figure 6(a) shows the original 84th frame of "Stefan" sequence (Group A) when QP value is 28 and Figures 6(b), 6(c), and 6(d) show the enlarged parts, indicated by solida and dotted lines in the original image, of the decoder output images with the proposed pre-processing, with the motion-adaptive bilateral filtering (Kim, Lee, Park, & Park, 2010), and without pre-processing, respectively. We can observe that characters 'BEL' in Figure 6(b) is more enhanced with less color artifacts than those in Figures 6(c) and 6(d). Also, legs of a player in Figure 6(b) are clearer than those of Figures 6(c) and 6(d) (with noticeable block artifacts).

Figure 7 shows the original 3rd frame of "Foreman" sequence (Group B) when QP value is 30 with H.263 video. Figures 7(b), 7(c), and 7(d) show the enlarged parts, indicated by solid and dotted lines in the original image, of the decoder output images with the proposed pre-processing, with the motion-adaptive bilateral filtering (Kim, Lee, Park, & Park, 2010), and without pre-processing, respectively. As shown in Figure 7(b), the decoder output image with the proposed pre-processing preserves edges and reduces block artifacts in homogeneous regions. Also ringing artifacts and false-color artifacts are reduced in Figure 7(b).

In addition, we also conduct experiments with H.264/AVC. To show the performance of the proposed pre-processing in H.264 video, we use CIF images with four QP values: 28, 32, 36, and 40 which are recommended in (Wu, Pan, Lim, Wu, Li, Lin, Rahardja, & Ko, 2005). With H.264 coding, the decoded output images with the proposed pre-processing show also better visual performance than with

Figure 6. Comparison of the decoder output images (H.263, 176×144, "Stefan", 84th frame, QP=28). (a) original image, (b) enlarged decoder output image with proposed pre-processing, (c) enlarged decoder output image with motion-adaptive bilateral filtering (Kim, Lee, Park, & Park, 2010), and (d) enlarged decoder output image without pre-processing.

| (a) | (b) | (c) | (d) |

H.263. Figures 8 and 9 show the comparison of the decoder output images with and without pre-processing in H.264. Figure 8(a) shows the original 7th frame of "Stefan" sequence (Group A) when QP value is 36. Figures 8(b), 8(c), and 8(d) show the enlarged parts, indicated by solida and dotted lines in the original image, of the decoder output images with the proposed pre-processing, with the motion-adaptive bilateral filtering (Kim, Lee, Park, & Park, 2010), and without pre-processing, respectively. As shown in Figure 8(b), detail of character 'n' in the image enclosed by a red rectangle is preserved. Also in Figure 8(b), images enclosed by a solid

Figure 7. Comparison of the decoder output images (H.263, 176×144, "foreman," 3rd frame, QP=30). (a) original image, (b) enlarged decoder output image with proposed pre-processing, (c) enlarged decoder output image with motion-adaptive bilateral filtering (Kim, Lee, Park, & Park, 2010), and (d) enlarged decoder output image without pre-processing.

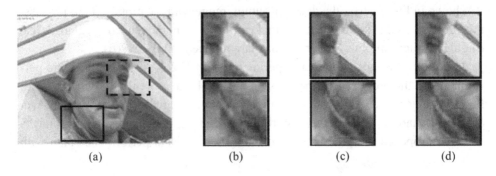

| (a) | (b) | (c) | (d) |

Figure 8. Comparison of the decoder output images (H.264, 176×144, "foreman," 7th frame, QP=36). (a) original image, (b) enlarged decoder output image with proposed pre-processing, (c) enlarged decoder output image with motion-adaptive bilateral filtering (Kim, Lee, Park, & Park, 2010), and (d) enlarged decoder output image without pre-processing.

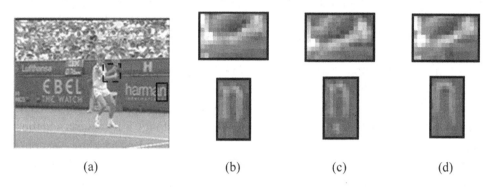

(a) (b) (c) (d)

line show that the result of the proposed method has clear boundaries with reduced block artifacts.

Figure 9(a) shows the original 39th frame of "Akiyo" sequence (Group D) when QP value is 40. Figures 9(b), 9(c), and 9(d) show the enlarged parts of the decoder output, indicated by solid and dotted lines in the original image, with the proposed pre-processing, with the motion-adaptive bilateral filtering (Kim, Lee, Park, & Park, 2010), and without pre-processing, respectively. As shown in Figure 9(b), we can see noticeable ringing and block artifacts near the left shoulder of the woman in the

Figure 9. Comparison of the decoder output images (H.264, 176×144, "akiyo," 39th frame, QP=40). (a) original image, (b) enlarged decoder output image with proposed pre-processing, (c) enlarged decoder output image with motion-adaptive bilateral filtering (Kim, Lee, Park, & Park, 2010), and (d) enlarged decoder output image without pre-processing.

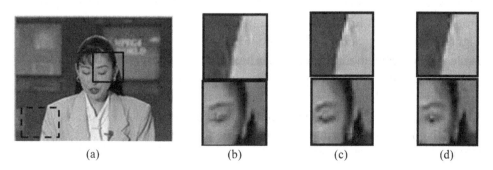

(a) (b) (c) (d)

images enclosed by a dotted line. Also, the images enclosed by a solid line show that block artifacts and color artifacts near the eyes of the woman are removed effectively and details are preserved better than in Figures 9(c) and 9(d).

We evaluate the decoded images that are filtered by conventional filters and the proposed filter as a pre-processing in terms of the objective quality by the peak signal to noise ratio (PSNR) (Ong, Yang, Lin, Lu, Yao, Lin, Rahardja, & Seng, 2006). Figure 10 shows RD curves for four sequences encoded by H.263. In this experiment, the proposed method is compared with low pass filter and spatio-temporal filter. Also we compare the method without filtering. In this experiment, we exclude result by the motion-adaptive bilateral filtering (Kim, Lee, Park, & Park, 2010). The motion-adaptive bilateral filter performs high-boost filtering that enhances the edges. High pass filtering generally increases the bit-rate with more image information and thus requires higher bit-rate on the same PSNR than other methods. Therefore, we compare four methods except for motion-adaptive bilateral filtering. Bold line with X symbol shows the performance of the proposed method, showing that the PSNR is higher than other methods at the same bit rate. Dotted line with small circle symbol shows the performance of low pass filter that is a 3×3 averaging filter. Also, dotted line with bigger circle symbol shows the performance of the spatio-temporal filter. This filter is used as averaging filter when motion occurs. Otherwise, the filter is used as temporal filter that gives the average value of two frames. The motion is detected according to the difference between two frames. In Figure 10, the proposed method shows indeed better performance than other methods. In Figures 10(b) and 10(c), the low pass filter shows better performance at some bit-rate. Especially, in high QP value, the proposed method shows better performance. Therefore in high QP value setting, artifacts are annoying a lot and artifacts can be suppressed by low pass filtering. Also, in small display device, users focus on the motion region, thus the filters that consider motion shows better performance.

Figure 11 shows RD curves for four sequences encoded by H.264. As in Figure 10, four methods are compared and bold line with X symbol shows the performance of the proposed method. Dotted line with small circle symbol shows the performance of low pass filter. Also, dotted line with bigger circle symbol shows the performance of the spatio-temporal filter. The proposed method shows that the PSNR of the proposed method is higher than those of other methods at the same bit-rate. In Figures 11(a), 11(c), and 11(d), the proposed method shows indeed better performance than other methods. Especially, in high QP value, most PSNR of the proposed method is higher than other methods. Meanwhile, performance without pre-processing is better than low pass filtering or spatial-temporal filtering in low QP value or high bit-rate. When the proposed method is applied to H.264, which has better compression performance than H.263, the performance of the proposed method is shown indistinctive.

Figure 10. Comparison of the average PSNR at various bit-rates (H.263): (a) mobile, (b) foreman, (c) salesman, and (d) claire

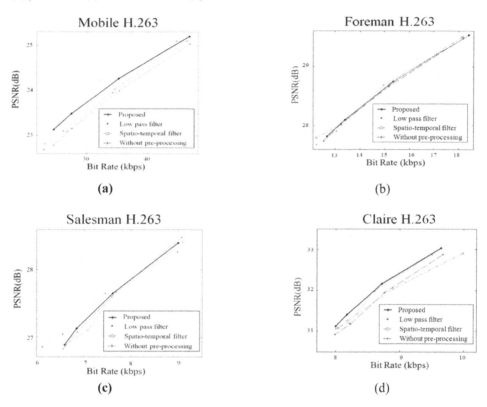

Table 2 shows performance comparison of decoder images in terms of the PSNR for H.263 video, whereas Table 4 for H.264 video. The proposed method is compared with four filtering methods. We compare method without any processing, motion-adaptive bilateral filter, low pass filter, and spatio-temporal filter. Low pass filter is averaging filter in 3×3 window. Spatio-temporal filter is used as averaging filter in the spatial domain exists between two adjacent frames, otherwise, as a temporal filter that uses the average value of three frames. The motion is detected according to the intensity difference between two adjacent frames. In Tables 3 and 4, we use bold type to highlight the largest PSNR value among five filtering methods. Most PSNR value of the proposed method is the highest value. Motion-adaptive bilateral filter (Kim, Lee, Park, & Park, 2010) and spatio-temporal filter show better performance than the methods without pre-processing and low pass filtering. Especially, in Table 3, the proposed method shows better performance with high QP values. In high QP value case, the compression is performed with a limited number of bits so that it is necessary to allocate the bit efficiently for reducing coding arti-

Figure 11. Comparison of the average PSNR at various bit-rates (H.264): (a) coastguard, (b) foreman, (c) salesman, and (d) claire

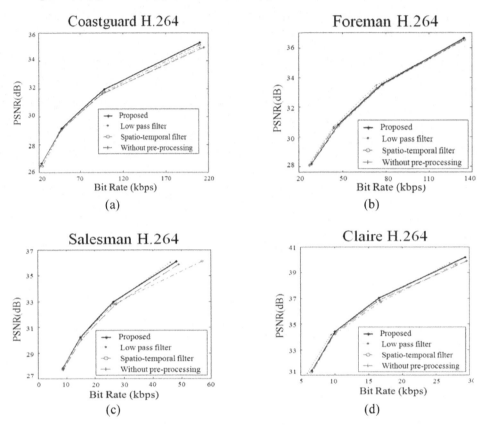

facts. Our pre-processing algorithm aims to reduce block artifacts, however, encoded images with low QP values may not have noticeable artifacts. As a result, as shown in Table 3, we can get a high PSNR improvement with pre-processing on the average, especially with high QP values. Table 4 shows the PSNR with H.264 video, which shows that the PSNR improvement by the proposed algorithm with high QP values is higher than with low QP values. In more detail, especially, PSNR improvement by the proposed algorithm for sequences in Groups A and C that contain complex background is large, because our algorithm considers not only motion but also spatial edginess for video enhancement.

Subjective quality measures are important factors to evaluate the video quality of sequences in various applications and many kinds of methods have been proposed (ITU-T Recommendation P.800., 1996; ITU-T Recommendation P.910., 1996). We evaluate the result of each method in terms of the subjective quality by the mean opinion score (MOS) (ITU-T Recommendation P.800., 1996). Especially, in the

Table 2. Performance comparison of the PSNR with/without pre-processing in H.263 video

Sequence	QP	Proposed	Motion-adaptive bilateral(Kim, Lee, Park, & Park, 2010)	Spatio-temporal filter	Low pass filter	Without pre-processing
Group A						
Mobile	20	**25.197**	25.039	25.099	25.105	25.055
	24	**24.264**	23.994	23.954	24.032	24.002
	28	**23.482**	23.152	23.103	23.100	23.157
	30	**23.132**	22.783	22.689	22.806	22.788
Bridge-close	20	28.566	28.564	28.600	28.620	**28.631**
	24	**27.925**	27.811	27.832	27.902	27.865
	28	**27.423**	27.297	27.299	27.307	27.339
	30	**27.200**	27.061	27.089	27.097	27.106
Coastguard	20	28.147	28.292	28.301	28.284	**28.303**
	24	27.421	27.472	27.445	27.437	**27.484**
	28	**26.822**	26.809	26.808	26.798	26.806
	30	**26.542**	26.531	26.439	26.536	26.529

proposed pre-processing method, PSNR value or performance of codec can be degraded by emphasizing enhancement in ROI region. The proposed method gives better performance as shown in Figures 10 and 11 and Tables 2 and 3, however, sometimes it gives poor performance. The proposed method has better subjective performance in a limited bit-rate range, thus we evaluate the performance in terms of the MOS. Table 4 shows the MOS of the proposed method, motion-adaptive bilateral filtering (Kim, Lee, Park, & Park, 2010), and the method without any pre-processing. In this experiment, the QP value is set to 20 in H.263 video and to 32 in H.264 video. The MOS tests are performed with 47 persons. The average MOS of 47 persons is used to evaluate the perceived subjective quality after decoding. To be a fair test, subjects are under the same environment. The MOS consists of five levels; scores 1, 2, 3, 4, and 5 refer to bad, poor, fair, good, and excellent, respectively. According to the criteria, people evaluate the subject quality of the sequence. As shown in Tables 2 and 3, most of decoder output sequences with the proposed method give higher PSNR values than those with other methods. As shown in Table 4, the proposed method also gives higher MOS values. However, in some cases, MOS value of the motion-adaptive bilateral filtering method (Kim, Lee, Park, & Park, 2010) is higher than that of the proposed method. It is because the motion-

Table 3. Performance comparison of the PSNR with/without pre-processing in H.264 video

Sequence	QP	Proposed	Motion-adaptive bilateral (Kim, Lee, Park, & Park, 2010)	Spatio-temporal filter	Low pass filter	Without pre-processing
Group A						
Mobile	28	34.179	**34.370**	34.097	34.109	34.120
	32	**30.073**	30.021	29.875	30.007	30.000
	36	**26.609**	26.192	26.572	26.552	26.560
	40	**23.643**	22.982	23.607	23.618	23.573
Bridge-close	28	35.782	**35.969**	35.384	35.437	35.299
	32	32.723	**32.896**	32.468	32.506	32.333
	36	**30.226**	30.113	30.037	30.086	29.967
	40	**28.248**	27.892	27.989	28.064	28.062
Coastguard	28	**35.294**	35.205	34.932	35.132	34.947
	32	**31.940**	31.803	31.597	31.747	31.627
	36	**29.152**	28.929	28.945	29.035	28.879
	40	**26.623**	26.320	26.337	26.452	26.443

adaptive bilateral filtering method contains high-boost filtering that preserves and emphasizes the edges. Even though the motion-adaptive bilateral filtering method gives better performance than other methods in terms of the MOS, it requires larger bit rates. As a result, the proposed method has better performance than the motion-adaptive bilateral filtering method under the limited bit stream condition. Experimental results show that the proposed method effectively enhances the subjective quality of video that is degraded by block artifacts.

Figures 12 and 13 show the PSNR comparison for 100 frames with H.263 and H.264 video, respectively. These figures show that the proposed method gives the highest PSNR value for 100 frames. In Figure 12, the PSNR is decreased periodically, which is a characteristic related to P-B frame mode of a codec used in our experiment. Tables 3 and 4 and Figures 12 and 13 show that the proposed method gives better performance than other methods in terms of the PSNR.

In summary, the proposed algorithm (with pre-processing) outperforms the existing methods (motion-adaptive bilateral algorithm and the method without pre-processing), in term of the visual quality, the PSNR (Tables 3 and 4), and MOS (Table 4). Small size of display device in mobile environment requires reducing

Table 4. Performance comparison of the MOS with/without pre-processing in H.263 and H.264 video

Sequence	H.263			H.264		
	Proposed	Motion-adaptive bilateral [10]	Without pre-processing	Proposed	Motion-adaptive bilateral [10]	Without pre-processing
Group A						
Mobile	**2.382**	2.297	2.255	**3.914**	3.574	3.829
Coastguard	2.553	**2.617**	2.489	3.787	**3.851**	3.553

artifacts while enhancing important edge information. The proposed pre-processing algorithms can be effectively used for efficient adaptive edge-preserving smoothing and detail enhancement of H.263 and H.264 video.

FUTURE RESEARCH

Further research will focus on the automatic selection of parameter values of the trilateral filter based on effective motion and spatial information.

CONCLUSION

Using trilateral filtering, we propose a new pre-processing method for edge-preserving smoothing and detail enhancement of H.263 and H.264 video. Three weights (domain, range, and temporal weights) are used to effectively reduce coding artifacts and to enhance spatial and temporal edges in decoder output video. Experimental results with various test sequences encoded by H.263 and H.264 show the effectiveness of the proposed method in terms of the PSNR and subjective visual quality (MOS). The proposed algorithm can be used as pre-processing for video enhancement of H.263, H.264, and MPEG-4 video.

ACKNOWLEDGMENT

This work was supported in part by PIXTREE.

Figure 12. PSNR comparison for 100 frames (H.263, QP=30): (a) mobile, (b) claire, and (c) akiyo

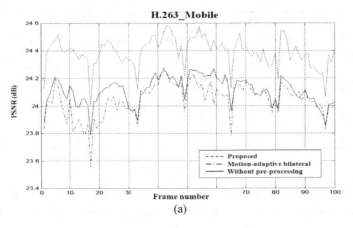

(a)

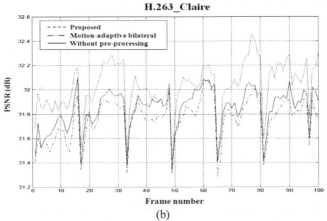

(b)

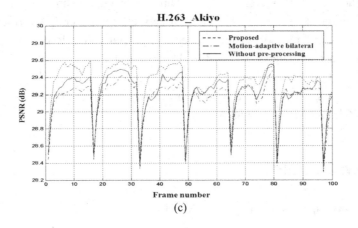

(c)

Figure 13. PSNR comparison for 100 frames (H.264, QP=28): (a) mobile, (b) claire, and (c) akiyo

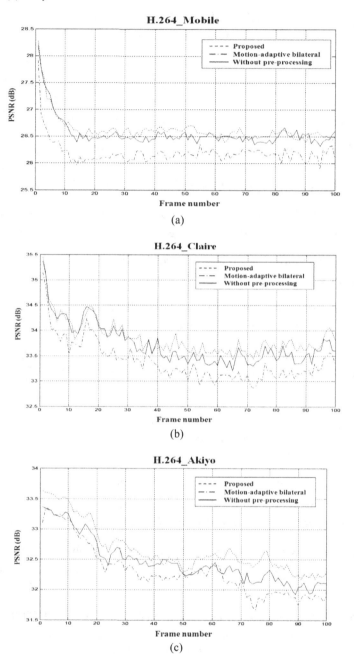

(a)

(b)

(c)

REFERENCES

Bennett, E. P., & McMillan, L. (2005). Video enhancement using per-pixel virtual exposures. *ACM Transactions on Graphics*, *24*(3), 845–852. doi:10.1145/1073204.1073272

Chai, D., Ngan, K. N., & Bouzerdoum, A. (2000). Foreground/background bit allocation for region-of-interest coding. In *Proceedings International Conference on Image Processing*, (pp. 438-441). Vancouver, Canada: IEEE.

Choi, H.-R., Lee, J. W., Park, R.-H., & Kim, J.-S. (2006). False contour reduction using directional dilation and edge preserving filtering. *IEEE Transactions on Consumer Electronics*, *52*(3), 1099–1109. doi:10.1109/TCE.2006.1706513

Duchowski, A. T., & Vertegaal, R. C. (2000). Eye-based interaction in graphical system: Theory and practice. In *Proceedings of ACM SIGGRAPH 2000*. ACM Press.

Etoh, M., & Yoshimura, T. (2005). Advances in wireless video delivery. *Proceedings of the IEEE*, *93*(1), 111–122. doi:10.1109/JPROC.2004.839605

ITU-T Recommendation P.800. (1996). *Methods for subjective determination of transmission quality*. Geneva, Switzerland: International Telecommunication Union.

ITU-T Recommendation P.910. (1996). *Subjective video quality assessment methods for multimedia applications*. Geneva, Switzerland: International Telecommunication Union.

Kim, J., & Jeong, J. (2007). Adaptive deblocking technique for mobile video. *IEEE Transactions on Consumer Electronics*, *53*(4), 1694–1702. doi:10.1109/TCE.2007.4429272

Kim, J.-H., Lee, J. W., Park, R.-H., & Park, M.-H. (2010). Adaptive edge-preserving smoothing and detail enhancement for video processing of H.263. In *Proceedings of the International Conference Consumer Electronics*, (pp. 337–338). IEEE.

Kim, S. D., Yi, J., Kim, H. M., & Ra, J. B. (1999). A deblocking filter with two separate modes in block-based video coding. *IEEE Transactions on Circuits and Systems for Video Technology*, *9*(1), 156–160. doi:10.1109/76.744282

List, P., Joch, A., Lainema, J., Bjontegaard, G., & Karczewicz, M. (2003). Adaptive deblocking filter. *IEEE Transactions on Circuits and Systems for Video Technology*, *13*(7), 614–619. doi:10.1109/TCSVT.2003.815175

Oguz, S. H., Hu, Y. H., & Nguyen, T. Q. (1998). Image coding ringing artifact reduction using morphological post-filtering. In *Proceedings IEEE Second Workshop Multimedia Signal Processing*, (pp. 628–633). IEEE Press.

Ong, E. P., Yang, X., Lin, W., Lu, Z., Yao, S., & Lin, X. (2006). Perceptual quality and objective quality measurements of compressed videos. *Journal of Visual Communication and Image Representation, 17*(4), 717–737. doi:10.1016/j.jvcir.2005.11.002

Pei, J., Lu, Z., & Xie, W. (2006). A method for IR point target detection based on spatial-temporal bilateral filter. In *Proceedings International Conference Pattern Recognition*, (pp. 846–849). IEEE.

Pham, T. Q., & Vliet, L. J. (2005). Separable bilateral filtering for fast video preprocessing. In *Proceedings of the IEEE International Conference Multimedia and Expo ICME 2005*, (pp. 454–457). IEEE Press.

Rijkse, K. (1996). H.263 video coding for low-bit-rate communication. *IEEE Communications Magazine, 34*(12), 42–45. doi:10.1109/35.556485

Su, J. K., & Mersereau, R. M. (2000). Motion estimation methods for overlapped block motion compensation. *IEEE Transactions on Image Processing, 9*(9), 1509–1521. doi:10.1109/83.862628

Sullivan, G. (2001). Recommended simulation common conditions for H.26L coding efficiency experiments on low resolution progressive scan source material. *Document VCEG-N81, 14th Meeting.*

Tomasi, C., & Manduchi, R. (1998). Bilateral filtering for gray and color images. In *Proceedings of the IEEE International Conference Computer Vision*, (pp. 839–846). IEEE Press.

Wan, S., Mrak, M., Ramzan, N., & Izquierdo, E. (2007). Perceptually adaptive joint deringing-deblocking filtering for scalable video transmission over wireless networks. *Signal Processing Image Communication, 22*(3), 266–276. doi:10.1016/j.image.2006.12.005

Webe, M., Milch, M., & Myszkowski, K. (2004). Spatio-temporal photon estimation using bilateral filtering . In *Proceedings Computer Graphics International 2004* (pp. 120–127). IEEE. doi:10.1109/CGI.2004.1309200

Wiegand, T., Sullivan, G. J., Bjntegaard, G., & Luthra, A. (2003). Overview of the H.264/AVC video coding standard. *IEEE Transactions on Circuits and Systems for Video Technology, 13*(7), 560–576. doi:10.1109/TCSVT.2003.815165

Wiegand, T., Sullivan, G. J., Bjøntegaard, G., & Luthra, A. (2003). *Draft ITU-T recommendation and final draft international standard of joint video specification.* ITU-T Rec. H.264/ISO/IEC 14496-10 AVC. Retrieved from http://www.itu.int

Wu, D., Pan, F., Lim, K. P., Wu, S., Li, Z. G., & Lin, X. (2005). Fast intermode decision in H.264/AVC video coding. *IEEE Transactions on Circuits System Video Technology, 15*(6), 953–958. doi:10.1109/TCSVT.2005.848304

Yu, Z., & Zhang, J. (2004). Video deblocking with fine-grained scalable complexity for embedded mobile computing. In *Proceedings of the 7th International Conference on Signal Processing*, (pp. 1173–1178). IEEE.

Zitova, B., & Flusser, J. (2003). Image registration methods: A survey. *Image and Vision Computing, 21*(11), 977–1000. doi:10.1016/S0262-8856(03)00137-9

ADDITIONAL READING

Bennett, E. P., Mason, J. L., & McMillan, L. (2007). Multispectral bilateral video fusion. *IEEE Transactions on Image Processing, 16*(5), 1185–1194. doi:10.1109/TIP.2007.894236

Duchowski, A. T., & Vertegaal, R. C. (2000). Eye-based interaction in graphical system: Theory and practice. In *Proceedings of ACM SIGGRAPH 2000,* (pp. 1–25). ACM Press.

Gonzalez, R. C., & Woods, R. E. (2010). *Digital image processing* (3rd ed.). Upper Saddle River, NJ: Pearson Education, Inc.

KEY TERMS AND DEFINITIONS

Bilateral Filter: A bilateral filter is a nonlinear filter that smoothes an image while preserving edges.

Codec: Related to IC chip for processing encoding or decoding data streaming signal.

MOS: Mean Opinion Score is subjective image quality measurement.

QP: Quantization Parameter, control quantity of quantization.

R-D Curve: Coding characteristics which shows quantization versus streaming rate.

ROI: Region of interest, selected region where user detect for special purpose.

Chapter 6
Thresholding Selection Based on Fuzzy Entropy and Bee Colony Algorithm for Image Segmentation

Yonghao Xiao
South China University of Technology, China & Foshan University, China

Weiyu Yu
South China University of Technology, China & Soochow University, China

Jing Tian
Wuhan University of Science and Technology, China

ABSTRACT

Image thresholding segmentation based on Bee Colony Algorithm (BCA) and fuzzy entropy is presented in this chapter. The fuzzy entropy function is simplified with single parameter. The BCA is applied to search the minimum value of the fuzzy entropy function. According to the minimum function value, the optimal image threshold is obtained. Experimental results are provided to demonstrate the superior performance of the proposed approach.

DOI: 10.4018/978-1-4666-3958-4.ch006

1. INTRODUCTION

Image segmentation is an important task where pixels with similar features (such as gray, color, texture, and shape) are classified into semantic objects or homogeneous regions. It serves as a key in image understand and pattern recognition and is a fundamental step toward high-level vision, which is significant for object recognition, image retrieval, video tracking, semantic analysis and other applications. In recent years, a large of segmentation methods have been developed, among all the existing segmentation techniques, thresholding technique is one of the most popular due to its simplicity and accuracy. The threshold processing plays an important role in the image segmentation (Sezgin & Sankur, 2004). In classical threshold segmentation (Sahoo, Soltani, Wong, et al., 1988; Pal & Pal, 1993; Sezgin & Sankur, 2004; Otsu, 1979), an image is usually segmented and classified to object and background according to threshold selection. The threshold segmentation is not suitable definitely when an image is complex. There have been some approaches based on threshold segmentation which give the optimum threshold, such as Otsu algorithm (Unnikrishnan, Pantofaru, & Hebert, 2007; Enyedi, Konyha, & Fazekas, 2005; Bilger, Kupferschlager, Muller-Schauenburg, et al., 2001; Otsu, 1979). One-dimensional Otsu algorithm can obtain better segmentation results, but it can't reflect the space-related information among the image pixels, it is difficult to obtain satisfactory segmentation results when the image has noise. To solve this problem, Liu (Liu & Li, 1993) proposed the two-dimensional histogram which is composed of the pixel gray-level distribution and neighborhood average gray-level distribution. Hou (Hou, Hu, & Nowinski, 2006) presented that the threshold obtained by otsu'method tends to get closer to the cluster with a larger variance or a larger quantity of pixels in an image. Hou also proposed a minimum class variance thresholding method which decides the optimal threshold based on the smallest variance of pixels within a class. There is some uncertainty when the image quality is not so good. The nature of this ambiguity in an image therefore arises from the uncertainty present. In order to decide whether a pixel can classify as a white or black, it is proposed to suggest a quantitative measure for fuzziness present in an image (Huang & Wang, 1995).

Entropy plays a significant role in image processing. The principle of entropy is to use uncertainty as a measure to describe the information contained in a source. Fuzzy entropy does not have the same meaning to information entropy, but rather provides a flexible description of the histogram. It is generally accepted that the histograms of most images follow multimodal distribution. There is many methods about entropy in image segmentation (Pal & Pal, 1989; Kapur, Sahoo, & Wong, 1985; Cheng, Chen, & Jiang, 2000). Pal (Pal & Pal, 1991) proposed an approach to measure the degree of resemblance between the template and the gray-scale image.

The classification status of the edge pixels in the template is modified in a way to maximize the Gray-scale Image Entropy. Cheng et al. (Cheng, Chen, & Jiang, 2000) presented a threshold approach by performing fuzzy partition on a two-dimensional histogram, which is based on the fuzzy relation and the maximum fuzzy entropy principle. Zhao et al. (Zhao, Fu, & Yan, 2001) designed a three-level threshold method for image segmentation. Fuzzy entropy through probability analysis, fuzzy partition and entropy theory is defined. Shelokar (Shelokar, Jayaraman, & Kulkarni, 2004) considered the fuzzy memberships as an indication, showing how strongly a gray value belongs to the background or to the foreground. There is obviously no guarantee of regular and simple conditions when segmenting natural images containing multiple objects with great variance of contents. A large number of previous works focused on segmenting images with distinct foreground will probably not be able to correctly detect objects from such images.

Swarm Intelligence (Bonabeau, Dorigo, & Theraulaz, 2001; Engelbrecht, 2005; Beni & Wang, 1989) has attracted many researcher's attention working on bioinformatics related problems in recent years. Bonabeau (Bonabeau, Dorigo, & Theraulaz, 1999) has first defined the swarm intelligence as "any attempt to design algorithms or distributed problem-solving devices inspired by the collective behavior of social insect colonies and other animal societies." Algorithms are motivated by the collective behavior of social insects (such as ant, bees and fish). These insects with very limited individual capability can cooperatively perform complex tasks necessary for their survival. For the past years there has been a slow but steady increase of research papers reporting the success of SI based search, clustering methods applied to the field of computational biology. Basic principles define the SI paradigm as follows (Milonas, 1994):

1. **Proximity Principle:** The swarm can carry out simple space and time computations.
2. **Quality Principle:** The swarm should be able to respond to quality factors in the environment.
3. **Principle of Diverse Response:** The swarm should not commit its activities along excessively narrow channels.
4. **Principle of Stability:** The swarm should not change its mode of behavior every time the environment changes.
5. **Principle of Adaptability:** The swarm must be able to change behavior mote when it is worth the computational price.

A swarm can be viewed as a group of agents cooperating to achieve some purposeful behavior and achieve some goal (Grosan, Abraham, & Monica, 2006).

This collective intelligence seems to emerge from what are often large groups of relatively simple agents. The agents use simple local rules to govern their actions and via the interactions of the entire group, the swarm achieves its objectives. An autonomous agent is a subsystem that interacts with its environment, which probably consists of other agents, but acts relatively independently from all other agents. The autonomous agent does not follow commands from a leader, or some global plan (Flake, 1999). Dorigo et al. (Sezgin & Sankur, 2004) proposed Artificial Ant Colony System as a new heuristic to solve combinatorial optimization problems. This new heuristic, called Ant Colony Optimization (ACO) has been found to be both robust and versatile in handling a wide range of combinatorial optimization problems. For instance, Malisia (Malisia & Tizhoosh, 2006) proposed an image binary segmentation method by adding ant pheromone information to original image data set based on ant colony algorithm and then clustering the data set with K-means algorithm. Yu proposed an Local Ant Colony Optimization for image binary segmentation (Yu, Zou, & Yu, 2010). Tao et al. (Tao, Jin, & Liu, 2007) used the ant colony optimization method to obtain the optimal parameters of the entropy-based object segmentation approach. Han (Han & Shi, 2007) presented a method for fuzzy pixel clustering in image segmentation using Ant Colony Algorithm. Moreover, they improved the algorithm by setting initial cluster centers based on image histogram information, thus greatly reducing computational complexity and running time.

Bee Colony Optimization (BCO) (Teodorovic & Lucic, 2006) has been development recently, the algorithm mimics the food foraging behavior of swarms of honey bees. A few models have been developed to model the intelligent behaviors of honeybee swarms and applied for solving combinatorial type problems (Tereshko & Lee, 2002; Tereshko & Loengarov, 2005; Wedde, Farooq, & Zhang, 2004). Yang (2005) developed a Virtual Bee Algorithm (VBA) to solve the numerical optimization problems. In VBA, a swarm of virtual bees are generated and started to move randomly. These bees interact when they find some target nectar corresponding to the values of food sources. The solution for the optimization problem can be obtained from the intensity of bee interactions.

This paper is organized as follows. In Section 2, bee colony feature first is introduced. In Section 3, minimum fuzzy entropy algorithm is described. In Section 4, BCO approach compare with fuzzy entropy is proposed to segment image via thresholding. In Section 5, we evaluate the performance of the proposed threshold approach using some standard images and compare it with others approach from the literature. Finally, Section 6 concludes this chapter.

2. BEE COLONY FEATURE

Bees perform tasks in an intelligent manner. Since the availability of the nectar sources around the hive varies in space and time, bees adapt its foraging behavior to the changes in the environment. For example, it is important to appropriately divide the worker, how many to explore new unknown sources, and how many to exploit the known food sources. Bee colony includes three parts:

1. **Food Sources:** The "profitability" of a food source is related to several factors such as its closeness to the nest, richness of food and the ease of extracting the energy from the source.
2. **Leader Bees:** Leader bees are associated with a specific food source they exploited. They carry information about the specific source such as its distance, direction from the hive and the profitability of the source. They share this information with the forager bees waiting in the hive by dancing which is an example of multiple interaction.
3. **Followed Bees:** onlookers and scouts. The scouts randomly search food sources and this behavior is a kind of fluctuations which is vital for self-organization; and the onlookers waiting in the hive find a food source by means of the information presented by employed foragers. The mean number of scouts is about 5~10% of the foragers (Seeley, 1995).

The exchange of information among bees is the most important occurrence in the formation of the collective knowledge. While examining the entire hive it is possible to distinguish between some parts that commonly exist in all hives. The most important part of the hive with respect to exchanging information is the dancing area. Communication among bees related to the quality of food sources takes place in the dancing area. This dance is called a waggle dance. Since information about all the current rich sources is available to an onlooker on the dance floor, probably it can watch numerous dances and decides to employ herself at the most profitable source. Employed foragers share their information with a probability proportional to the profitability of the food source, and the sharing of this information through waggle dancing is longer in duration. Hence, the recruitment is proportional to the profitability of the food source.

At the beginning, a potential forager will start as unemployed forager. That bee will have no knowledge about the food sources around the nest. There are two possible options for such a bee:

1. It can be a scout and starts searching around the nest spontaneously for a food.
2. It can be a recruit after watching the waggle dances and starts searching for a food source (in Figure 1).

3. MINIMUM FUZZY ENTROPY

3.1. Fuzzy Entropy

The fuzzy entropy is defined as

$$H(I) = \sum_{i=1}^{C} H(B) \tag{1}$$

Here

Figure 1. Behavior of honey bee foraging for nectar

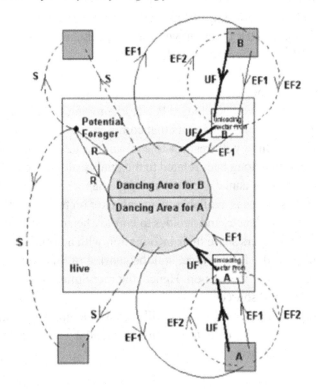

$$H(B) = -\sum_{j=0}^{J-1} \frac{h(j)}{\mu_i(j)P'(B_i)} \log \frac{h(j)}{\mu_i(j)P'(B_i)} \qquad (2)$$

where

$$P'(B_i) = -\sum_{j=0}^{J-1} \frac{h(j)}{\mu_i(j)} \qquad (3)$$

Equation 2 defines the entropy of the distribution:

$$\frac{h(j)}{\mu_i(j)P'(B_i)}$$

and it represent the distribution of the quotients of the grayscale histogram and the fuzzy membership. then Equation 2 just becomes the traditional entropy which is regarded as one of the best approaches to thresholding, so the novel entropy contains Kapur's entropy in itself and introduces fuzzy concept to treat with the natural fuzziness of image thresholding.

3.2. Fuzzy Membership Function

The definition of fuzzy membership is the kernel of applications of fuzzy set theory. It is believed that the membership describes the certainty whether an element belongs to the fuzzy set or not. The membership also describes the contribution of an element to the fuzzy set, which means the fuzzy set is constituted by all elements weighted by their memberships. For most images, the grayscale histogram follows multimodal distribution, i.e., the histogram shows different peaks (Pal & Pal, 1993), which can be explained by ineluctable noises in images. It is assumed that the peak value represents the major gray of an object, and other values around it represent the impact of noises.

3.3. Image Minimum Fuzzy Entropy

Natural images generally suffer from environment noise and slight color change. The first or second order differential operators such as 'Sobel,' 'Prewitt,' 'Canny' are used as edge detectors to estimate image edge. Since edge detection operators will amplify the noise, filtering is a necessary step to reduce noise effect in general.

In this case, the segmented results produces heavily over-segmented. Noise such as salt and pepper will be removed before segmenting it.

An original image is segmented into the object E_o and the background E_b. E_o is a group of pixels with high gray levels, and E_b with the low gray levels. $\varphi = \{E_o, E_b\}$ has unknown probabilistic partition P_o and P_b. Pixels of an image are classified into 'o' or 'b', the corresponding probability $p_{o/k}$ or $p_{b/k}$.

The fuzzy memberships function μ_o and μ_b are showed on Figure 2, they are also given by

$$\mu_o(k) = \begin{cases} 0, & k \leq a \\ \dfrac{(k-a)^2}{(c-a)*(b-a)}, & a < k \leq b \\ 1 - \dfrac{(k-c)^2}{(c-a)*(c-b)}, & b < k \leq c \\ 1, & k > c \end{cases} \tag{4}$$

$$\mu_b(k) = \begin{cases} 1, & k \leq a \\ 1 - \dfrac{(k-a)^2}{(c-a)*(b-a)}, & a < k \leq b \\ \dfrac{(k-c)^2}{(c-a)*(c-b)}, & b < k \leq c \\ 0, & k > c \end{cases} \tag{5}$$

The membership functions $\mu_o(k)$, $\mu_b(k)$ can be used to approximate the conditional probability $p_{o/k}$ and $p_{b/k}$, then the following equations hold:

$$P_o = \sum_{k=0}^{255} p_k * p_{o/k} = \sum_{k=0}^{255} p_k * \mu_o(k)$$

$$P_b = \sum_{k=0}^{255} p_k * p_{b/k} = \sum_{k=0}^{255} p_k * \mu_b(k) \tag{6}$$

The fuzzy entropy function is defined as:

Figure 2. Fuzzy membership functions graph

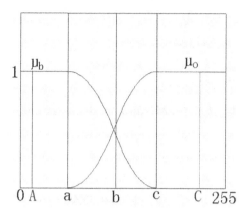

$$H\left(a,b,c\right) = -\sum_{k=0}^{255} \frac{p_k * u_o\left(k\right)}{P_o} * \ln\left(\frac{p_k * u_o\left(k\right)}{P_o}\right)$$
$$-\sum_{k=0}^{255} \frac{p_k * u_b\left(k\right)}{P_b} * \ln\left(\frac{p_k * u_b\left(k\right)}{P_b}\right)$$

(7)

Here the three parameters a, b, c satisfy the condition $0 \leq a \leq b \leq c \leq 255$.

In reference (Liu & Li, 1993), maximal $H\left(a,b,c\right)$ is searched in (a, b, c) space, when $H\left(a,b,c\right)$ achieves the maximum value, the corresponding parameters a, b and c formulate optimal solve, and are used to calculate threshold of image segmentation.

In this paper, a new minimum fuzzy entropy algorithm is proposed. Based on fuzzy entropy equation (4), the parameter a and c can be given by equation (8) and (9)

$$a = A, \quad if \; 0 \leq p_k \leq P_t \,,$$
$$k = 0, 1, 2, \cdots, A-1 \; and \; p_A > P_t$$

(8)

$$c = C, \quad if \; 0 \leq p_k \leq P_t \,,$$
$$k = 255, 254, \cdots, C+1 \; and \; p_C > P_t$$

(9)

$P_t \geq 0$ is a very small constant. If set $P_t > 0$, the influence of isolate pixels such as pulse noise are neglected. The fuzzy entropy can be modified as follow:

$$H(b) = -\sum_{k=A}^{C} \frac{p_k * u_o(k)}{P_o} * \ln\left(\frac{p_k * u_o(k)}{P_o}\right)$$
$$-\sum_{k=A}^{C} \frac{p_k * u_b(k)}{P_b} * \ln\left(\frac{p_k * u_b(k)}{P_b}\right)$$

(10)

Here $b \in \Re$ and $A \le b \le C$. Minimizing the fuzzy entropy $H(b)$

$$H_{opt}(B) = \min(H(b))$$

(11)

then optimal solve B is obtained. The optimal fuzzy membership functions are also obtained by substituting (A, B, C) in equation (4) and (5).

Then the segmentation threshold T is the intersection point of the optimal $\mu_o(k)$ and $\mu_b(k)$ curve. T can be given as follow:

$$T(A,B,C) = \begin{cases} A + \sqrt{(C-A)*(B-A)/2} \\ (A+C)/2 \le B \le C \\ C - \sqrt{(C-A)*(C-B)/2} \\ A \le B \le (A+C)/2 \end{cases}$$

(12)

4. BEE COLONY OPTIMIZATION ALGORITHM

In this paper, we consider each possible solution $x = (A, b, C)$ as one bee, the optimal solution of fuzzy function $H(b)$ is corresponds to the best bee.

The overall framework of the fuzzy entropy BCA approach can be shown in Figure 3. Where VOFS denotes the value of food source, NBFS denotes neighborhood of high value food source.

Algorithm begins by setting initial BCA parameters generating N bees randomly, including total bees, number of leader bees, followed bees and scout bees, radium of neighbor, number of circulation. Then all bees are assigned as scout and fly out for searching food source. When they fly back the hive, the Value Of Food Sources (VOFS) which they found are computed and sorted.

If VOFS is high, the correspond bee is reassigned as leader bee to search neighbor of itself food source; if VOFS is middle, the correspond bee is reassigned as follow bee to search neighbor of leader-bee's food source, which food source is selected

Figure 3. BCO-based and fuzzy entropy image segment overview

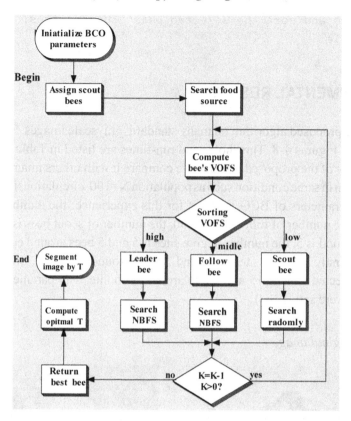

via the transition rule; the others keep as scout bee to search food source randomly. Then circulation times K minus 1, if K>0 keep circulation, else step out circulation and return the best bee. And then the threshold T is computed according to best bee, the image can be segmented by the threshold T.

The algorithm is listed as follows:

```
1. Initial the parameters of bees' population.
2. Assign all bees as scout bees to randomly forage food
sources.
3. Evaluate the values of the food sources searched by
population.
4. Sort the values of the food sources.
5. While (stopping criterion not met).
6. Assign work to leader bees/follow bees/scout bees according
to VOFS.
```

```
7. Select the bees with best VOFS from each patch.
8. Evaluate and sort the selected bees' food sources.
9. End while.
```

5. EXPERIMENTAL RESULTS

We evaluate proposed algorithm on many standard, grayscale images. Some results are shown in Figures 4-8. Thresholds and run-times are listed in Table 1. To verify the efficiency of the proposed method, we compare it with others image segmentation algorithm in same condition such as population N=100, circulation times K=100. The other parameters of BCO were set for this experience: the number of leader bees is 40, the number of follow bees is 50, the number of scout bees is 10, the size of neighborhood is 5, the number of elite sites is 5 and 5 bees around each site. The number of firstly selected sites is 20 and 3 bees around each site, the number of secondly selected sites is 15 and 1 bee around each site. The parameter of fuzzy entropy P_t were set $P_t = 0$.

Figure 4 Original image

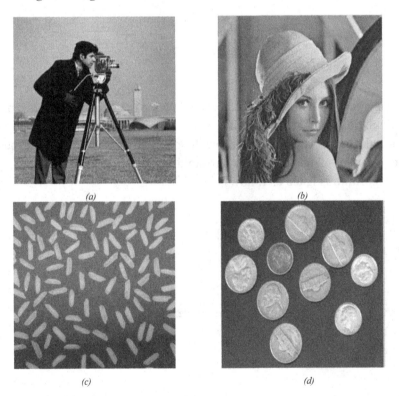

(a)

(b)

(c)

(d)

Figure 5. 1-D Otsu segmentation results

(a)

(b)

(c)

(d)

Figure 6. ACO segmentation results

(a)

(b)

(c)

(d)

Figure 7. Fish colony segmentation results

Figure 8. BCO segmentation results

Table 1. Thresholds and run-times of different thresholding methods for some grayscale image

	1-D otsu method	Cheng method	Fish colony method	ACO method	Proposed method
Coin	120	85 / 5.342s	128/ 0.281s	81 / 24.320s	91 / 0.359s
Lena	114	132/ 4.273s	116/ 1.359s	121/ 24.320s	122 / 0.296s
Peppers	101	115/ 6.245s	103/ 0.835s	133/ 24.290s	119 / 0.421s
Camerman	88	85 / 5.345s	90/ 0.375s	83 / 24.897s	84 / 0.343s
Saturn	80	84 / 5.435s	71/ 0.571s	81 /24.976s	65 / 0.670s
rices	120	116 /4.356s	133/ 0.234s	114/ 22.917s	113 / 0.312s

Figure 4-8 show four images threshold with the proposed method and other algorithm. Figure 9 shows image histogram and fuzzy membership function. Intersection of membership function is desire threshold. Table 1 shows threshold and consume time.

Figure 9. Segmentation threshold and probability distribution

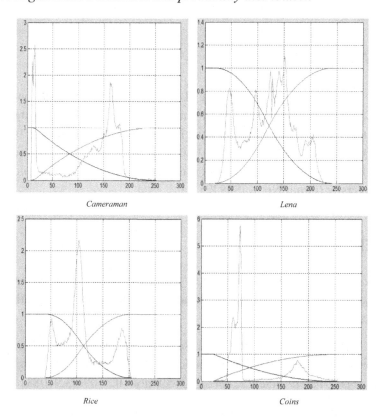

Cameraman

Lena

Rice

Coins

Experiments results show that our approach can decrease consume time, while the performance of ant colony optimal algorithm is slow. Table 1 show that the proposed method is much faster than others except for the Ostu's.

6. CONCLUSION

The automatic segmenting semantic object from the background is still a challenge in image segmentation. Entropy-based method is a wide-studied and effective threshold strategy. In recent years, there have been numerous applications of fuzzy entropies in image segmentation. In this paper, we compare the proposed Bee Algorithm based on Fuzzy Entropy (FEBCA) segmentation method with other approaches. FEBCA is successfully applied in image segmentation. The results of the performance evaluation show that the proposed fuzzy entropy segmentation method provides best segmentation performance. The experiment results show that the implementation of the proposed fuzzy entropy principle by FEBCA has more highly effective and performance, consume time is shorter obviously. Our ongoing and further works include clustering validity in our approach, adaptive determination for the clustering number and fast bee colony algorithm.

ACKNOWLEDGMENT

This work was supported by the National Natural Science Foundation of China (Grant No. 60872123, 60972133), the Joint Fund of the National Natural Science Foundation and the Guangdong Provincial Natural Science Foundation (Grant No. U0835001), the Fundamental Research Funds for the Central Universities, SCUT, Provincial Key Laboratory for Computer Information Processing Technology, Soochow University (Grant No. KJS0922).

REFERENCES

Beni, G., & Wang, U. (1989). *Swarm intelligence in cellular robotic systems*. Paper presented at the NATO Advanced Workshop on Robots and Biological Systems. Tuscany, Italy.

Bilger, K., Kupferschlager, J., & Muller-Schauenburg, W. (2001). Threshold calculation for segmented attenuation correction in PET with histogram fitting. *IEEE Transactions on Nuclear Science, 48*(1), 43–50. doi:10.1109/23.910831

Bonabeau, E., Dorigo, M., & Theraulaz, G. (1999). *Swarm intelligence: From natural to artificial systems*. Oxford, UK: Oxford University Press.

Bonabeau, E., Dorigo, M., & Theraulaz, G. (2001). Swarm intelligence: From natural to artificial systems. *Journal of Artificial Societies and Social Simulation, 4*(1).

Cheng, H. D., Chen, Y. H., & Jiang, X. H. (2000). Thresholding using two dimensional histogram and fuzzy entropy principle. *IEEE Transactions on Image Processing, 9*(4), 732–735. doi:10.1109/83.841949

Cheng, H. D., Chen, Y. H., & Jiang, X. H. (2000). Thresholding using twodimensional histogram and fuzzy entropy principle. *IEEE Transactions on Image Processing, 9*(4), 732–735. doi:10.1109/83.841949

Engelbrecht, A. P. (2005). *Fundamentals of computational swarm intelligence*. New York, NY: Wiley.

Enyedi, B., Konyha, L., & Fazekas, K. (2005). Threshold procedures and image segmentation. In *Proceedings of the 47th International Symposium*, (pp. 29-32). ELMAR.

Flake, G. (1999). *The computational beauty of nature*. Cambridge, MA: MIT Press.

Grosan, C., Abraham, A., & Monica, C. (2006). *Swarm intelligence in data mining*. Berlin, Germany: Springer.

Han, Y. F., & Shi, P. F. (2007). An improved ant colony algorithm for fuzzy clustering in image segmentation. *Neurocomputing, 70*, 665–671. doi:10.1016/j.neucom.2006.10.022

Hou, Z., Hu, Q., & Nowinski, W. L. (2006). On minimum variance thresholding. *Pattern Recognition Letters, 27*(14), 1732–1743. doi:10.1016/j.patrec.2006.04.012

Huang, L. K., & Wang, M. J. J. (1995). Image thresholding by minimizing the measures of fuzziness. *Pattern Recognition, 28*(1), 41–51. doi:10.1016/0031-3203(94)E0043-K

Kapur, J. N., Sahoo, P. K., & Wong, A. K. C. (1985). A new method for graylevel picture thresholding using the entropy of the histogram. *Computer Vision Graphics and Image Processing, 29*, 273–285. doi:10.1016/0734-189X(85)90125-2

Liu, J.-Z., & Li, W.-Q. (1993). The automatic thresholding of graylevel pictures via two-dimensional Otsu method. *Acta Automatica Sinica, 19*(1), 101–105.

Malisia, A. R., & Tizhoosh, H. R. (2006). Image thresholding using ant colony optimization. In *Proceedings of the 3rd Canadian Conference on Computer and Robot Vision*, (pp. 26-29). IEEE.

Milonas, M. M. (1994). Swarms, phase transitions, and collective intelligence. In Langton, C. G. (Ed.), *Artificial Life III*. Reading, MA: Addison Wesley.

Otsu, N. (1979). A threshold selection method from gray level histograms. *IEEE Transactions on Systems, Man, and Cybernetics, 9*(1), 62–66. doi:10.1109/TSMC.1979.4310076

Otsu, N. (1979). A threshold selection method from gray level histograms. *IEEE Transactions on Systems, Man, and Cybernetics, 9*(1), 62–66. doi:10.1109/TSMC.1979.4310076

Pal, N. R., & Pal, S. K. (1989). Object-background segmentation using new definitions of entropy. *IEEE Proceedings, 136*(4), 284-295.

Pal, N. R., & Pal, S. K. (1991). Entropy: A new definition and its applications. *IEEE Transactions on Systems, Man, and Cybernetics, 21*(5), 1260–1270. doi:10.1109/21.120079

Pal, N. R., & Pal, S. K. (1993). A review on image segmentation techniques. *Pattern Recognition, 26*(2), 1277–1294. doi:10.1016/0031-3203(93)90135-J

Pal, N. R., & Pal, S. K. (1993). A review on image segmentation techniques. *Pattern Recognition, 26*(9), 1277–1294. doi:10.1016/0031-3203(93)90135-J

Sahoo, P. K., Soltani, S., & Wong, A. K. C. (1988). A survey of threshold techniques. *Computer Vision Graphics and Image Processing, 41*(2), 233–260. doi:10.1016/0734-189X(88)90022-9

Seeley, T. D. (1995). *The wisdom of the hive*. Cambridge, MA: Harvard University Press.

Sezgin, M., & Sankur, B. (2004). Survey over image thresholding techniques and quantitative performance evaluation. *Journal of Electronic Imaging, 13*(1), 146–165. doi:10.1117/1.1631315

Sezgin, M., & Sankur, B. (2004). Survey over image thresholding techniques and quantitative performance evaluation. *Journal of Electronic Imaging, 13*(1), 146–168. doi:10.1117/1.1631315

Shelokar, P. S., Jayaraman, V. K., & Kulkarni, B. D. (2004). An ant colony approach for clustering. *Analytica Chimica Acta, 59*, 187–195. doi:10.1016/j.aca.2003.12.032

Tao, W., Jin, H., & Liu, L. (2007). Object segmentation using ant colony optimization algorithm and fuzzy entropy. *Pattern Recognition Letters, 28*, 788–796. doi:10.1016/j.patrec.2006.11.007

Teodorovic, D., & Lucic, P. (2006). Goran bee colony optimization: Principles and applications. In *Proceedings of the 8th Seminar on Neural Network Applications in Electrical Engineering, NEUREL,* (pp. 51-156). NEUREL.

Tereshko, V., & Lee, T. (2002). How information mapping patterns determine foraging behaviour of a honey bee colony. *Open Systems & Information Dynamics, 9,* 181–193. doi:10.1023/A:1015652810815

Tereshko, V., & Loengarov, A. (2005). Collective decision-making in honey bee foraging dynamics. *Computing and Information Systems Journal, 9*(3).

Tereshko, V., & Loengarov, A. (2005). Collective decision-making in honey bee foraging dynamics. *Computing and Information Systems Journal,* 1352-4049.

Unnikrishnan, R., Pantofaru, C. E., & Hebert, M. (2007). Toward objective evaluation of image segmentation algorithms. *IEEE Transactions on Pattern Analysis and Machine Intelligence, 29*(6), 929–943. doi:10.1109/TPAMI.2007.1046

Wedde, H. F., Farooq, M., & Zhang, Y. (2004). BeeHive: An efficient fault-tolerant routing algorithm inspired by honey bee behavior, ant colony, optimization and swarm intelligence. In *Proceedings of the 4th International Workshop.* Brussels, Belgium: ANTS.

Yang, X. S. (2005). Engineering optimizations via nature-inspired virtual bee algorithms. *Lecture Notes in Computer Science, 3562,* 317. doi:10.1007/11499305_33

Yu, W., Zou, R., & Yu, Z. (2010). Image segmentation based on local ant colony optimization. *Computer Applications, 30*(5), 1344–2346.

Zhao, M., Fu, A. M. N., & Yan, H. A. (2001). Technique of three-level thresholding based on probability partition and fuzzy 3-partition. *IEEE Transactions on Fuzzy Systems, 9*(3), 469–479. doi:10.1109/91.928743

Chapter 7
Image Denoising via 2-D FIR Filtering Approach

Jingyu Hua
Zhejiang University of Technology, China

Wankun Kuang
Zhejiang University of Technology, China

ABSTRACT

Image denoising has received much concern for decades. One of the simplest methods for image denoising is the 2-D FIR lowpass filtering approach. Firstly, the authors make a comparative study of the conventional lowpass filtering approach, including the classical mean filter and three 2-D FIR LowPass Filters (LPF) designed by McClellan transform. Then an improved method based on learning method is presented, where pixels are filtered by five edge-oriented filters, respectively, facilitated to their edge details. Differential Evolution Particle Swarm Optimization (DEPSO) algorithm is exploited to refine those filters. Computer simulation demonstrates that the proposed method can be superior to the conventional filtering method, as well as the modern Bilateral Filtering (BF) and the Stochastic Denoising (SD) method.

INTRODUCTION

Visual information transmitted in the form of digital image is becoming a major means of communication in modern age, which are widely used in the application such as television, magnetic resonance imaging, astronomy and other exploration research, etc. However, those images are often corrupted by the imperfect instruments, blurred by the noise in transmission or compression. Thus, how to recover

DOI: 10.4018/978-1-4666-3958-4.ch007

the original visual information as much as possible has become a major concern for decades. Generally, the deblurring issue can be viewed as a denoising problem and typical noise models include the Gaussian noise, the salt and pepper noise, the speckle noise and the Brownian noise (Lim, 1990). In this chapter, we focus on the lowpass filtering approach on denoising the image corrupted by the Gaussian noise but via a new perspective.

BACKGROUND

So far, there are two basic approaches to image denoising, spatial filtering methods and transform domain filtering methods (Lalitha & Mrityunjaya, 2011). A conventional way to remove noise from image data is to employ spatial filters, which can be further divided into two categories. The first one category is linear spatial filters, such as the mean filter and the Wiener filter. The mean filter is a sliding spatial window filter that replaces the center element in the window with the average of all pixel in the same window, where the larger the mask size, the more noise filtered as well as the more blurred of the image. The Wiener filter is a popular adaptive filter based on assumptions of known statistical characteristics of the signal and noise, which requirements usually cannot be fulfilled. The second category is non-linear spatial filters, such as the median filter. Similar to the mean filter, the median filters replace the center pixel of the window with the computed median. In recent, the improved filter, such as weighted median filter, relaxed median filter are proposed.

The transform domain filtering methods contains the frequency domain and the wavelet domain. The former often use the lowpass filters for denoising. By reducing the high frequency components while preserving the low frequency components, lowpass filtering reduces a large amount of noise at the expense of reducing a small amount of signal (Lim, 1990). Thus, the lowpass filtering approach is quite coarse. Contrary to the simple spatial or frequency domain method, wavelet transform method is localized not only in frequency domain but also in spatial domain (Potnis, Somkuwar, & Sapre, 2010), which makes it more flexible and efficient. Varies of wavelet-based methods have been proposed. For example, the VISUShrink method (Donoho & Johnstone, 1994) exploits the fact that signal energy becomes more concentrated into fewer coefficients in the transform domain while noise energy does not which enables the separation of signal from noise. And the Wavelet Coefficient Model approach (Romberg, Hyeokho, & Baraniuk, 2001) identifies close correlation of signal at different resolutions by observing the signal across multiple resolutions which produces excellent output but is computationally much more complex and expensive.

All the methods mentioned above are non-data adaptive in nature. Breakthrough made in 1994, when P. Comon presented a new method, Independent Component Analysis (ICA) (Hoyer, 1999), which is data adaptive and can generate promising results. Its significance lies in the fact that denoising of images is also dependent on the image (type) which is to be denoised.

MAIN FOCUS OF THE CHAPTER

Firstly, we made a brief introduction of a popular and effective method to evaluate the image quality, i.e., the Structural SIMilarity Index (SSIM), which laid the foundation of all the evaluation of the subsequent sections. Then, conventional 2-D FIR lowpass filtering approaches, both the mean filter and other LPFs designed by McClellan transform are investigated. However, conventional approaches do not take into consideration the local details of the corrupted image. To tackle this issue, we present a method to design five edge-oriented 2-D FIR LPFs, where the pixels are grouped into five classes according to edge details before they have been filtered and DEPSO algorithm is exploited to refine those filters.

Image Quality Measurement

The Peak Signal-to-Noise Ratio (PSNR) is one of the simplest methods for measuring the quality of images. However, as is shown in (Wang, Bovik, Sheikh, & Simoncelli, 2004), noisy images share the same PSNRs may differ a lot on the visual quality. That implies that PSNR is not very well matched to perceived visual quality.

In (Wang, Bovik, Sheikh, & Simoncelli, 2004), Wang proposed a new framework, i.e., SSIM, to tackle this issue, which is generated by multiplying three sub-measurements, including the luminance comparison $l(x,y)$ characterized by the mean intensity μ_x and μ_y, the signal contrast $c(x,y)$ characterized by the deviation σ_x, σ_y and σ_{xy} and the structure comparison $s(x,y)$ characterized by the covariance σ_{xy}. The SSIM can be expressed as

$$
\begin{aligned}
SSIM(\boldsymbol{x}, \boldsymbol{y}) &= l(\boldsymbol{x}, \boldsymbol{y}) \mathrm{g} c(\boldsymbol{x}, \boldsymbol{y}) \mathrm{g} s(\boldsymbol{x}, \boldsymbol{y}) \\
&= \frac{(2\mu_x\mu_y + C_1)(2\sigma_{xy} + C_2)}{(\mu_x^2 + \mu_y^2 + C_1)(\sigma_x^2 + \sigma_y^2 + C_2)} \\
C_1 &= (K_1 M)^2 \\
C_2 &= (K_2 M)^2
\end{aligned}
$$
(1)

where M is the dynamic range of the pixel values (255 for 8-bit grayscale images), K_1 and K_2 are constants, with typical value 0.01 and 0.03 respectively. Of course, the larger SSIM is, the better the test image is. Particularly, $s(x,y)$ is a variable that has characterized the PSNR information. Thus, in this study, we use the SSIM instead of PSNR to evaluate the image quality.

Conventional Lowpass Filters for Image Denoising

The energy of a typical image is primarily concentrated in its low-frequency components (Lim, 1990). Thus, an intuitive way to denoise is filtering the noisy image with a 2-D lowpass FIR filter, which reduces the high-frequency components while preserving the low-frequency components.

2-D FIR Filters

The frequency response of $h(m,n)$ with a support in a $(2L+1)\times(2L+1)$ square defined by $-L \leq m, n \leq L$ can be expressed as (Lim, 1990)

$$H(\omega_1, \omega_2) = \sum_{m=-L}^{L} \sum_{n=-L}^{L} h(m,n) e^{-j(m\omega_1 + n\omega_2)} \tag{2}$$

In image processing, the zero-phase filters $h(m,n)$ are preferred (Lim, 1990). Firstly, the image data to be processed are real, which call for the realness of the coefficient $h(m,n)$. Secondly, non-linear phase distorts the different frequency components, equivalently the signal shape on the spatial domain, such as blurring. And finally, the implementations can be simplified if coefficients $h(m,n)$ satisfy some symmetry properties. One of the popular schemes is twofold-symmetry,

$$h(m,n) = h(-m,-n) \tag{3}$$

Thus, only $2L^2+2L+1$ coefficients are independent. And the design task turns to find the suitable $2L^2+2L+1$ coefficients. Denoting the input pixel as $y_I(m,n)$ and output pixel as $y_O(m,n)$, then

$$y_O(m,n) = \sum_{l_1=-L}^{L} \sum_{l_2=-L}^{L} y_I(l_1, l_2) h(m-l_1, n-l_2) \tag{4}$$

Denoising using Lowpass FIR Filters

Mean Filters

The mean filter is a sliding spatial window filter that replaces the center element in the window with the average of all pixel in the same window, where the larger the mask size, the more noise filtered as well as the more blurred of the image. As for the mean filter with support size $N \times N$ ($N = 2L+1$), all the coefficients equals to $1/N^2$. It is obvious that mean filter is a typical kind of FIR LPFs.

2-D FIR Lowpass Filters

However, once the support size is specified, cutoff frequency of the mean filter is determined. To design the more general LPFs, one can resort to McClellan transform (Lim, 1990), where the typical McClellan transform matrix T is set to

$$T = \frac{1}{8} \begin{bmatrix} 1 & 2 & 1 \\ 2 & -4 & 2 \\ 1 & 2 & 1 \end{bmatrix} \tag{5}$$

and the prototype One-Dimensional (1-D) FIR filters can be design by classical *Remez* algorithm.

Proposed Method for Designing Denoising Filters

In (Zhang, 2011), Zhang propose to classify the whole image into five groups according to its edge direction and then to design five 2-D FIR filters. Difficulties arise when it comes to design the five filters, equivalently, to specify the suitable frequency responses, for which are not known as priors. To tackle this issue, we resort to learning method. Namely, via training the system (five filters) with the noisy image and noiseless images, the filter coefficients that generate the best denoising performance are selected. The computation core of the learning method is the DEPSO algorithm (Hao, Guo, & Huang, 2007).

Edge Classifier

By exploiting the Prewitt criterion (Gonzalez & Woods, 2008), we divide the pixels into five classes according to its edge differences, viz., one non-edge class and four edge classes, which is decided by the direction of the gradient $G(l_1,l_2)$. The definition of $G(l_1,l_2)$ can be as follows:

$$G(l_1,l_2) = \sqrt{[G_x(l_1,l_2)]^2 + [G_y(l_1,l_2)]^2} \tag{6}$$

where $G_x(l_1,l_2)$ and $G_y(l_1,l_2)$ denotes the horizontal gradient and the vertical gradient respectively. If $G(l_1,l_2)$ is smaller than a pre-specified value *Gate*, then pixel (l_1,l_2) belongs to the non-edge classes. The other four classes can be grouped by judging

$$\alpha(l_1,l_2) = \tan^{-1}[G_x(l_1,l_2)/G_y(l_1,l_2)] \tag{7}$$

In (Zhang, 2011), Zhang proposed to judge $\alpha(l_1,l_2)$ directly. However, there exist too many pixels in one image thus executing the arctangent arithmetic in (7) for each pixel would result in heavy computation load. To overcome the computational difficulty, we proposed to replace the arctangent arithmetic operation with the simple comparison operation as is shown in Figure 1, because the logical operation is much more efficient than the arctangent arithmetic operation.

DEPSO Algorithm for FIR Filter Designing

DEPSO is an efficient optimization algorithm which combines the advantages of the Differential Evolution (DE) and the Particle Swarm Optimization (PSO). By utilizing the differential information, the DE algorithm owns good ability in exploring local search and maintaining the diversity. But it suffers from the stability problem due to the lacking of global information (Hao, Guo, & Huang, 2007). PSO

Figure 1. Edge classifier

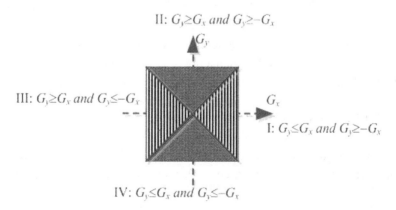

is inspired by the cooperation behavior of bird flocks, which enables it to make use of the global information. But it is often premature because the diversity decreases dramatically as the iteration goes on (Storn & Price, 1995). Obviously, DE and PSO complement each other. Combined with their advantages, DEPSO executes either DE or PSO algorithm according to a pre-specified probability, which tends to be more efficient and robust.

Since five 2-D FIR filters are needed in this scheme, the total number of the filter coefficients is $5(2L^2+2L+1)$. Thus, the i-th particle can be represent as

$$X_i = [a(1), a(2), ..., a[5(2L^2+2L+1)]]] \tag{8}$$

By exploiting the symmetry property (3), the first filter $h_1(m,n)$ can be obtained by rearranging the first group elements in X_i, whose total number is $(2L^2+2L+1)$. And the other four filters can be produced respectively by the subsequent group elements in a similar way. To evaluate the quality of the particle X_i, we take SSIM as the fitness function

$$f_i = \text{SSIM}(y_{i1}, y_{i2}) \tag{9}$$

where y_{i1} represents the noiseless image, while y_{i2} represents the filtered image. The filtered image y_{i2} can be generated by combining the five classes pixels filtered by the five filters $h_1(m,n)$, $h_2(m,n)$, ..., $h_5(m,n)$ respectively. The algorithm can be described as follows:

Algorithm

1. Initialize a $P \times [5(2L^2+2L+1)]$ population array of particles with random positions and velocities. All the elements in population X and velocity V is kept within $[-1/N^2, 1/N^2]$, where P is the population size.
2. Evaluate the SSIM performances of all the particles. And then initialize the personal best agent *pbest* and global agent *gbest*.
3. For each particle, generate a random number R uniformly distributed in the interval $[0,1]$. If R is smaller than a pre-specified constant, i.e., the cross constant CR, then change the position according to the DE strategy:

$$X_i(k) = X_i(k) + \lambda \cdot [gbest - X_i(k)] + F \cdot [X_{r1}(k) - X_{r2}(k)] \tag{10}$$

where λ and F are additional control variables, $r1$ and $r2$ are random indexes within $[1,P]$ that differ from i (Storn & Price, 1995). Otherwise, update the position and velocity with

$$V_i(k) = c\{V_i(k) + c_1 \bullet rand \bullet [gbest - X_i(k)]$$
$$+c_2 \bullet rand \bullet [pbest - X_i(k)]\} \tag{11}$$
$$X_i(k) = X_i(k) + V_i(k)$$

where χ is the constriction factor, *rand* is also a random number uniformly distributed in the interval [0,1], c_1 and c_2 are learning factors (Hao, Guo, & Huang, 2007).

4. Evaluate the SSIM performances of all the particles and update *pbest* and *gbest*.
5. If the number of iteration meets *MaxCnt*, go to step *6*); else go to step *2*).
6. Stop.

Simulation Results

All the test images are retrieved from (Gonzalez, 2008). The means of the Gaussian noise is set to 0 and the variances are set to 10, 20, and 30 respectively. To make the comparison more significant, all support size of the 2-D FIR filters are set to 5×5. The cutoff frequencies (ω_p, ω_s) of three prototype 1-D FIR filters equal to $(0.2\pi, 0.4\pi)$, $(0.4\pi, 0.6\pi)$, and $(0.6\pi, 0.8\pi)$, respectively. Parameter *Gate* in the edge classifier is set to the mean value of all pixels in one image. Additional parameters in the DEPSO algorithm in this example are given as Table 1.

Algorithm terminates while the maximum iteration times reached.

To make the comparison significant, the images processed by the modern BF method (Tomasi & Manduchi, 1998) and the SD method (Estrada, Fleet, & Jepson, 2009) are listed. As for the BF method, half-size of the Gaussian is set to 21, the spatial-domain standard deviation is set to 4 and the intensity-domain standard deviation is set to 0.2. As for the SD method, the standard deviation of the noise process is set to 0.2, the stopping threshold for random walks is set to 0.0001 and the number of trials per pixel is set to 25. Those parameters are all chosen by referring (Estrada, Fleet, & Jepson, 2009). The numerical SSIM performances of the filtered images by the four LPFs are given in *Table 2~4*. Sample filtered Lena images with variance $\sigma = 30$ are shown in *Figure 2* (a)~(j).

Table 1. Parameters of DEPSO algorithm

Parameters	P	CR	λ	F	χ	c_1	c_2	MaxCnt
Value	30	0.5	0.9	0.5	0.729	2.05	2.05	1000

Table 2. Denoising performances of images with variance σ = 10

Test Images	Performances (SSIM)								
	Noisy	LPF1	LPF2	LPF3	Mean	Median	BF (fixed)	SD (fixed)	Proposed
Lena	0.6135	0.8201	0.8035	0.7494	0.8197	0.8245	0.8228	0.8229	0.8768
Jetplane	0.5976	0.8535	0.8772	0.7562	0.8442	0.8509	0.8583	0.8303	0.8756
Lake	0.6906	0.7775	0.7980	0.7768	0.7539	0.7595	0.7780	0.8399	0.8340
Livingroom	0.7170	0.7139	0.7902	0.8046	0.6693	0.6972	0.7033	0.8464	0.8069
Mandril	0.7916	0.7007	0.8788	0.8905	0.6318	0.6495	0.6445	0.8743	0.8240
Peppers	0.6302	0.7765	0.7350	0.7099	0.7776	0.7831	0.7941	0.8087	0.8176
Pirate	0.6804	0.7572	0.8000	0.7902	0.7362	0.7556	0.7410	0.8402	0.8334
Walkbridge	0.8173	0.6298	0.7699	0.8520	0.5832	0.6098	0.6503	0.8803	0.7728
Woman_Blonde	0.6481	0.7417	0.7517	0.7430	0.7361	0.7404	0.7703	0.8211	0.8144
Woman_Darkhair	0.5265	0.8888	0.8104	0.7104	0.9070	0.8944	0.8972	0.8082	0.8875

Table 3. Denoising performances of images with variance σ = 20

Test Images	Performances (SSIM)								
	Noisy	LPF1	LPF2	LPF3	Mean	Median	BF (fixed)	SD (fixed)	Proposed
Lena	0.3443	0.7530	0.6443	0.5041	0.7732	0.7475	0.7716	0.4390	0.7971
Jetplane	0.3478	0.7873	0.7879	0.5129	0.7935	0.7679	0.8004	0.4400	0.8112
Lake	0.4418	0.7330	0.6972	0.5771	0.7199	0.7010	0.7471	0.5226	0.7563
Livingroom	0.4562	0.6704	0.6687	0.6057	0.6405	0.6367	0.6897	0.5377	0.7040
Mandril	0.5538	0.6687	0.7805	0.7270	0.6108	0.6051	0.6550	0.6199	0.6997
Peppers	0.3506	0.7163	0.5886	0.4793	0.7362	0.7150	0.7529	0.4457	0.7529
Pirate	0.4121	0.7057	0.6617	0.5718	0.7011	0.6882	0.7157	0.5009	0.7458
Walkbridge	0.5848	0.6066	0.6970	0.7046	0.5666	0.5721	0.6600	0.6486	0.6499
Woman_Blonde	0.3733	0.6841	0.6012	0.5109	0.6967	0.6748	0.7384	0.4625	0.7311
Woman_Darkhair	0.2498	0.8075	0.6219	0.4265	0.8462	0.7997	0.8246	0.3578	0.8409

Scrutinizing into Table 2~4, we can see that the SSIMs of the Gaussian noise corrupted images degenerate drastically with the increase of the variance σ. Fortunately, the image quality is improved significantly after the LPF filtering. And the improvement is more evident in the large variance cases.

Table 4. Denoising performances of images with variance σ = 30

Test Images	Performances (SSIM)								
	Noisy	LPF1	LPF2	LPF3	Mean	Median	BF (fixed)	SD (fixed)	Proposed
Lena	0.2225	0.6721	0.5109	0.3579	0.7115	0.6585	0.5574	0.2569	0.7311
Jetplane	0.2389	0.7115	0.6864	0.3775	0.7321	0.6743	0.5849	0.2718	0.7495
Lake	0.3126	0.6771	0.6046	0.4473	0.6761	0.6328	0.5926	0.3470	0.6965
Livingroom	0.3118	0.6141	0.5544	0.4612	0.6001	0.5715	0.5575	0.3471	0.6368
Mandril	0.3958	0.6252	0.6766	0.5865	0.5806	0.5556	0.5720	0.4303	0.6219
Peppers	0.2233	0.6420	0.4639	0.3378	0.6801	0.6348	0.5607	0.2584	0.6950
Pirate	0.2739	0.6417	0.5381	0.4234	0.6542	0.6144	0.5585	0.3102	0.6809
Walkbridge	0.4236	0.5741	0.6158	0.5723	0.5423	0.5301	0.5917	0.4594	0.5805
Woman_Blonde	0.2411	0.6124	0.4730	0.3630	0.6432	0.5983	0.5530	0.2746	0.6670
Woman_Dark-hair	0.1450	0.7140	0.4788	0.2769	0.7712	0.6903	0.5653	0.1796	0.7809

Figure 2. Denoising results of sample Lena image with variance σ = 30

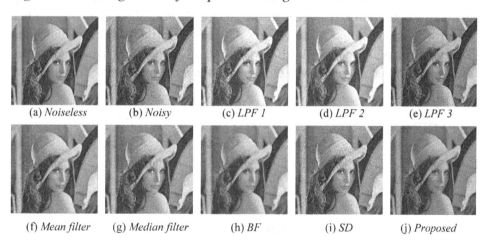

(a) *Noiseless* (b) *Noisy* (c) *LPF 1* (d) *LPF 2* (e) *LPF 3*

(f) *Mean filter* (g) *Median filter* (h) *BF* (i) *SD* (j) *Proposed*

As for the conventional lowpass filtering approaches, the mean filter yields the best performance. The LPF1 is second but close to the mean filter, even outperforms the mean filter in some cases. LPF2 performs well in the cases with $\sigma = 10$, but it deteriorated in cases corresponding to $\sigma = 20$ and $\sigma = 30$. In addition, LPF3 is the worst. As for the modern approaches, both BF and SD performs well in the cases that $\sigma = 10$, but their performances deteriorated drastically with the increase of variances. However, our proposed techniques yield the best performance.

FUTURE RESEARCH DIRECTIONS

By the combination of two different methods, i.e., the DE algorithm and the PSO algorithm, DEPSO algorithm exploits the good properties of different methods. This combined algorithm can be regarded as a hybrid algorithm, which has been receiving lots of concerns in swarm-based optimization field. Thus, on one hand, new PSO based hybrid algorithm can be used to generate the filter coefficients instead of the DEPSO algorithm in the view of optimization algorithm.

On the other hand, image denoising is a challenge problem due to the fact that the denoising algorithms are strong noise type and image type related. Thus, to develop the data-adaptive algorithm is of great significance. The ICA method marked a new era of image denoising, and further study can be developing other data-adaptive algorithm analogous to ICA and other brand new data-adaptive algorithms.

CONCLUSION

In this chapter, we presented a denoising method through the 2-D FIR filtering approach, where coefficients are generated by the DEPSO algorithm. Training the system with noisy and noiseless images, the generated filter helps to yield better visual quality than the conventional lowpass filtering approach, the classical mean filter, median filter, and even wiener filter, and the modern BF and SD method.

REFERENCES

Donoho, D. L., & Johnstone, I. M. (1994). Ideal spatial adaption via wavelet shrinkage. *Biometrika, 81*(3), 425–455. doi:10.1093/biomet/81.3.425

Estrada, F., Fleet, D., & Jepson, A. (2009). Stochastic image denoising. *British Machine Vision Conference*. Retrieved November 20, 2011, from http://www.cs.utoronto.ca/~strider/Denoise/

González, R. C. (2008). *Standard test images*. Retrieved November 20, 2011, from http://www.ece.utk.edu/~gonzalez/ipweb2e/downloads/standard_test_images/standard_test_images.zip

González, R. C., & Woods, R. E. (2008). *Digital image processing*. Englewood Cliffs, NJ: Prentice Hall.

Hao, Z. F., Guo, G. H., & Huang, H. (2007). A particle swarm optimization algorithm with differential evolution over continuous spaces. In *Proceedings of the International Conference on Machine Learning and Cybernetics*, (vol. 2, pp. 1031-1035). IEEE.

Hoyer, P. (1999). *Independent component analysis in image denoising*. (Master Degree Dissertation). Helsinki University of Technology. Helsinki, Finland. Retrieved November 20, 2011, from http://www.cs.helsinki.fi/u/phoyer/papers/ps/dippa.ps

Lalitha, Y. S., & Mrityunjaya, V. L. (2011). A novel approach noise filtration for MRI images sample in medical image processing. *International Journal of Computer Science and Communication, 2*(2), 359–363.

Lim, J. S. (1990). *Two-dimensional signal and image processing*. Englewood Cliffs, NJ: Prentice Hall.

Potnis, A., Somkuwar, A., & Sapre, S. D. (2010). A review on natural image denoising using independent component analysis (ica) technique. *Advances in Computational Research, 2*(1), 6–14.

Romberg, J. K., Hyeokho, C., & Baraniuk, R. G. (2001). Bayesian tree-structured image modeling using wavelet-domain hidden Markov models. *IEEE Transactions on Image Processing, 10*(7), 1056–1068. doi:10.1109/83.931100

Storn, R., & Price, K. (1995). *Differential evolution - A simple and efficient adaptive scheme for global optimization over continuous spaces*. ICSI Technical Report TR-95-012. Retrieved August 16, 2011, from http://www.icsi.berkeley.edu/~storn/TR-95-012.pdf

Tomasi, C., & Manduchi, R. (1998). Bilateral filtering for gray and color images. In *Proceedings of the International Conference on Computer Vision*, (pp. 839-846). IEEE.

Wang, Z., Bovik, A. C., Sheikh, H. R., & Simoncelli, E. P. (2004). Image quality assessment: From error visibility to structural similarity. *IEEE Transactions on Image Processing, 13*(4), 600-612. Retrieved November 20, 2011, from http://www.ece.uwaterloo.ca/~z70wang/research/ssim/

Zhang, S. (2011). Image denoising using FIR filters designed with evolution strategies. In *Proceedings of the 2011 3rd International Workshop on Intelligent Systems and Applications (ISA)*, (pp. 1-4). IEEE.

ADDITIONAL READING

Bacchelli, Silvia, & Papi, S. (2006). Image denoising using principal component analysis in the wavelet domain. *Journal of Computational and Applied Mathematics, 189*(1-2), 606–621. doi:10.1016/j.cam.2005.04.030

Baker, S., & Kanade, T. (2002). Limits on super-resolution and how to break them. *IEEE Transactions on Pattern Analysis and Machine Intelligence, 24*(9), 1167–1183. doi:10.1109/TPAMI.2002.1033210

Bell, A. J., & Sejnowski, T. J. (1997). The "independent components" of natural scenes are edge filters. *Vision Research, 37*(23), 3327–3338. doi:10.1016/S0042-6989(97)00121-1

Bronstein, M. M., Bronstein, A. M., Zibulevsky, M., & Zeevi, Y. Y. (2005). Blind deconvolution of images using optimal sparse representations. *IEEE Transactions on Image Processing, 14*(6), 726–736. doi:10.1109/TIP.2005.847322

Buades, A., Coll, B., & Morel, J. M. (2005). A review of image denoising algorithms, with a new one. *Multiscale Modeling & Simulation, 4*(2), 490–530. doi:10.1137/040616024

Cardoso, J. F., & Laheld, B. H. (1996). Equivariant adaptive source separation. *IEEE Transactions on Signal Processing, 44*(12), 3017–3030. doi:10.1109/78.553476

Chatterjee, P., & Milanfar, P. (2010). Is denoising dead? *IEEE Transactions on Image Processing, 19*(4), 895–911. doi:10.1109/TIP.2009.2037087

Chatterjee, P., & Milanfar, P. (2011). Practical bounds on image denoising: From estimation to information. *IEEE Transactions on Image Processing, 20*(5), 1221–1233. doi:10.1109/TIP.2010.2092440

Chen, M., Xu, M., & Franti, P. (2011). Adaptive context-tree-based statistical filtering for raster map image denoising. *IEEE Transactions on Multimedia, 13*(6), 1195–1207. doi:10.1109/TMM.2011.2166538

Deka, B., & Bora, P. K. (2011). Removal of random-valued impulse noise using sparse representation. In *Proceedings of the National Conference on Communications*, (pp. 1-5). IEEE.

Dong, W., Zhang, L., Shi, G., & Wu, X. (2011). Image deblurring and super-resolution by adaptive sparse domain selection and adaptive regularization. *IEEE Transactions on Image Processing, 20*(7), 1838–1857. doi:10.1109/TIP.2011.2108306

Elad, M., & Aharon, M. (2006). Image denoising via sparse and redundant representations over learned dictionaries. *IEEE Transactions on Image Processing, 15*(12), 3736–3745. doi:10.1109/TIP.2006.881969

Felsberg, M. (2011). Autocorrelation-driven diffusion filtering. *IEEE Transactions on Image Processing, 20*(7), 1797–1806. doi:10.1109/TIP.2011.2107330

Gao, H., & Xu, W. (2011). Particle swarm algorithm with hybrid mutation strategy. *Applied Soft Computing, 11*(8), 5129–5142. doi:10.1016/j.asoc.2011.05.046

Goossens, B., Pizurica, A., & Philips, W. (2009). Removal of correlated noise by modeling the signal of interest in the wavelet domain. *IEEE Transactions on Image Processing, 18*(6), 1153–1165. doi:10.1109/TIP.2009.2017169

Hae, J. S., Chatterjee, P., Takeda, H., & Milanfar, P. (2007). A comparison of some state of the art image denoising methods. In *Proceedings of the Forty-First Asilomar Conference on Signals, Systems and Computers*, (pp. 518-522). Asilomar.

Hammond, D. K., & Simoncelli, E. P. (2008). Image modeling and denoising with orientation-adapted Gaussian scale mixtures. *IEEE Transactions on Image Processing, 17*(11), 2089–2101. doi:10.1109/TIP.2008.2004796

Heechan, P., Martin, G. R., & Yao, Z. (2007). Image denoising with directional bases. In *Proceedings of the IEEE International Conference on Image Processing*, (pp. I301-I304). IEEE Press.

Hirakawa, K., & Parks, T. W. (2005). Image denoising for signal-dependent noise. In *Proceedings of the IEEE International Conference on Acoustics, Speech, and Signal Processing*, (Vol. 2, pp. 29-32). IEEE Press.

Hyvärinen, A. (1999). A fast and robust fixed-point algorithms for independent component analysis. *IEEE Transactions on Neural Networks, 10*(3), 626–634. doi:10.1109/72.761722

Hyvärinen, A., Hurri, J., & Hoyer, P. O. (2009). *Natural image statistics - A probabilistic approach to early computational vision*. Retrieved November 20, 2011, from http://www.naturalimagestatistics.net/

Kathiravan, S., Raja, N. G., & Kumar, R. A. (2011). An investigation on image denoising technique using pixel-component-analysis. *Innovative Systems Design and Engineering, 2*(4), 233–241.

Kervrann, C., & Bourlanger, J. (2006). Optimal spatial adapation for patchbased image denoising. *IEEE Transactions on Image Processing, 15*(10), 2866–2878. doi:10.1109/TIP.2006.877529

Lin, Z., & Shum, H. Y. (2004). Fundamental limits of reconstruction-based super-resolution algorithms under local translation. *IEEE Transactions on Pattern Analysis and Machine Intelligence, 26*(1), 83–97. doi:10.1109/TPAMI.2004.1261081

Luisier, F., Blu, T., & Unser, M. (2011). Image denoising in mixed Poisson-Gaussian noise. *IEEE Transactions on Image Processing, 20*(3), 696–708. doi:10.1109/TIP.2010.2073477

Muresan, D. D., & Parks, T. W. (2003). Adaptive principal components and image denoising. In *Proceedings of the International Conference on Image Processing*, (Vol. 1, pp. I101-I104). IEEE.

Peyre, G. (2011). A review of adaptive image representations. *IEEE Journal of Selected Topics in Signal Processing, 5*(5), 896–911. doi:10.1109/JSTSP.2011.2120592

Poli, R., Kennedy, J., & Blackwell, T. (2007). Particle swarm optimization - An overview. *Swarm Intelligence, 1*(1), 33–57. doi:10.1007/s11721-007-0002-0

Robinson, D., & Milanfar, P. (2004). Fundamental performance limits in image registration. *IEEE Transactions on Image Processing, 13*(9), 1185–1199. doi:10.1109/TIP.2004.832923

Scharcanski, J., Jung, C. R., & Clarke, R. T. (2002). Adaptive image denoising using scale and space consistency. *IEEE Transactions on Image Processing, 11*(9), 1092–1101. doi:10.1109/TIP.2002.802528

Zhang, S., Tang, T., Wu, C., Xi, N., & Wang, G. (2010). A novel image denoising method using independent component analysis and dual-tree complex wavelet transform. In *Proceedings of the International Conference on Wireless Communications Networking and Mobile Computing*, (pp. 1-4). IEEE.

KEY TERMS AND DEFINITIONS

2D-FIR Filters: Two dimensional finite response filters.

DEPSO: Differential evolution particle swarm optimization, which combines the differential evolution algorithm with particle swarm algorithm.

Edge Classifier: An algorithm that groups the pixels into several classes according to certain criterion.

Image Denoising: Reducing the noise in the corrupted image as much as possible.

Linear Phase: The phase response is a linear function of time t.

Lowpass Filter: Filters that attenuate the high frequency components while preserve the low frequency components of input signals.

Mean Filter: Averaging FIR filter that all the coefficients share the same value.

Chapter 8

Optimization of Image Zernike Moments Shape Feature Based on Evolutionary Computation

Maofu Liu
Wuhan University of Science and Technology, China

Huijun Hu
Wuhan University of Science and Technology, China

ABSTRACT

The image shape feature can be described by the image Zernike moments. In this chapter, the authors point out the problem that the high dimension image Zernike moments shape feature vector can describe more detail of the original image but has too many elements making trouble for the next image analysis phases. Then the low dimension image Zernike moments shape feature vector should be improved and optimized to describe more detail of the original image. Therefore, the optimization algorithm based on evolutionary computation is designed and implemented in this chapter to solve this problem. The experimental results demonstrate the feasibility of the optimization algorithm.

DOI: 10.4018/978-1-4666-3958-4.ch008

INTRODUCTION

With the development and maturity of the image acquisition and storage technology, especially the sharp emergency and increment of Web images in the social networking service environment, Web users and humans are deluged by a great quantity of image data. They need the techniques and tools to efficiently retrieve, analyze, and understand the image data. Then the image feature which can be used to represent the image becomes more and more important. In fact, the image feature extraction and description is the most critical phase in the image retrieval, image analysis, and image understanding.

The image features include text, color, texture, shape, edge, shadows, temporal detail, and so on (Foschi, Kolippakkam, Huan, et al., 2002) and the image shape feature plays a very fundamental and important role in image analysis and understanding, so an effective and efficient shape descriptor is the key component of the image shape feature extraction and representation.

There are two types of image shape feature descriptors: contour-based and region-based shape feature descriptors. The region-based shape feature descriptors, for example the moment, are more reliable for shapes that have complex boundaries, because they rely on not only the contour pixels but also all pixels constituting the shapes (Teh & Chin, 1988).

The moments, especially geometric moment, centric moment, orthogonal invariance moments, have already been used in image shape description and content-based image retrieval (Teh & Chin, 1988; Liao & Pawlak, 1996; Mukundan & Pang, 2002; Pang, Andrew, David, et al., 2004). The Zernike moment, one kind of the orthogonal invariance moments, is the most commonly used technique in image shape feature extraction and description. Many researchers have paid much more attention to its invariant characteristics, including translation invariance, rotation invariance and scale invariance (Liao & Pawlak, 1996, 1997; Kim & Kim, 2000; Palak & Subbalakshmi, 2004; Chalechale, Naghdy, & Mertins, 2005; Kamila, Mahapatra, & Nanda, 2005).

After the computation of the Zernike moments to the original image, the image shape feature vector can be obtained. In fact, much higher order of the Zernike moments are used, more detail of the original image shape can be described. On the other hand, given the image Zernike moments shape feature vector and using the image reconstruction technique, the reconstructed image based on the Zernike moments shape feature vector of the original image can be turned out.

The reconstructed image will contain more detail of the original image and be closer to the original image as the order is higher, but the dimension of the Zernike moments shape feature vector also will be higher. If the order of the Zernike moment is 20, 25, 30, 35, 40, and 45, the dimension of the Zernike moments shape feature vector will correspondingly be 121, 182, 256, 342, 441, and 552.

If wanting to describe more detail of the original image shape, higher order of the Zernike moment will be used and higher dimension of the image Zernike moments shape feature vector will be obtained. The high dimension of the feature vector will make trouble to the next phases of image analysis, so the researchers have to solve the problem that the more detail can be described via the lower order of the Zernike moment and lower dimension of image Zernike moments shape feature vector.

In the chapter, the optimization algorithm based on evolutionary computation is designed and the low dimension image Zernike moments shape feature vector will be improved and optimized to describe more detail of the original image.

ZERNIKE MOMENTS

Definition

In mathematics, a moment is, loosely speaking, a quantitative measure of the shape of a set of points. For example, the second moment is widely used and measures the width of a set of points in a particular sense in one dimension or higher dimensions, especially the shape of a cloud of points. Other moments describe other aspects of a distribution such as how the distribution is skewed from its mean, or peaked.

In image processing, computer vision and related fields, an image moment is a certain particular weighted average (moment) of the image pixels' intensities, or a function of such moments, usually chosen to have some attractive property or interpretation. Image moments are useful to describe objects after segmentation.

For a two-dimensional continuous function $f(x, y)$, the raw moment of order ($p + q$) is defined as:

$$M_{pq} = \int\limits_{-\infty}^{\infty} \int\limits_{-\infty}^{\infty} x^p x^q f(x, y) dx dy \tag{1}$$

where $p, q = 0, 1, 2, \dots$. If adapt this to grayscale image with pixel intensities $I(x, y)$, the moments of raw image M_{pq} are calculated by the following formula.

$$M_{pq} = \sum_x \sum_y x^p y^q I(x, y) \tag{2}$$

In some cases, this may be calculated by considering the image as a probability density function, i.e., by dividing the above by $\sum_x \sum_y I(x,y)$.

A uniqueness theorem states that if $f(x,y)$ is piecewise continuous and has nonzero values only in a finite part of the x-y plane, moments of all orders exist, and the moment sequence M_{pq} is uniquely determined by $f(x,y)$. Conversely, the moment sequence M_{pq} also uniquely determines $f(x,y)$. In practice, the image is summarized with functions of a few lower order moments.

Based on the raw moments, the central moments, with the characteristic of translational invariant, can be defined as:

$$\mu_{pq} = \int\limits_{-\infty}^{\infty}\int\limits_{-\infty}^{\infty} (x - \bar{x})(y - \bar{y})f(x,y)dxdy \tag{3}$$

where $\bar{x} = M_{10}\big/M_{00}$ and $\bar{y} = M_{01}/M_{00}$ are the components of the centroid.

If $f(x,y)$ is a digital image $I(x,y)$, then the central moments can be defined as the following formula.

$$\mu_{pq} = \sum_x \sum_y (x - \bar{x})^p (y - \bar{y})^q I(x,y) \tag{4}$$

The central moments of order up to 3 are as follows.

$$
\begin{aligned}
\mu_{00} &= M_{00} \\
\mu_{10} &= 0 \\
\mu_{10} &= 0 \\
\mu_{11} &= M_{11} - \bar{x}M_{01} = M_{11} - \bar{y}M_{10} \\
\mu_{20} &= M_{20} - \bar{x}M_{10} \\
\mu_{02} &= M_{02} - \bar{y}M_{01} \\
\mu_{21} &= M_{21} - 2\bar{x}M_{11} - \bar{y}M_{20} + 2\bar{x}^2 M_{01} \\
\mu_{12} &= M_{12} - 2\bar{y}M_{11} - \bar{x}M_{02} + 2\bar{y}^2 M_{10} \\
\mu_{30} &= M_{30} - 3\bar{x}M_{20} + 2\bar{x}^2 M_{10} \\
\mu_{03} &= M_{03} - 3\bar{y}M_{02} + 2\bar{y}^2 M_{01}
\end{aligned}
\tag{5}
$$

Moments η_{pq} where $(p+q) \geq 2$ can be constructed to be invariant to both translation and changes in scale by dividing the corresponding central moment by the properly scaled $(00)^{th}$ moment, using the following formula.

$$\eta_{pq} = \frac{\mu_{pq}}{\mu_{00}^{(1+\frac{p+q}{2})}} \tag{6}$$

It is possible to calculate moments which are invariant under translation, changes in scale, and also rotation. Most frequently used are the Hu set of invariant moments.

$$
\begin{aligned}
H_1 =\ & \eta_{20} + \eta_{02} \\
H_2 =\ & (\eta_{20} - \eta_{02})^2 + (2\eta_{11})^2 \\
H_3 =\ & (\eta_{30} - 3\eta_{12})^2 + (3\eta_{21} - \eta_{03})^2 \\
H_4 =\ & (\eta_{30} + \eta_{12})^2 + (\eta_{21} + \eta_{03})^2 \\
H_5 =\ & (\eta_{30} - 3\eta_{12})(\eta_{30} + \eta_{12})[(\eta_{30} + \eta_{12})^2 \\
& -3(\eta_{21} + \eta_{03})^2] + \\
& (3\eta_{21} - \eta_{03})(\eta_{21} + \eta_{03})[3(\eta_{30} + \eta_{12})^2 \\
& -(\eta_{21} + \eta_{03})^2] \\
H_6 =\ & (\eta_{20} - \eta_{02})[(\eta_{30} + \eta_{12})^2 - (\eta_{21} + \eta_{03})^2] \\
& +4\eta_{11}(\eta_{30} + \eta_{12})(\eta_{21} + \eta_{03}) \\
H_7 =\ & (3\eta_{21} - \eta_{03})(\eta_{30} + \eta_{12})[(\eta_{30} + \eta_{12})^2 \\
& -3(\eta_{21} + \eta_{03})^2] - \\
& (\eta_{30} - 3\eta_{12})(\eta_{21} + \eta_{03})[3(\eta_{30} + \eta_{12})^2 \\
& -(\eta_{21} + \eta_{03})^2]
\end{aligned}
\tag{7}
$$

Here, we use Zernike moment to represent and describe the shape feature of the image. Zernike moment is a kind of orthogonal complex moments and its kernel is a set of Zernike complete orthogonal polynomials defined over the interior of the unit disc in the polar coordinates space (Ye & Peng, 2002; Hasan, 2012). Let $f(x,y)$ be the image intensity function, and the two-dimensional Zernike moment of order m with repetition n is defined as:

$$Z_{mn} = \frac{m+1}{\pi} \iint_{x^2+y^2 \leq 1} f(x,y)[V_{mn}(x,y)]^* \, dx\, dy \tag{8}$$

$$m \geq 0$$

where $[V_{mn}(x,y)]^*$ is the complex conjugate representation of $V_{mn}(x,y)$, and both m and n are integer and the relation between m and n can be described as:

$$(m-|n|) \text{ is even and } |n| \leq m \tag{9}$$

In the polar coordinates space, the two-dimensional Zernike moment can be defined as:

$$Z_{mn} = \frac{m+1}{\pi} \int_0^{2\pi} \int_0^1 f(r,\theta) V_{mn}(r,\theta) r dr d\theta \tag{10}$$

$$r \leq 1$$

where $r = \sqrt{x^2 + y^2}$ and $\theta = \tan^{-1}(y/x)$.

The Zernike polynomial $V_{mn}(r,\theta)$ is defined as:

$$V_{mn}(r,\theta) = R_{mn}(r) \exp(jn\theta) \tag{11}$$

where $j = \sqrt{-1}$, and the orthogonal radial polynomial $R_{mn}(r)$ is given by

$$R_{mn}(r) = \sum_{s=0}^{\frac{m-|n|}{2}} (-1)^s \frac{(m-s)!}{s!(\frac{m+|n|}{2} - s)!(\frac{m-|n|}{2} - s)!} r^{m-2s} \tag{12}$$

For the computer digital image, let $P(x,y)$ be the intensity of the image pixel, and the formula (1) can be represented as:

$$Z_{mn} = \frac{m+1}{\pi} \sum_x \sum_y P(x,y)[V_{mn}(x,y)]^* \tag{13}$$

$$x^2 + y^2 \leq 1$$

The image shape feature extracted and described by the Zernike moments is not sensitive to the noises and the values of the Zernike moments are hardly redundant because the kernel of the Zernike moment is the vector of the orthogonal radial polynomials. The low order Zernike moments can represent the whole shape of the original image and the high order Zernike moments can describe the detail. So the shape feature of the image can be represented by a vector of the values of the Zernike moments.

The different order of the Zernike moments can be computed via the formula (6) according to the variance of the order. In the same way, the different values of the Zernike moments can be calculated according to the variance of the repetition in the case of the order invariance. The results can be looked on as the Zernike moments vector of the specified original image shape feature.

The Zernike moments vector Z of the image shape feature can be given easily after sorted the values of the Zernike moments each order firstly ascending and then sorted those of each repetition ascending according to the order (Ma, Zhang, & Yan, 2011; Signh, Walia, & Mittal, 2012; Liu, He, & Ye, 2007; Liu, Hu, Zhong, et al., 2008).

$$Z = < z_1, z_2, z_3, ..., z_i, ... >$$ (14)

Image Reconstruction

The Zernike moments vector can represent and describe the image shape feature. In fact, the image can also be reconstructed from the Zernike moments feature vector via the inverse transformation of the Zernike moment in the unit disc because it is only the mapping transformation from the image intensive space to the Zernike moment space.

The image reconstruction can be defined as:

$$\hat{P}(r, \theta) = \sum_{m=0}^{m_{\max}} \sum_n Z_{mn} V_{mn}(r, \theta)$$ (15)

where $\hat{P}(r, \theta)$ is the reconstructed image and $m_{\max}$ is the maximum of the order of the Zernike moment. It is proved that the reconstructed image is the same as the original image while $m_{\max}$ is infinite in theory.

If expand the formula (8) and use some theorems and equations, the following formula is given in Box 1.

With the dimension increment of the image Zernike moments shape feature vector, more detail of the original image shape can be reconstructed from the Zernike moments feature vector, but the high dimension Zernike moments shape feature

Table 1. The order of the Zernike moment and the responding dimension of the image Zernike moments shape feature vector

Order	10	11	12	13	14	15
Dimension	36	42	49	56	64	72

Box 1.

$$
\begin{aligned}
\hat{P}(r,\theta) &= \sum_{m=0}^{m_{\max}} \sum_{n<0} Z_{mn} V_{mn}(r,\theta) + \sum_{m=0}^{m_{\max}} \sum_{n\geq 0} Z_{mn} V_{mn}(r,\theta) \\
&= \sum_{m=0}^{m_{\max}} \sum_{n>0} Z_{m(-n)} V_{m(-n)}(r,\theta) + \sum_{m=0}^{m_{\max}} \sum_{n\geq 0} Z_{mn} V_{mn}(r,\theta) \\
&= \sum_{m=0}^{m_{\max}} \sum_{n>0} Z_{mn}^{*} V_{mn}^{*}(r,\theta) + \sum_{m=0}^{m_{\max}} \sum_{n\geq 0} Z_{mn} V_{mn}(r,\theta) \\
&= \sum_{m} \left[\sum_{n>0} \left[Z_{mn}^{*} V_{mn}^{*}(r,\theta) + Z_{mn} V_{mn}(r,\theta) \right] + Z_{m0} V_{m0}(r,\theta) \right] \quad (16) \\
&= \sum_{m} \left[\sum_{n>0} \left\{ \left[\mathrm{Re}[Z_{mn}] - j\,\mathrm{Im}[Z_{mn}] \right] R_{mn}(r) \left[\cos(n\theta) - j\sin(n\theta) \right] \right. \right. \\
&\quad + \left. \left[\mathrm{Re}[Z_{mn}] + j\,\mathrm{Im}[Z_{mn}] \right] R_{mn}(r) \left[\cos(n\theta) + j\sin(n\theta) \right] \right\} \\
&\quad + \left. \left[\mathrm{Re}[Z_{m0}] + j\,\mathrm{Im}[Z_{m0}] \right] R_{m0}(r) \right]
\end{aligned}
$$

The final result can be represented as:

$$
\hat{P}(r,\theta) = \sum_{m} \left\{ \sum_{n>0} \left[C_{mn}\cos(n\theta) + S_{mn}\sin(n\theta) \right] R_{mn}(r) + \frac{C_{m0}}{2} R_{m0}(r) \right\} \quad (17)
$$

$$
C_{mn} = 2\,\mathrm{Re}(Z_{mn}) = \frac{2m+2}{\pi} \sum_{x}\sum_{y} P(r,\theta) R_{mn}(r)\cos(n\theta) \quad x^2 + y^2 \leq 1 \quad (18)
$$

$$
S_{mn} = -2\,\mathrm{Im}(Z_{mn}) = \frac{-2m-2}{\pi} \sum_{x}\sum_{y} P(r,\theta) R_{mn}(r)\sin(-n\theta) \quad x^2 + y^2 \leq 1 \quad (19)
$$

vector is a trouble for the next image analysis phases. The lower dimension one should be improved or optimized to describe more detail of the original image.

Feature Evaluation

According to the definition of the Zernike moment, the values of the Zernike moments of each order least than $m_{\max}$ can be calculated of the image once the maximum of the order $m_{\max}$ is specified. Then the Zernike moments shape feature set Z of the original image can be given. Correspondingly, if the Zernike moments shape feature set Z of the original image is known, the image can be reconstructed based on the principle of the image reconstruction mentioned above.

Of course, there is some difference between the reconstructed image and the original image. The difference can be measured via the dissimilarity degree between the reconstructed image and the original image.

$$H(P,\hat{P}) = \sum_r \sum_\theta | P(r,\theta) - \hat{P}(r,\theta) | \tag{20}$$

where $P(r,\theta)$ and $\hat{P}(r,\theta)$ are the original image and the reconstructed image respectively and $H(P,\hat{P})$ is the dissimilarity degree. The meaning of the dissimilarity degree is the number of the pixels not reconstructed completely if the original image is a binary one.

In fact, after the image reconstruction mentioned above, the reconstructed image should be taken the further processes, such as image quantifying, intensive equalization and thresholding.

According to difference between the reconstructed image and the original image, the image reconstruction ratio RR can be defined as:

$$RR = (1 - \frac{H(P,\hat{P})}{\sum_r \sum_\theta P(r,\theta)}) \times 100\% \tag{21}$$

The image reconstruction ratio can be used to evaluate the description ability of the image Zernike moments shape feature.

OPTIMIZATION ALGORITHM BASE ON EVOLUTIONARY COMPUTATION

A number of search techniques have been developed for researching optimization problems and evolutionary computation is one of them. Evolutionary computation uses computational models of evolutionary processes as key elements in the design and implementation of computer-based problem solving systems (Spears, Jong, Baeck, Thomas, et al., 1993) and is based on principles of biological evolution, such as natural selection and genetic inheritance.

In computer science, evolutionary computation is a subfield of artificial intelligence, more particularly computational intelligence, which involves combinatorial optimization problems. Evolutionary computation uses iterative progress, such as growth or development in a population. This population is then selected in a guided random search using parallel processing to achieve the desired end. Such processes are often inspired by biological mechanisms of evolution. As evolution can produce highly optimized processes and networks, it has many applications in computer science.

Evolutionary algorithms form a subset of evolutionary computation in which they generally only involve techniques implementing mechanisms inspired by biological evolution such as reproduction, mutation, recombination, natural selection, and survival of the fittest. Candidate solutions to the optimization problem play the role of individuals in a population, and the cost function determines the environment within which the solutions should be survived. Evolution of the population then takes place after the repeated application of the above operators. In this process, there are two main forces that form the basis of evolutionary systems, i.e., recombination and mutation create the necessary diversity and thereby facilitate novelty, while selection acts as a force increasing quality.

Many aspects of such an evolutionary process are stochastic. Changed pieces of information due to recombination and mutation are randomly chosen. On the other hand, selection operators can be either deterministic, or stochastic. In the latter case, individuals with a higher fitness have a higher chance to be selected than individuals with a lower fitness, but typically even the weak individuals have a chance to become a parent or to survive.

Evolutionary computation works surprisingly well for complicated, large, multi-dimensional search spaces (Foster, 1996), so evolutionary computation can also be used to improve and optimize the low dimension image Zernike moments shape feature vector to describe more detail of the original image, so optimization algorithm based on evolutionary computation is designed and implemented to solve the problem mentioned above.

There are several critical phases in the optimization algorithm based on evolutionary computation, such as encoding representation, initial population, fitness function, genetic operators, selection strategy, termination condition, and so on. The optimization algorithm based on evolutionary computation of image Zernike moments shape feature vector is represented in Figure 1.

In this optimization algorithm, a very direct encoding representation is taken. For 10-order Zernike moment, there are 36 elements in the image Zernike moments shape feature vector and one 37-dimensional vector is used to represent it. The fore 36 dimensions represent each element of the feature vector and the last dimension is the fitness of the feature vector. The fitness of the feature vector is calculated by one fitness function, which is defined by formula (22) and can represent the similarity between the original image and the reconstructed image.

Figure 1. Evolutionary computation based optimization algorithm

---

Algorithm: Evolutionary computation based optimization algorithm of image Zernike moments shape feature vector

Input: The order of the image Zernike shape feature vector needed to be optimized (*order*);
 The original testing image (*destImage*);
 The maximum number of the optimization generations (*maxGen*).

Output: The best image Zernike shape feature vector in final population (*best*);
 The reconstructed image based the best the image Zernike shape feature vector in
 final population (*rectImage*);
 The fitness of best the image Zernike shape feature vector (*fitValue*).

Step 1: Initialize the breeding population *endPop* which size is 20, the number of recurrent generation *gen*, the maximum number of the optimization generations *maxGen*, the recurrent best individual *best*;

Step 2: Generate the starting population *startPop* which size is 10;

Step 3: Repeat

Step 4: If (*gen*=1) then turning to Step 5;

Step 5: Select 9 individuals from *endPop* to *startPop* using roulette wheel selection, then put *best* in *startPop*;

Step 6: Put all individuals of the *startPop* in *endPop*, initialize the loop variable *i*=1
 While (*i*<10)
  Stochastic select one individual and put it in *endPop* after mutation;

Step 7: Select the best individual from *endPop* to *best*;

Step 8: *Gen*=*Gen*+1;

Step 9: Until (*Gen*=*maxGen*);

Step 10: Output the result of *best*, *rectImage*, *fitValue*.

$$fitValue = 1 - \frac{\sum_r \sum_\theta | (P(r,\theta)) - \hat{P}(r,\theta) |}{\sum_r \sum_\theta P(r,\theta)} \qquad (22)$$

The initial image Zernike moments shape feature vector is looked on as the first individual in the initial population which scale is 10 and the genetic operation on the first individual is used to generate the other individuals. There are three basic genetic operators, that is reproduction, crossover and mutation and the mutation operation is used in this optimization algorithm. One individual is modified via its specific element multiplied by a random.

The selection strategy is roulette wheel selection and the termination condition is specifying the maximum number of the optimization generations. In fact, the threshold of the fitness of the best individual of each generation can also be used as the termination condition.

In this optimization algorithm, there are many other functions, such as termination condition function, initial population function, population mutation function, individual selection function, fitness function, and so forth.

The time complexity of the optimization algorithm is mainly due to the digital image processing on the assumption that the dimension of the image Zernike moments shape feature vector is k, the scale of the evolutionary population is l, the number of the generations is m and the size of the digital image matrix is $n \times n$. In this optimization algorithm, the image reconstruction based on the image Zernike moments shape feature vector and the computation of the fitness are both related to the digital image processing. With l scale of the evolutionary population and m evolutionary generations, the image reconstruction implements (ml) times, and every image construction needs (kn^2) elementary computations, so there are $(mlkn^2)$ elementary computations in the all image reconstruction. The fitness must be calculated after the image construction and the fitness function is based on every pixel of the digital image and there are n^2 comparisons, so there are totally (mln^2) comparisons for l scale of the evolutionary population and m evolutionary generation. Generally speaking, l and k are much less than m and n. If m is ultimately equal to n, the time complexity of the image reconstruction and the fitness function are both $O(mn^2)$ and the whole optimization algorithm has time complexity $O(n^3)$. If m is much less than n, the whole optimization algorithm has time complexity $O(n^2)$.

EXPERIMENT RESULTS

In the chapter, many experiments in the MATLAB environments have been made on the trademark image database ITEM S8, the MPEG-7 standard testing image database which has around 3000 trademark logo images (ISO/IEC JTC1/SC29/WG11/N2467, 1998). The experiment results of mark1279 trademark image in the trademark logo image database are listed to demonstrate the feasibility of the optimization algorithm and the experiment results of the other trademark images used in the experiments have the same conclusion.

The image of the Figure 2 is the testing image, i.e., the original mark1279 trademark image. The Figure 3 is the reconstructed intensive images based on the Zernike moments shape feature set of the original image. We use the magnitude of

Figure 2. The testing image

Figure 3. The reconstructed images based on Zernike moments shape feature set

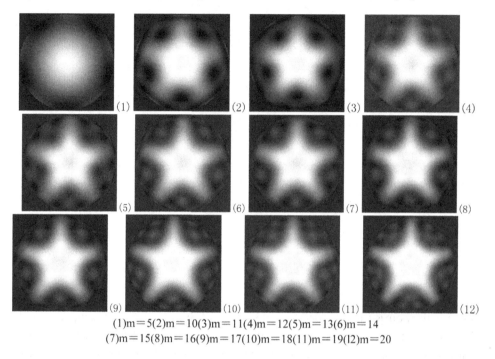

(1)m＝5(2)m＝10(3)m＝11(4)m＝12(5)m＝13(6)m＝14
(7)m＝15(8)m＝16(9)m＝17(10)m＝18(11)m＝19(12)m＝20

the complex Zernike moments value as the Zernike moments value for convenient calculation in the following experiments, which does not affect the experiment results (Mukundan & Pang, 2002).

From the results mentioned above, the conclusion is easily driven that the reconstructed image is very close to the original image when the order of the Zernike moment is 19. The reconstructed image will contain more detail of the original image and be closer to the original image as the order is higher.

The detail of the reconstruction ratios between the original image and the reconstructed images are showed in the Figure 4. There are 110 values in the image Zernike moments shape feature set when the order of the Zernike moment is 19. The fluctuation of the reconstruction ratios between moment order 19 and moment order 20 is mainly attributes to the further processes, especially the threshold value selection.

The comparative experiment is made between Zernike moment descriptor and Fourier descriptor since Fourier descriptor is usually used to represent and describe image shape feature. The Fourier descriptor matrix has the same size as the original image. The trademark image mark1279 and its Fourier descriptor matrix have the same size 111×111, and the size is obviously much more than 110. If only adopting the top 110 elements of the Fourier descriptor matrix, the image reconstruction

Figure 4. The reconstruction ratio of Zernike moments shape feature set (m=5,10~20)

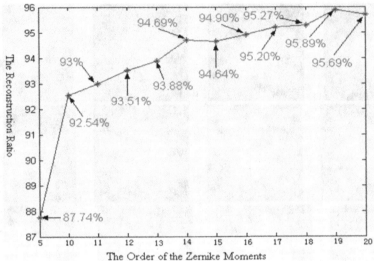

based on the Fourier descriptor does not work at all. When selecting the top 20×111 elements of the Fourier descriptor matrix, the reconstructed image based on the Fourier descriptor is shown in Figure 5(a) and apparently only part of the whole original testing image and much worse than Figure 3(11). Only when selecting the top 30×111 elements of the Fourier descriptor matrix, the shape of the original testing image can be approximately reconstructed, and the reconstructed result is listed in Figure 5(b) and also much worse than Figure 3(11).

The same reconstruction and comparative experiments results can be made on the other images in the trademark image database ITEM S8.

The values of the Zernike moments of the testing image are illustrated in Figure 6 when the value of the order is from 0 to 19. There are totally 110 values in the Figure 6.

The Figure 7 is the reconstructed images using the best individual of each evolutionary generation after implementing the optimization algorithm based on the evolutionary computation mentioned above. The order of the Zernike moment used in the image Zernike moments shape feature vector is from 10 to 15 in Figure 3 and

Figure 5. The reconstructed image based on Fourier descriptor

(a)   (b)

Figure 6. The values of Zernike moments of the testing image (m=0~19)

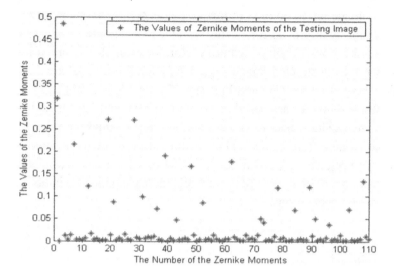

Figure 7. Table 1 lists the order of the Zernike moment from 10 to 15 and the re-sponding dimension of the image Zernike moments shape feature vector.

In the process of implementing optimization algorithm, the maximum number of the optimization generations is 100.

Figure 7. The reconstructed images using the best individual of each evolutionary generation after implementing the optimization algorithm based on evolutionary computation

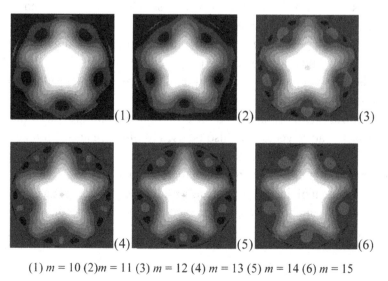

(1) $m = 10$ (2)$m = 11$ (3) $m = 12$ (4) $m = 13$ (5) $m = 14$ (6) $m = 15$

From the results mentioned above, the conclusion is easily driven that the reconstructed image based on the optimized image Zernike moments shape feature vector is obviously improved comparing with the reconstructed image based on the original Zernike moments shape feature vector, for example, Figure 3(4) to Figure 7(3). In fact, the constructed image Figure 7(5) and Figure 7(6) are very close to the testing image Figure 3(11) and Figure 3(12). For Figure 7(5) and Figure 7(6), the reconstructed images are based on 64-dimensional and 72-dimensional image Zernike moments shape feature vectors respectively. Comparing with 19 order of the Zernike moment for Figure 3(11), the dimension of image Zernike moments shape feature vector is reduced from 110 to 64 or 72. Of course, the accuracy of the optimization will be improved more while increasing the maximum number of the optimization generations.

CONCLUSION

Image analysis is the process to extract useful semantic information or knowledge from the complicated image database or data set and the significant method to understand the huge amounts of the images.

The image feature extraction and description is the critical phase in the image analysis. The image shape feature is a very important one and can be represented and described by the image Zernike moments shape feature vector. The paper points out the problem that the high dimension image Zernike moments shape feature vector can describe more detail of the image but has too many elements in the vector and it will make trouble for the next image analysis phases. So the low dimension image Zernike moments shape feature vector should be improved and optimized to describe more detail of the image.

For optimization problem, the evolutionary computation is a good choice. The optimization algorithm based on evolutionary computation is designed and implemented in the following section in the chapter. The experimental results demonstrate the feasibility of the solution.

The optimization algorithm based on evolutionary computation of the Zernike moments shape feature vector can also be used to improve and optimize the other orthogonal invariance moments shape feature vector, such as Legendre moment, Pseudo-Zernike moment, Fourier-Mellon moment, and so on.

The development of the image analysis technique can also make a great progress on image retrieval, image coding, image recognition, and so forth.

REFERENCES

Belkasim, S., Hassan, E., & Obeidi, T. (2004). Radial Zernike moment invariants. In *Proceeding of the Fourth International Conference on Computer and Information Technology*, (pp. 790-795). IEEE.

Chalechale, A., Naghdy, G., & Mertins, A. (2005). Sketch-based image matching using angular partitioning. *IEEE Transactions on Systems, Man, and Cybernetics. Part A, Systems and Humans, 35*(1), 28–41. doi:10.1109/TSMCA.2004.838464

Chong, C. W., Raveendran, P., & Mukundan, R. (2003). Translation invariants of Zernike moments. *Pattern Recognition, 36*(8), 1765–1773. doi:10.1016/S0031-3203(02)00353-9

Foschi, G., Kolippakkam, D., Huan, L., et al. (2002). Feature extraction for image mining. In *Proceedings of 8th International Workshop on Multimedia Information Systems*, (pp. 103-109). IEEE.

Foster, J. A. (1996). *Introduction to evolutionary computation*. Retrieved April 4, 1996, from http://people.ibest.uidaho.edu/~foster/Talks/intro-ec.pdf

Hasan, S. Y. (2012). Study of Zernike moments using analytical Zernike polynomials. *Advances in Applied Science Research, 3*(1), 583–590.

ISO/IEC JTC1/SC29/WG11/N2467. (1998). *Description of MPEG-7 content set*. Retrieved from http://www.tnt.uni-hannover.de/project/mpeg/audio/public/mpeg7/w2467.html

Kamila, K., Mahapatra, S., & Nanda, S. (2005). Invariance image analysis using modified Zernike moments. *Pattern Recognition Letters, 26*(6), 747–753. doi:10.1016/j.patrec.2004.09.026

Kim, W.-Y., & Kim, Y.-S. (2000). A region-based shape descriptor using zernike moments. *Signal Processing Image Communication, 16*, 95–102. doi:10.1016/S0923-5965(00)00019-9

Liao, S. X., & Pawlak, M. (1996). On image analysis by moments. *IEEE Transactions on Pattern Analysis and Machine Intelligence, 18*(3), 254–266. doi:10.1109/34.485554

Liao, S. X., & Pawlak, M. (1997). Image analysis with zernike moment descriptors. In *Proceedings of IEEE Canadian Conference on Electrical and Computer Engineering*, (vol. 2, pp. 700–703). IEEE Press.

Liu, M., He, Y., & Ye, B. (2007). Image Zernike moments shape feature evaluation based on image reconstruction. *Geo-Spatial Information Science, 10*(3), 191–195. doi:10.1007/s11806-007-0060-x

Liu, M., Hu, H., & Zhong, M. (2008). Evolutionary computation based optimization of image Zernike moments shape feature vector. *Wuhan University Journal of Natural Sciences, 13*(2), 151–158. doi:10.1007/s11859-008-0206-1

Ma, Z. M., Zhang, G., & Yan, L. (2011). Shape feature descriptor using modified Zernike moments. *Pattern Analysis & Applications, 14*(1), 9–22. doi:10.1007/s10044-009-0171-0

Mukundan, R., & Pang, A. (2002). Stereo image analysis: A new approach using orthogonal moment functions. In *Proceedings of Asian Technology Conference in Mathematics*, (pp. 513-522). IEEE.

Palak, A., & Subbalakshmi, P. (2004). Rotation and cropping resilient data hiding with Zernike moments. In *Proceeding of International Conference on Image Processing*, (vol. 4, pp. 2175-2178). IEEE.

Pang, H., Andrew, B., & David, L. (2004). Palmprint verification with moments. *Journal of WSCG, 12*(3), 325–332.

Seo, J. S., & Yoo, C. D. (2006). Image watermarking based on invariant regions of scale-space representation. *IEEE Transactions on Signal Processing, 54*(4), 1537–1549. doi:10.1109/TSP.2006.870581

Signh, C., Walia, E., & Mittal, N. (2012). Rotation invariant complex Zernike moments features and their applications to human face and character recognition. *Computer Vision, 5*(5), 255–265.

Spears, W. M., Jong, K. A., Baeck, T., et al. (1993). An overview of evolutionary computation. In *Proceeding of European Conference on Machine Learning*, (vol. 667, pp. 442-459). IEEE.

Teh, C., & Chin, T. (1988). On image analysis by the method of moments. *IEEE Transactions on Pattern Analysis and Machine Intelligence, 10*(4), 496–513. doi:10.1109/34.3913

Ye, B., & Peng, J. (2002). Improvement and invariance analysis of Zernike moments using as a region-based shape descriptor. *Journal of Pattern Recognition and Image Analysis, 12*(4), 419–428.

Ye, B., & Peng, J. (2002). Invariance analysis of improved Zernike moments. *Journal of Optics. A, Pure and Applied Optics, 4*(6), 606–614. doi:10.1088/1464-4258/4/6/304

Chapter 9
Dimension Reduction of Local Manifold Learning Algorithm for Hyperspectral Image Classification

Sheng Ding
Wuhan University, China &
Wuhan University of Science and Technology, China

Li Chen
Wuhan University of Science and Technology, China

Jun Li
Wuhan University of Science and Technology, China

ABSTRACT

This chapter addresses the problems in hyperspectral image classification by the methods of local manifold learning methods. A manifold is a nonlinear low dimensional subspace that is supported by data samples. Manifolds can be exploited in developing robust feature extraction and classification methods. The manifold coordinates derived from local manifold learning (LLE, LE) methods for multiple data sets. With a proper selection of parameters and a sufficient number of features, the manifold learning methods using the k-nearest neighborhood classification results produced an efficient and accurate data representation that yields higher classification accuracies than linear dimension reduction (PCA) methods for hyperspectral image.

DOI: 10.4018/978-1-4666-3958-4.ch009

1. INTRODUCTION

Airborne hyperspectral sensors have the capability of providing detailed measurements of the earth surface with very high-spectral resolutions. This makes them powerful when dealing with applications requiring discrimination between subtle differences in ground covers (e.g., plant type differentiation, material quantification, and target detection). However, the large dimensional data spaces (up to several hundred) generated by these sensors can result in degraded classification accuracies. This is due to the curse of dimensionality (Hughes effect) characterizing of this type of data (Bazi & Melgani, 2006; Campbell & Wynee, 2011; Melgani & Bruzzone, 2004; Ritter & Urcid, 2011). Over the past years, various solutions dealing with the classification of hyperspectral images have been proposed to improve the classification of hyperspectral remote sensing imagery (Bazi & Melgani, 2006; Melgani & Bruzzone, 2004). Dimension reduction play key role in the processing of hyperpsectral imagery classification. Traditional dimensionality reduction is important in many domains, since it mitigates the curse of dimensionality and other undesired properties of high-dimensional spaces (Jimenez & Landgrebe, 1997). As a result, dimensionality reduction facilitates classification, visualization, and compression of high-dimensional data. In general, dimensionality reduction was performed using linear techniques such as Principal Components Analysis (PCA) (Pearson, 1901), factor analysis (Spearman, 1904), and classical scaling (Torgerson, 1952). However, these linear techniques cannot adequately handle complex nonlinear data. Motivated by the lack of a systematic comparison of dimensionality reduction techniques, this paper presents a comparative study of the most important linear dimensionality reduction technique (PCA), and two nonlinear dimensionality reduction techniques. The aims of the chapter are (1) to investigate to what extent novel nonlinear dimensionality reduction techniques outperform the traditional PCA on real-world datasets and (2) to identify the inherent weaknesses of the nonlinear dimensionality reduction techniques. The investigation is performed by both a theoretical and an empirical evaluation of the dimensionality reduction techniques. The identification is performed by a careful analysis of the empirical results on a selection of real world hyperspectral datasets.

In this paper, two local manifold learning methods which are widely used in the machine learning community are investigated in a collaborative study for classification of hyperspectral data. These two local manifold learning methods (LLE, LE) are applied to two hyperspectral data sets that differ in acquisition characteristics (airborne vs. spaceborne), ground resolution, number of spectral bands, and scene characteristics. The manifold coordinates are compared to the coordinates of the original data and linear feature extraction methods using the k-nearest neighborhood classification results.

2. DIMENSION REDUCTION AND MANIFOLD LEARNING

2.1. Dimension Reduction

Dimension Reduction (DR) has been used to mitigate the issues of high interband spectral correlation and the Hughes phenomenon for classification of hyperspectral data. The resultant features not only require reduced data storage and computation, but also produce a more robust and accurate classifier. Several unsupervised and supervised linear feature extraction methods have been applied to hyperspectral data. Unsupervised methods include projection pursuit (Ifarraguerri & Chang, 2000), wavelet transforms (Bruce, Hoger, & Li, 2002), and independent component analysis (Wang & Chang, 2006). Supervised methods include penalized discriminant analysis (Yu, Ostland, Gong, & Pu, 1999), best-bases feature extraction (Kumar, Ghosh, & Crawford, 2001), and non-parametric weighted feature extraction (Kuo & Landgrebe, 2004). Recently, the impact of feature selection has been also investigated with respect to Support Vector Machines (SVM) which do not necessarily require a separate feature selection and extraction step (Pal & Foody, 2010). Although the SVM classifier is well known for its robustness to high dimensionality, removal of irrelevant features can still improve the performance of an SVM classifier for some hyperspectral data. Principal Components Analysis (PCA) is a linear technique for dimensionality reduction, which means that it performs dimensionality reduction by embedding the data into a linear subspace of lower dimensionality. Although there exist various techniques to do so, PCA is by far the most popular (unsupervised) linear technique. Therefore, in our comparison, we only include PCA. PCA constructs a low-dimensional representation of the data that describes as much of the variance in the data as possible. This is done by finding a linear basis of reduced dimensionality for the data, in which the amount of variance in the data is maximal.

The Maximum Noise Fraction (MNF) transform was proposed first in (Green, Berman, Switzer, & Craig, 1988) for noise removal, where a set of features was obtained from linear combinations of original spectral bands in such a way that the new features maximize the signal to noise ratio. Application of the transform isolates the noise in residual bands which are discarded, thereby reducing the dimension of the data. In Greco, Diani, and Corsini (2006), classification of AVIRIS data was performed using the maximum likelihood (ML) classifier based on MNF based feature extraction results. The method produced higher classification accuracies than those obtained by Principal Component Analysis (PCA). The MNF method (Green, Berman, Switzer, & Craig, 1988) is mathematically equivalent to noise-adjusted principal component analysis (Lee, Woodyatt, & Berman, 1990).

Various feature extraction methods were proposed to overcome shortcomings of PCA and MNF. Segmented PCA (Jia & Richards, 1999) tackles the problem by constructing subgroups of highly correlated spectral bands, then applying PCA to each subgroup and performing feature selection. Kaewpijit et al. (Kaewpijit, le Moigne, & El-Ghazawi, 2003) addressed two shortcomings of PCA, computation and the susceptibility to outliers, using a wavelet decomposition approach. The wavelet method was applied to scenes acquired by the AVIRIS and AISA sensors, and classification experiments were performed with ML, minimum distance, and parallelpiped classifiers. For these experiments, the wavelet features produced comparable or better classification results with reduced computational complexity. Independent Component Analysis (ICA) proposed in (Wang & Chang, 2006) seeks to improve discrimination of subtle materials in high spectral resolution of hyperspectral data using mutual information instead of the second-order statistics employed by PCA and MNF. Performance of ICA was evaluated in (Wang & Chang, 2006) for endmember extraction and data compression, where the experiment results showed that ICA produced better results than PCA and the MNF method.

Nonlinear feature extraction methods, namely manifold learning, have been investigated recently to accommodate the nonlinear characteristics of hyperspectral data. Nonlinear methods investigated for the classification of hyperspectral data include Curvilinear Component Analysis (CCA) (Lennon, Mercier, Mouchot, & Hubert-Moy, 2001), isometric feature mapping (Isomap) (Bachmann, Ainsworth, & Fusina, 2005), local linear embedding (LLE) (Mohan, Sapiro, & Bosch, 2007; Ma, Crawford, & Tian, 2010), kernel ortho-normalized partial least squares (KPLS) (Arenas-Garcia & Camps-Valls, 2008), diffusion geometric coordinates (He, Zhang, Wang, & Li, 2009), kernel PCA (KPCA) (Fauvel, Chanussot, & Benediktsson, 2009), and Local Tangent Space Alignment (LTSA) (Ma, Crawford, & Tian, 2010). Although manifold learning methods have yielded improved results for the classification of hyperspectral data, blind of use of the methods often results in unsatisfactory results compared to those of simple linear methods. Performance of manifold learning methods needs to be investigated with respect to factors such as (1) dimension of manifold coordinates, (2) selection of free parameters, (3) number of classes, and (4) scene characteristics. Overall patterns of manifold coordinates also differ between global manifold learning methods (e.g. Isomap and KPCA) and local methods (e.g. LLE, LE, LTSA). Whereas global methods preserve the overall shape of a manifold by considering pairwise spectral relationships between all samples, but local methods primarily focus on a spectrally local space in which the global structure is formed through the local connections. Investigation of these factors would be informative for robust application of various manifold learning methods.

2.2. Local Manifold Learning

Nonlinear manifold learning methods are broadly characterized as global or local approaches. Global manifold methods retain the fidelity of the overall topology of the data set, but have greater computational overhead for large data sets, while local methods preserve local geometry and are computationally efficient because they only require sparse matrix computations. Although global manifolds seek to preserve geometry across all scales of the data and have less tendency to overfit the data, which is beneficial for generalization in classification, local methods may yield good results for data sets which have significantly different sub-manifolds. In the paper, we use two local manifold methods for dimension reduction.

The two local manifold learning methods are investigated in this study: Locally Linear Embedding (LLE), and Laplacian Eigenmaps (LE). All two methods are initiated by constructing a nearest neighborhood for each data point, and the local structures are then used to obtain a global manifold. According to the framework, by solving the eigenvalue problem $LY = \lambda BY$, the embedding Y is provided by the eigenvectors corresponding to the 2~(p+1) smallest eigenvalues (the eigenvector that corresponds to the smallest zero eigenvalue is a unit vector with equal elements and is discarded).

2.2.1. Locally Linear Embedding (LLE)

In LLE (Bachmann, Ainsworth, & Fusina, 2005), the local properties of each neighborhood are represented by the linear coeficients that best reconstruct each data point from its neighbors. Let $F \in R^{n \times n}$ be composed of the reconstruction coeficients of all the data points, which is obtained by minimizing the reconstruction error according to

$$e(f_i) = \left\| x_i - \sum_i f_{ij} x_{ij} \right\|^2 \quad s.t. \sum_j f_{ij} = 1 \tag{1}$$

where f_{ij} denotes the reconstruction weight of x_i from its j-th neighbor x_{ij}. The embedding is then obtained by retaining these coefficients in the low dimensional space via the objective function:

$$\Phi(Y) = \sum_i \left\| y_i - \sum_j f_{ij} y_j \right\|^2$$

$$s.t. \frac{1}{n} \sum_i y_i y_j^T = I, \sum_i y_i = 0$$

(2)

which can be minimized by solving the problem:

$$Y^* = \arg\min_{YBY^T=I} tr(YLY^T)$$

where I is the identify matrix. where the Laplacian matrix $L = (I - F^T)(I - F)$, constraint matrix $B = I$, and the similarity matrix $W = F + F^T - F^T F$.

In LLE, the local properties of the data manifold are constructed by writing the high-dimensional datapoints as a linear combination of their nearest neighbors. In the low-dimensional representation of the data, LLE attempts to retain the reconstruction weights in the linear combinations as good as possible. The popularity of LLE has led to the proposal of linear variants of the algorithm (Mohan, Sapiro, & Bosch, 2007; Ma, Crawford, & Tian, 2010), and to successful applications to, e.g., superresolution (He, Zhang, Wang, & Li, 2009) and sound source localization (Arenas-Garcia & Camps-Valls, 2008). However, there also exist experimental studies that report weak performance of LLE. In (Arenas-Garcia & Camps-Valls, 2008), LLE was reported to fail in the visualization of even simple synthetic biomedical datasets. In (Fauvel, Chanussot, & Benediktsson, 2009), it is claimed that LLE performs worse than Isomap in the derivation of perceptual-motor actions.

2.2.2. Laplacian Eigenmaps (LE)

In LE, the weighted neighborhood graph of each data point is obtained by calculating the pairwise distances between neighbors, where the distance is normally calculated using a Gaussian kernel function with parameter. Let $W \in R^{n \times n}$ be the adjacency matrix that summarizes the neighborhood relations. The embedding Y is obtained by minimizing the distances between each data point and its neighbors in the low dimensional space:

$$\Phi(Y) = \sum_{i,j} \left\| y_i - y_j \right\|^2 W_{ij} \quad s.t. YDY^T = I$$

(3)

which is analogous to (3.2) with L = D -W and B = D. It is also equivalent (up to scaling) to the eigenvalue decomposition of the normalized graph Laplacian matrix defined by $D^{-1/2}(D - W) D^{-1/2}$ (Fauvel, Chanussot, & Benediktsson, 2009).

3. EXPERIMENT AND RESULTS

3.1. Remotely Sensed Data for Comparative Experiments

Two hyperspectral remotely sensed data sets which are commonly used to evaluate classification methods were analyzed in this comparative study. The data were acquired by sensors covering approximately the same range of wavelengths in the visible and short wave infrared portions of the spectrum in 10-nm spectral bands at spatial resolutions from 2-30 m. Spectral signatures of classes are complex and often overlapping, and spatial patterns include natural vegetation and agricultural fields in both fragmented and regular geometric patterns. Site and class related information is listed in Table 1. Important characteristics of each data set are summarized in the remainder of this section.

Table 1. Class labels and number of labeled samples

ID	Class name	ID	Class name
1	Water (158)	1	Alfalfa (54)
2	Willow swamp (243)	2	Corn - No till (1434)
3	Cabbage palm hammock (256)	3	Corn – Min till (834)
4	Cabbage palm/oak(252)	4	Corn (234)
5	Slash pine (161)	5	Grass/pasture (497)
6	Oak/broadleaf hammock (229)	6	Grass/trees (747)
7	Hardwood swamp (105)	7	Grass/pasture-mowed (26)
8	Graminoid marsh (431)	8	Hay- windrowed (489)
9	Spartina marsh (520)	9	Oats (20)
10	Cattail marsh (404)	10	Soy – No till (968)
11	Salt marsh (419)	11	Soy – Min till (2468)
12	Mud flats (503)	12	Soy – clean (614)
13	Water (927)	13	Wheat (212)
		14	Woods (1294)
		15	Bldg-grass-trees-drives (380)
		16	Stone-steel towers (95)

3.2. Kennedy Space Center Aviris Data (KSC)

Airborne hyperspectral data were acquired by the NASA AVIRIS sensor at 18-m spatial resolution over Kennedy Space Center during March, 1996. Noisy and water absorption bands were removed, leaving 176 features for 13 wetland and upland classes of interest. Cabbage Palm Hammock (Class 3) and Broad Leaf/Oak Hammock (Class 6) are upland trees, Willow Swamp (Class 2), Hardwood Swamp (Class 7), Graminoid Marsh (Class 8), and Spartina Marsh (Class 9) are trees and grasses in wetlands. Their spectral signatures are mixed and often exhibit only subtle differences. Results for all 13 classes and for these difficult classes are reported for the manifold learning experiments. The data was acquired from an altitude of 20 km and has a spatial resolution of 18 m. After removing low SNR bands and water absorption, a total of 176 bands remains for analysis. The dataset has 13 classes representing the various land cover types of the environment (Munoz-Mari, Bruzzone, & Cramps-Valls, 2007; Camps-Valls, Gomez-Chova, Munoz-Mari, Martinez-Ramon, & Rojo-Alvarez, 2008).

For classification purposes, 13 classes representing the various land cover types that occur in this environment were defined for the site (Table 1). Classes 4 and 6 represent mixed classes. Figure 1 shows and RGB composition with the labeled classes highlighted. The interest in this class is motivated because of its intrinsic complexity, it is underrepresented and it can be confused with similar subclasses in the scene.

Figure 1. RGB composition of the data acquired over the KSC (Kennedy space center)

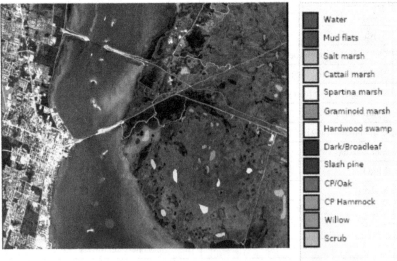

3.3. Indian Pine Aviris Data (IND PINE)

The Indiana Indian Pine (IND PINE) 16-class data set was acquired by the NASA AVIRIS sensor in June, 1992 at 20-m spatial resolution (AVIRIS, 1992). The scene is primarily comprised of agricultural fields with regular geometry, providing an opportunity to evaluate the impact of within-class variability at medium spatial resolution. This data set was chosen because its ground truth is available, so that the classification accuracy can easily be evaluated. The data consists of 145×145 pixels with 220 bands. The number of bands is initially reduced to 200 by removing bands covering water absorption and noisy bands. The original ground truth has actually 16 classes (see Figure 2).

3.4. Experimental Results

Focusing on issues related to dimensionality reduction rather than performance related to classifiers, the k-Nearest-Neighbor (kNN) method with k=1 was used as the common base classifier. Some experiments are performed by dimensionality reduction methods for hyperspectral data. All labeled data sets were randomly sampled to provide 50% training and 50% testing samples, with 10 replications of each experiment. The same data points for each of the two data sets were used for each dimensionality reduction method to provide consistent comparisons. Classification results are provided for the two local manifold learning methods (LLE and LE), and compared to a linear dimensionality reduction methods (PCA). The base classifier was k-NN with k=1 in all experiments. Results are also included for the original data both for similarities based on spectral angle, as spectral angle is often preferred for classification of hyperspectral data.

Figure 2. RGB composition and ground truth of the IND PINE data

Experimental results for KSC and IND PINE data are provided to illustrate performance of the various dimensionality reduction methods for all classes. For these two local methods p ranges from 5 to 100. Figure 3 contains plots of experimental results obtained from the 1NN-SAM classifier, over a range of the parameter values for the respective methods. Figure 3 and Figure 4 indicates that LLE outperforms PCA and 1NN -SAM for both sets of KSC data and IND PINE dataset. but requires significantly larger p(> 30) to obtain these results. The mean values of the kappa statistics are plotted as a function of dimension for each nonlinear learning method and for PCA, and compared to those obtained using the original full dimensional data with 1NN-SAM(Spectral Angle Mapper, SAM). Several trends are suggested by these results. Similar results were observed in experiments using the IND PINE data (see Figure 4).

Figure 3. LLE for KSC dataset

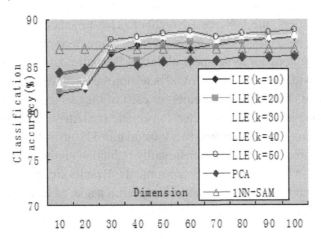

Figure 4. LLE for IND PINE dataset

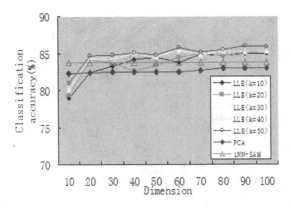

Figure 5 and Figure 6 indicates that LE outperforms PCA and 1NN-SAM for KSC data and IND PINE data. For the multi-class problem, the highest accuracy is achieved for p = 60 .This denote that the more complex the data,the more features are needed to describe the data structure. In general, the larger value of k, better classification results is achieved for the parameters k. k = 10 and k=20 has less effective on the classification of the two dataset, other values of k can get a similar good results, indicating that in the hyperspectral image classification, LLE in the larger range of the parameter k is not sensitive to classification accuracy.

In general, small values of k need more bands to achieve good classification results, because small k to the neighborhood structure is relatively small, and de-

Figure 5. LE for KSC dataset

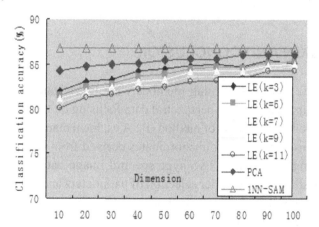

Figure 6. LE for IND PINE dataset

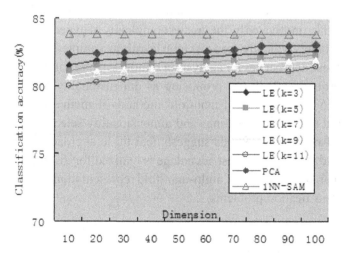

scribe more details of the data structure, so they need more bands to complete describe the local structure. Larger k values will smooth some of the details, but might be better to take into account the data of the global structure, and with a small amount of band, we can better describe the data structure information.

From Figure 5 and Figure 6, we can see LE achieve lower accuracies than PCA and 1NN-SAM for the multi-category classification. The best results are obtained for k = 3. For all the data categories, classification of LE get worse result than the PCA and the effect of 1NN-SAM, but when the band number is enough, LE achieve similar result compared with the PCA and 1NN-SAM effect. In addition, 1NN-SAM classification is best for all the two datasets. For all categories of data, 20-30 band are need to achieve a stable classification usually. For the parameters k, and small values of k (k = 3,5) perform better result, this is different with LLE algorithm (large k value is better).

4. DISCUSSION AND CONCLUSION

We can conclude manifold learning methods were investigated specifically with respect to their application to hyperspectral data focusing on the (a) parameter values, (b) dimensionality, (c) type of method (PCA vs. local manifold). Classification was performed using the manifold coordinates derived from two local (LLE, LE) manifold learning methods for two hyperspectral image data sets with differing class characteristics. With a proper selection of parameters and a sufficient number of features, the manifold learning methods produced an efficient, accurate data representation that yields higher classification accuracies than linear dimension reduction method (PCA).

The goal of this study was to investigate the characteristics of nonlinear manifold learning methods for dimensionality reduction in classification of hyperspectral data. The study was also motivated by the greater complexity of hyperspectral data relative to example data sets typically used machine learning examples, which could impact the value of these approaches for analysis of remote sensing data. Overall, nonlinear manifold learning methods are promising as dimensionality reduction methods. However, PCA can outperform manifold methods if methods are implemented without regard to parameter settings and dimensionality selection. Computational complexity of nonlinear methods suggests that these approaches should be used judiciously and that their greatest advantage is realized for discriminating difficult classes. Further, investigation of multi-manifold representations may have merit for supervised classification problems.

ACKNOWLEDGMENT

This research was supported by National Natural Science Foundation of China under Grant (NO.61273303).

REFERENCES

Arenas-Garcia, J., & Camps-Valls, G. (2008). Efficient kernel orthonormalized PLS for remote sensing applications. *IEEE Transactions on Geoscience and Remote Sensing, 46*(10), 2872–2881. doi:10.1109/TGRS.2008.918765

AVIRIS. (1992). *NW Indiana's indian pines 1992 data set.* Retrieved from ftp://ftp. ecn.purdue.edu/biehl/MultiSpec/92AV3C

Bachmann, C. M., Ainsworth, T. L., & Fusina, R. A. (2005). Exploiting manifold geometry in hyperspectral imagery. *IEEE Transactions on Geoscience and Remote Sensing, 43*(3), 441–454. doi:10.1109/TGRS.2004.842292

Bazi, Y., & Melgani, F. (2006). Toward an optimal SVM classification system for hyperspectral remote sensing images. *IEEE Transactions on Geoscience and Remote Sensing, 44*(11), 3374–3385. doi:10.1109/TGRS.2006.880628

Bruce, L. M., Koger, C. H., & Li, J. (2002). Dimensionality reduction of hyperspectral data using discrete wavelet transform feature extraction. *IEEE Transactions on Geoscience and Remote Sensing, 40*(10), 2331–2338. doi:10.1109/TGRS.2002.804721

Campbell, J. B., & Wynee, R. H. (2011). *Introduction to remote sensing* (5th ed.). New York, NY: The Guilford Press.

Camps-Valls, G., & G'omez-Chova, L., Mu~noz-Mar'ı, J., Mart'ınez-Ram'on, M., & Rojo-' Alvarez, J. L. (2008). Kernelbased framework for multi-temporal and multi-source remote sensing data classification and change detection. *IEEE Transactions on Geoscience and Remote Sensing, 46*(11), 1822–1835. doi:10.1109/ TGRS.2008.916201

Fauvel, M., Chanussot, J., & Benediktsson, J. A. (2009). Kernel principal component analysis for the classi_cation of hyperspectral remote sensing data over urban areas. *EURASIP Journal on Advances in Signal Processing, 11.*

Greco, M., Diani, M., & Corsini, G. (2006). Analysis of the classification accuracy of a new MNF based feature extraction algorithm. *Image and Signal Processing for Remote Sensing XII, 6365*(1).

Green, A. A., Berman, M., Switzer, P., & Craig, M. D. (1988). A transformation for ordering multispectral data in terms of image quality with implications for noise removal. *IEEE Transactions on Geoscience and Remote Sensing, 26*(1), 65–74. doi:10.1109/36.3001

He, J., Zhang, L., Wang, Q., & Li, Z. (2009). Using diffusion geometric coordinates for hyperspectral imagery representation. *IEEE Geoscience and Remote Sensing Letters, 6*(4), 767–771. doi:10.1109/LGRS.2009.2025058

Ifarraguerri, A., & Chang, C. (2000). Unsupervised hyperspectral image analysis with projection pursuit. *IEEE Transactions on Geoscience and Remote Sensing, 38*(6), 2529–2538. doi:10.1109/36.885200

Jia, X., & Richards, J. A. (1999). Segmented principal components transformation for efficient hyperspectral remote-sensing image display and classification. *IEEE Transactions on Geoscience and Remote Sensing, 37*(1), 538–542. doi:10.1109/36.739109

Jimenez, L. O., & Landgrebe, D. A. (1997). Supervised classification in high-dimensional space: Geometrical, statistical, and asymptotical properties of multivariate data. *IEEE Transactions on Systems, Man, and Cybernetics, 28*(1), 39–54.

Kaewpijit, S., Le Moigne, J., & El-Ghazawi, T. (2003). Automatic reduction of hyperspectral imagery using wavelet spectral analysis. *IEEE Transactions on Geoscience and Remote Sensing, 41*(4), 863–871. doi:10.1109/TGRS.2003.810712

Kumar, S., Ghosh, J., & Crawford, M. M. (2001). Best-bases feature extraction algorithms for classification of hyperspectral data. *IEEE Transactions on Geoscience and Remote Sensing, 39*, 1368–1379. doi:10.1109/36.934070

Kuo, B., & Landgrebe, D. A. (2004). Nonparametric weighted feature extraction for classi_cation. *IEEE Transactions on Geoscience and Remote Sensing, 42*(5), 1096–1105. doi:10.1109/TGRS.2004.825578

Lee, J. B., Woodyatt, A. S., & Berman, M. (1990). Enhancement of high spectral resolution remote-sensing data by a noise-adjusted principal components transform. *IEEE Transactions on Geoscience and Remote Sensing, 28*(3), 295–304. doi:10.1109/36.54356

Lennon, M., Mercier, G., Mouchot, M. C., & Hubert-Moy, L. (2001). Curvilinear component analysis for nonlinear dimensionality reduction of hyperspectral images. *Image and Signal Processing for Remote Sensing VII, 4541*, 157–168. doi:10.1117/12.454150

M. Fauvel, Chanussot, J., & Benediktsson, J. A. (2009). Kernel principal component analysis for the classification of hyperspectral remote sensing data over urban areas. *EURASIP Journal on Advances in Signal Processing.*

Ma, L., Crawford, M. M., & Tian, J. (2010). Local manifold learning-based k-nearest neighbor for hyperspectral image classification. *IEEE Transactions on Geoscience and Remote Sensing, 48*(11), 4099–4109.

Melgani, F., & Bruzzone, L. (2004). Classification of hyperspectral remote sensing images with support vector machine. *IEEE Transactions on Geoscience and Remote Sensing, 42*(10), 1778–1790. doi:10.1109/TGRS.2004.831865

Mohan, A., Sapiro, G., & Bosch, E. (2007). Spatially coherent nonlinear dimensionality reduction and segmentation of hyperspectral images. *IEEE Geoscience and Remote Sensing Letters, 4*(2), 206–210. doi:10.1109/LGRS.2006.888105

Mu~noz-Mar'ı, J., Bruzzone, L., & Camps-Valls, G. (2007). A support vector domain description approach to supervised classification of remote sensing images. *IEEE Transactions on Geoscience and Remote Sensing, 45*(8), 2683–2692. doi:10.1155/2009/783194

Pal, M., & Foody, G. M. (2010). Feature selection for classi_cation of hyperspectral data by SVM. *IEEE Transactions on Geoscience and Remote Sensing, 48*(5), 2297–2307. doi:10.1109/TGRS.2009.2039484

Pearson, K. (1901). On lines and planes of closest fit to systems of points in space. *Philosophical Magazine, 2*, 559–572. doi:10.1080/14786440109462720

Ritter, G. X., & Urcid, G. (2011). A latex matrix method for hyperspectral image unmixing. *Information Science, 181*, 1787–1803. doi:10.1016/j.ins.2010.03.022

Spearman, C. (1904). General intelligence objectively determined and measured. *The American Journal of Psychology, 15*, 206–221. doi:10.2307/1412107

Torgerson, W. S. (1952). Multidimensional scaling I: Theory and method. *Psychometrika, 17*, 401–419. doi:10.1007/BF02288916

Wang, J., & Chang, C. (2006). Independent component analysis-based dimensionality reduction with applications in hyperspectral image analysis. *IEEE Transactions on Geoscience and Remote Sensing, 44*(6), 1586–1600. doi:10.1109/TGRS.2005.863297

Wang, J., & Chang, C. (2006). Independent component analysis-based dimensionality reduction with applications in hyperspectral image analysis. *IEEE Transactions on Geoscience and Remote Sensing, 44*(6), 1586–1600. doi:10.1109/TGRS.2005.863297

Yu, B., Ostland, M., Gong, P., & Pu, R. (1999). Penalized discriminant analysis of in situ hyperspectral data for conifer species recognition. *IEEE Transactions on Geoscience and Remote Sensing, 37*(5), 2569–2577. doi:10.1109/36.789651

Compilation of References

A, B., & Hogg, D. (1994). Learning flexible models from image sequence. In *Proceedings in Euro Conference Computing Visual Journal*, (pp. 299-308). IEEE.

Aggarwal, J. K., & Cai, Q. (1999). Human motion analysis: A review. *Computer Vision and Image Understanding*, *73*, 428–440. doi:10.1006/cviu.1998.0744

Ahmad, M., & Lee, S. W. (2006). Human action recognition using multi-view image sequences features. In *Proceedings of the 7th International Conference on Automatic Face and Gesture Recognition*. IEEE.

Ahmad, M., & Lee, S. W. (2008). Human action recognition using shape and CLG-motion flow from multi-view image sequences. *Pattern Recognition*, *41*(7), 2237–2252. doi:10.1016/j.patcog.2007.12.008

Ahn, J. H. (2009). Human tracking and silhouette extraction for human - Robot interaction systems. *Pattern Analysis & Applications*, *12*, 167–177. doi:10.1007/s10044-008-0112-3

Amer, A., & Regazzoni, C. (2005). Introduction to the special issue on video object processing for surveillance applications. *Real-Time Imaging*, *11*, 167–171. doi:10.1016/j.rti.2005.06.001

Andrade, E., Blunsden, S., & Fisher, R. (2005). Simulation of crowd problems for computer vision. In *Proceedings of the First International Workshop on Crowd Simulation*. IEEE.

Anusuya, M. A., & Katti, S. K. (2009). Speech recognition by machine: A review. *International Journal of Computer Science and Information Security*, *6*(3), 181–205.

Arenas-Garcia, J., & Camps-Valls, G. (2008). Efficient kernel orthonormalized PLS for remote sensing applications. *IEEE Transactions on Geoscience and Remote Sensing*, *46*(10), 2872–2881. doi:10.1109/TGRS.2008.918765

Arulampalam, M. S., Maskell, S., Gordon, N., & Clapp, T. (2002). A tutorial on particle filters for online nonlinear/non-gaussian bayesian tracking. *IEEE Transactions on Signal Processing*, *50*(2), 174–188. doi:10.1109/78.978374

AVIRIS. (1992). *NW Indiana's indian pines 1992 data set*. Retrieved from ftp://ftp.ecn.purdue.edu/biehl/MultiSpec/92AV3C

Ayers, D., & Shah, M. (1998). Monitoring human behavior in an office environment. In *Proceedings of the Intepprretation of Visual Motion*, (pp. 65-72). IEEE.

Compilation of References

Babu, R. V. (2001). Compressed domain action classification using HMM. *Pattern Recognition Letters*, *23*(10), 1203–1213. doi:10.1016/S0167-8655(02)00067-3

Bachmann, C. M., Ainsworth, T. L., & Fusina, R. A. (2005). Exploiting manifold geometry in hyperspectral imagery. *IEEE Transactions on Geoscience and Remote Sensing*, *43*(3), 441–454. doi:10.1109/TGRS.2004.842292

Barbu, T. (2011). An automatic face detection system for RGB images. *International Journal of Computers, Communications & Control*, *4*(1), 21–32.

Bazi, Y., & Melgani, F. (2006). Toward an optimal SVM classification system for hyperspectral remote sensing images. *IEEE Transactions on Geoscience and Remote Sensing*, *44*(11), 3374–3385. doi:10.1109/TGRS.2006.880628

Belkasim, S., Hassan, E., & Obeidi, T. (2004). Radial Zernike moment invariants. In *Proceeding of the Fourth International Conference on Computer and Information Technology*, (pp. 790-795). IEEE.

Ben-Arie, J. (2002). Human activity recognition using multidimensional indexing. *IEEE Transactions on Pattern Analysis and Machine Intelligence*, *24*, 1091–1104. doi:10.1109/TPAMI.2002.1023805

Benedek, C., & Sziranyi, T. (2008). Bayesian foreground and shadow detection in uncertain frame rate surveillance videos. *IEEE Transactions on Image Processing*, *17*, 608–621. doi:10.1109/TIP.2008.916989

Beni, G., & Wang, U. (1989). *Swarm intelligence in cellular robotic systems*. Paper presented at the NATO Advanced Workshop on Robots and Biological Systems. Tuscany, Italy.

Bennett, E. P., & McMillan, L. (2005). Video enhancement using per-pixel virtual exposures. *ACM Transactions on Graphics*, *24*(3), 845–852. doi:10.1145/1073204.1073272

Bilger, K., Kupferschlager, J., & Muller-Schauenburg, W. (2001). Threshold calculation for segmented attenuation correction in PET with histogram fitting. *IEEE Transactions on Nuclear Science*, *48*(1), 43–50. doi:10.1109/23.910831

Blake, A., & Isard, M. (1998). *Active contours*. London, UK: Springer-Verlag. doi:10.1007/978-1-4471-1555-7

Blumensath, T., & Davies, M. E. (2009). Iterative hard thresholding for compressed sensing. *Applied and Computational Harmonic Analysis*, *27*(3), 265–274. doi:10.1016/j.acha.2009.04.002

Blunsden, S., Fisher, R., & Andrade, E. (2006). *Recognition of coordinated multi agent activities: The individual vs the group*. Technical Report No. EDI-INF-RR-0830. Edinburgh, UK: The University of Edinburgh.

Bobick, A. F., & Wilson, A. D. (1995). A state-based technique for the summarization and recognition of gesture. In *Proceedings of International Conference on Computer Vision*. IEEE.

Bobick, A., & Davis, J. (1996). Real-time recognition of activity using temporal templates. In *Proceedings of IEEE Workshop on Applications of Computer Vision*. IEEE Press.

Bobick, A., & Davis, J. (2001). The recognition of human movement using temporal templates. *IEEE Transactions on Pattern Analysis and Machine Intelligence*, *23*(3), 257–267. doi:10.1109/34.910878

Bonabeau, E., Dorigo, M., & Theraulaz, G. (1999). *Swarm intelligence: From natural to artificial systems*. Oxford, UK: Oxford University Press.

Bonabeau, E., Dorigo, M., & Theraulaz, G. (2001). Swarm intelligence: From natural to artificial systems. *Journal of Artificial Societies and Social Simulation, 4*(1).

Brand, M., et al. (1997). *Coupled hidden markov models for complex action recognition*. Paper presented at the IEEE Computer Society Conference on Computer Vision and Pattern Recognition. New York, NY.

Breen, A. (1992). Speech synthesis models: A review. *Electronics & Communication Engineering Journal, 4*(1), 19–31. doi:10.1049/ecej:19920006

Brubaker, M. (2010). Physics-based person tracking using the anthropomorphic walker. *International Journal of Computer Vision, 87*, 140–155. doi:10.1007/s11263-009-0274-5

Bruce, L. M., Koger, C. H., & Li, J. (2002). Dimensionality reduction of hyperspectral data using discrete wavelet transform feature extraction. *IEEE Transactions on Geoscience and Remote Sensing, 40*(10), 2331–2338. doi:10.1109/TGRS.2002.804721

Buxton, H., & Gong, S. (1995). Visual surveillance in a dynamic and uncertain world. *Artificial Intelligence, 78*(1-2), 431–459. doi:10.1016/0004-3702(95)00041-0

Caillette, F. (2008). Real-time 3-D human body tracking using learnt models of behaviour. *Computer Vision and Image Understanding, 109*, 112–125. doi:10.1016/j.cviu.2007.05.005

Campbell, J. B., & Wynee, R. H. (2011). *Introduction to remote sensing* (5th ed.). New York, NY: The Guilford Press.

Campbell, J. P. (1997). Speaker recognition: A tutorial. *Proceedings of the IEEE, 85*(9), 1437–1462. doi:10.1109/5.628714

Camps-Valls, G., & G'omez-Chova, L., Mu~noz-Mar'ı, J., Mart'ınez-Ram'on, M., & Rojo-' Alvarez, J. L. (2008). Kernelbased framework for multi-temporal and multi-source remote sensing data classification and change detection. *IEEE Transactions on Geoscience and Remote Sensing, 46*(11), 1822–1835. doi:10.1109/TGRS.2008.916201

Castel, C., et al. (1996). *What is going on? A high level interpretation of sequences of images*. Paper presented at the the European Conference on Computer Vision. London, UK.

Celik, M. V. (2002). Video authentication with self recovery. In *Proceedings of Security and Watermarking of Multimedia Contents 4* (*Vol. 4314*, pp. 531–541). IEEE. doi:10.1117/12.465311

Chai, D., Ngan, K. N., & Bouzerdoum, A. (2000). Foreground/background bit allocation for region-of-interest coding. In *Proceedings International Conference on Image Processing*, (pp. 438-441). Vancouver, Canada: IEEE.

Chalechale, A., Naghdy, G., & Mertins, A. (2005). Sketch-based image matching using angular partitioning. *IEEE Transactions on Systems, Man, and Cybernetics. Part A, Systems and Humans, 35*(1), 28–41. doi:10.1109/TSMCA.2004.838464

Compilation of References

Chan, C. H., Goswami, B., Kittler, J., & Christmas, W. (2012). Local ordinal contrast pattern histograms for spatiotemporal, lip-based speaker authentication. *IEEE Transactions on Information Forensics and Security, 7*(2), 602–612. doi:10.1109/TIFS.2011.2175920

Chang, I. C., & Lin, H. C. (1996). Ribbon-based motion analysis of human body movements. In *Proceedings of the 13th International Conference on Pattern Recognition.* IEEE.

Chengalvarayan, R. (1999). Robust energy normalization using speech/non-speech discriminator for German connected digit recognition. [Budapest, Hungary: EUROSPEECH.]. *Proceedings of EUROSPEECH, 1999,* 61–64.

Cheng, H. D., Chen, Y. H., & Jiang, X. H. (2000). Thresholding using two dimensional histogram and fuzzy entropy principle. *IEEE Transactions on Image Processing, 9*(4), 732–735. doi:10.1109/83.841949

Chen, X., Hero, A., & Savarese, S. (2012). Multimodal video indexing and retrieval using directed information. *IEEE Transactions on Multimedia, 14*(1), 3–16. doi:10.1109/TMM.2011.2167223

Cheung, Y.-M., Liu, X., & You, X. (2012). A local region based approach to lip tracking. *Conference on Pattern Recognition and image. Analysis, 45*(9), 3336–3347.

Chibelushi, C., Gandon, S., Mason, J., Deravi, F., & Johnston, R. (1996). Design issues for a digital audio-visual integrated database. In *Proceedings of the IEEE Colloquium on Integrated Audio-Visual Processing for Recognition, Synthesis and Communication,* (pp. 1-7). IEEE Press.

Chibelushi, C. C., Deravi, F., & Mason, J. S. (2002). A review of speech-based bimodal recognition. *IEEE Transactions on Multimedia, 4*(1), 23–37. doi:10.1109/6046.985551

Chieu, H., et al. (2006). Activity recognition from physiological data using conditional random fields. In *Proceedings of the Singapore-MIT Alliance Computer Science Program.* MIT.

Chiou, G., & Hwang, J.-N. (1997). Lip-reading from color video. *IEEE Transactions on Image Processing, 6,* 1192–1195. doi:10.1109/83.605417

Choi, H.-R., Lee, J. W., Park, R.-H., & Kim, J.-S. (2006). False contour reduction using directional dilation and edge preserving filtering. *IEEE Transactions on Consumer Electronics, 52*(3), 1099–1109. doi:10.1109/TCE.2006.1706513

Chong, C. W., Raveendran, P., & Mukundan, R. (2003). Translation invariants of Zernike moments. *Pattern Recognition, 36*(8), 1765–1773. doi:10.1016/S0031-3203(02)00353-9

Cohen, L. D. (1991). On active contour models and balloons. *Computing Visual Imaging Understanding, 53*(2), 211–218. doi:10.1016/1049-9660(91)90028-N

Collins, R. T., et al. (2000). *A system for video surveillance and monitoring: VSAM final report.* Technical Report No. CMU-RI-TR-00-12. Pittsburgh, PA: Carnegie Mellon University.

Craver, S., Memon, N., Yeo, B., & Yeung, N. M. (1998). Resolving rightful ownerships with invisible watermarking techniques: Limitations, attacks, and implications. *IEEE Journal on Selected Areas in Communications, 16*(4), 573–586. doi:10.1109/49.668979

Cross, D., & Mobasseri, B. G. (2002). Water marking for self authentication of compressed video. In *Proceedings of the IEEE International Conference on Image Processing*. Rochester: IEEE Press.

D, G. S., & Hennecke, M. (1996). *Speechreading by humans and machines*. Berlin, Germany: Springer.

Diffie, W., & Hellman, M. E. (1976). New directions in cryptography. *IEEE Transactions on Information Theory, 22*(6), 644–654. doi:10.1109/TIT.1976.1055638

Ditmann, J., Steinmetz, A., & Steinmetz, R. (1999). Content based digital signature for motion pictures authentication and content fragile watermarking. In *Proceedings of the IEEE International Conference on Multimedia Computing and Systems*, (vol. 2, pp. 209-213). IEEE Press.

Dittman, J., Mukharjee, A., & Steinbach, M. (2000). Media independent watermarking classification and the need for combining digital video and audio watermarking for media authentication. In *Proceedings of the International Conference on Information Technology: Coding and Computing*. IEEE Press.

Do, T. T., Gan, L., Nguyen, N., & Tran, T. D. (2008). Sparsity adaptive matching pursuit algorithm for practical compressed sensing. In *Proceedings of the 2008 42nd Asilomar Conference on Signals, Systems and Computers*, (pp. 581–587). Asilomar.

Donoho, D. L. (2006). Compressed sensing. *IEEE Transactions on Information Theory, 52*(4), 1289–1306. doi:10.1109/TIT.2006.871582

Donoho, D. L., & Johnstone, I. M. (1994). Ideal spatial adaption via wavelet shrinkage. *Biometrika, 81*(3), 425–455. doi:10.1093/biomet/81.3.425

Donoho, D., Drori, I., Tsaig, Y., & Starck, J. (2006). *Sparse solution of underdetermined linear equations by stagewise orthogonal matching pursuit*. Palo Alto, CA: Stanford University.

Duchowski, A. T., & Vertegaal, R. C. (2000). Eye-based interaction in graphical system: Theory and practice. In *Proceedings of ACM SIGGRAPH 2000*. ACM Press.

Du, J., Hu, Y., & Jiang, H. (2011). Boosted mixture learning of gaussian mixture hidden markov models based on maximum likelihoof for speech recognition. *IEEE Transactions on Audio, Speech, and Language Processing, 19*(7), 2091–2100. doi:10.1109/TASL.2011.2112352

Duong, T. V., et al. (2005). *Activity recognition and abnormality detection with the switching hidden semi-Markov model*. Paper presented at the IEEE Computer Society Conference on Computer Vision and Pattern Recognition. New York, NY.

Duong, T. V. (2009). Efficient duration and hierarchical modeling for human activity recognition. *Artificial Intelligence, 173*(7-8), 830–856. doi:10.1016/j.artint.2008.12.005

Dupont, S., & Luettin, J. (2000). Audio-visual speech modeling for continuous speech recognition. *IEEE Transactions on Multimedia, 2*(3), 141–151. doi:10.1109/6046.865479

Duta, R., & Hart, P. (1973). *Pattern classification and scene analysis*. New York, NY: Wiley.

Compilation of References

Elgammal, A. (2002). Background and foreground modeling using nonparametric kernel density estimation for visual surveillance. *Proceedings of the IEEE, 90*, 1151–1163. doi:10.1109/JPROC.2002.801448

Engelbrecht, A. P. (2005). *Fundamentals of computational swarm intelligence.* New York, NY: Wiley.

Enyedi, B., Konyha, L., & Fazekas, K. (2005). Threshold procedures and image segmentation. In *Proceedings of the 47th International Symposium,* (pp. 29-32). ELMAR.

Estrada, F., Fleet, D., & Jepson, A. (2009). Stochastic image denoising. *British Machine Vision Conference.* Retrieved November 20, 2011, from http://www.cs.utoronto.ca/~strider/Denoise/

Etoh, M., & Yoshimura, T. (2005). Advances in wireless video delivery. *Proceedings of the IEEE, 93*(1), 111–122. doi:10.1109/JPROC.2004.839605

Eveno, N., Caplier, A., & Coulon, P.-Y. (2004). Accurate and quasi-automatic lip tracking. *IEEE Transactions on Circuits and Systems for Video Technology, 14,* 706–715. doi:10.1109/TCSVT.2004.826754

Fallon, M., & Godsill, S. (2012). Acoustic source localization and tracking of a time-varying number of speakers. *IEEE Transactions on Audio, Speech, and Language Processing, 20*(4), 1409–1415. doi:10.1109/TASL.2011.2178402

Fang, Y., Wang, Y., & Tan, T. (2004). Improving face detection through fusion of contour and region information. *Chinese Journal of Computer, 27,* 482–491.

Farid, H. (2006). Digital doctoring: How to tell the real from fake. *Significance, 3*(4), 162–166. doi:10.1111/j.1740-9713.2006.00197.x

Farmer, J., Casdagli, M., Eubank, S., & Gibson, J. (1991). State-space reconstruction in the presence of noise. *Physica D. Nonlinear Phenomena, 51*(1-3), 52–98. doi:10.1016/0167-2789(91)90222-U

Fauvel, M., Chanussot, J., & Benediktsson, J. A. (2009). Kernel principal component analysis for the classi_cation of hyperspectral remote sensing data over urban areas. *EURASIP Journal on Advances in Signal Processing, 11.* Mu~noz-Mar'ı, J., Bruzzone, L., & Camps-Valls, G. (2007). A support vector domain description approach to supervised classification of remote sensing images. *IEEE Transactions on Geoscience and Remote Sensing, 45*(8), 2683–2692.

Flake, G. (1999). *The computational beauty of nature.* Cambridge, MA: MIT Press.

Fook, C., Hariharan, M., Yaacob, S., & Adom, A. (2012). A review: Malay speech recognition and audio visual speech recognition. In *Proceedings of the International Conference on Biomedical Engineering,* (pp. 479-484). IEEE.

Foschi, G., Kolippakkam, D., Huan, L., et al. (2002). Feature extraction for image mining. In *Proceedings of 8th International Workshop on Multimedia Information Systems,* (pp. 103-109). IEEE.

Foster, J. A. (1996). *Introduction to evolutionary computation.* Retrieved April 4, 1996, from http://people.ibest.uidaho.edu/~foster/Talks/intro-ec.pdf

Friedman, N., & Russell, S. (1997). *Image segmentation in video sequences: A probabilistic approach.* Paper presented at the Thirteenth Conference on Uncertainty in Artificial Intelligence. New York, NY.

G. K. L. C. (2009). Robust computer voice recognition using improved MFCC algorithm. In *Proceedings of the IEEE International Conference on New Trends in Information and Service Science*, (pp. 835-840). IEEE Press.

Gennaro, R., & Rohatgi, P. (1997). How to sign digital stream. [Crypto.]. *Proceedings of Crypto, 1997*, 180–197.

Geradts, Z. J., & Bijhold, J. (1999). Forensic video investigation with real time digitized uncompressed video image sequences. In *Proceedings of the Investigation and Forensic Science Technologies.* IEEE.

González, R. C. (2008). *Standard test images*. Retrieved November 20, 2011, from http://www.ece.utk.edu/~gonzalez/ipweb2e/downloads/standard_test_images/standard_test_images.zip

González, R. C., & Woods, R. E. (2008). *Digital image processing*. Englewood Cliffs, NJ: Prentice Hall.

Goyani, M., Dave, N., & Patel, N. (2010). Preformance analysis of lip synchronization using LPC, MFCC and PLP speech parameters. In *Proceedings of the IEEE International Conference on Computational Intelligence and Communication Networks*, (pp. 582-587). IEEE Press.

Greco, M., Diani, M., & Corsini, G. (2006). Analysis of the classification accuracy of a new MNF based feature extraction algorithm. *Image and Signal Processing for Remote Sensing XII, 6365*(1).

Green, A. A., Berman, M., Switzer, P., & Craig, M. D. (1988). A transformation for ordering multispectral data in terms of image quality with implications for noise removal. *IEEE Transactions on Geoscience and Remote Sensing, 26*(1), 65–74. doi:10.1109/36.3001

Grosan, C., Abraham, A., & Monica, C. (2006). *Swarm intelligence in data mining*. Berlin, Germany: Springer.

Guerrini, F., Leonardi, R., & Migliorati, P. (2004). A new video authentication template based on bubble random sampling. In *Proceedings of the European Signal Processing Conference 2004*. IEEE.

Guo, Y., et al. (1994). *Understanding human motion patterns*. Paper presented at the IEEE International Conference on Pattern Recognition. New York, NY.

Hager, G. D., & Belhumeur, P. N. (1998). Efficient region tracking with parametric models of geometry and illumination. *IEEE Transactions on Pattern Analysis and Machine Intelligence, 20*, 1025–1039. doi:10.1109/34.722606

Han, Y. F., & Shi, P. F. (2007). An improved ant colony algorithm for fuzzy clustering in image segmentation. *Neurocomputing, 70*, 665–671. doi:10.1016/j.neucom.2006.10.022

Haritaoglu, I., Harwood, D., & Davis, L. S. (2000). W4: Real-time surveillance of people and their activities. *IEEE Transactions on Pattern Analysis and Machine Intelligence, 22*, 809–830. doi:10.1109/34.868683

Hasan, S. Y. (2012). Study of Zernike moments using analytical Zernike polynomials. *Advances in Applied Science Research, 3*(1), 583–590.

Hauzia, A., & Noumeir, R. (2007). Methods for image authentication: A survey. *Proceedings of the Multimedia Tools and Applications, 39*, 1–46. doi:10.1007/s11042-007-0154-3

He, D., Sun, O., & Tian, Q. (2003). A semi fragile object based video authentication system. In *Proceedings of IEEE ISCAS 2003*. Bangkok, Thailand: IEEE Press.

Compilation of References

He, J., Zhang, L., Wang, Q., & Li, Z. (2009). Using diffusion geometric coordinates for hyperspectral imagery representation. *IEEE Geoscience and Remote Sensing Letters*, *6*(4), 767–771. doi:10.1109/LGRS.2009.2025058

Hermansky, H. (1990). Perceptual linear predictive (PLP) analysis of speech. *Acoustical Society of America Journal*, *87*, 1738–1752. doi:10.1121/1.399423

Honig, S. F., Hacker, G., Brugnara, C., & Fabio. (2005). Revising perceptual linear prediction. In *Proceedings of INTERSPEECH-2005*, (pp. 2997-3000). INTERSPEECH.

Hossan, M., Memon, S., & Gregory, M. (2010). A novel approach for MFCC feature extraction. In *Proceedings of the International Conference on Signal Processing and Communication Systems*, (pp. 1-5). IEEE.

Hou, Z., Hu, Q., & Nowinski, W. L. (2006). On minimum variance thresholding. *Pattern Recognition Letters*, *27*(14), 1732–1743. doi:10.1016/j.patrec.2006.04.012

Hoyer, P. (1999). *Independent component analysis in image denoising*. (Master Degree Dissertation). Helsinki University of Technology. Helsinki, Finland. Retrieved November 20, 2011, from http://www.cs.helsinki.fi/u/phoyer/papers/ps/dippa.ps

Hu, D. H., & Yang, Q. (2008). CIGAR: Concurrent and interleaving goal and activity recognition. In *Proceedings of the National Conference on Artificial Intelligence*. IEEE.

Huang, H., & Makur, A. (2011). Backtracking-based matching pursuit method for sparse signal reconstruction. *IEEE Signal Processing Letters*, *18*(7), 391–394. doi:10.1109/LSP.2011.2147313

Huang, L. K., & Wang, M. J. J. (1995). Image thresholding by minimizing the measures of fuzziness. *Pattern Recognition*, *28*(1), 41–51. doi:10.1016/0031-3203(94)E0043-K

Ifarraguerri, A., & Chang, C. (2000). Unsupervised hyperspectral image analysis with projection pursuit. *IEEE Transactions on Geoscience and Remote Sensing*, *38*(6), 2529–2538. doi:10.1109/36.885200

Isard, M., & Blake, A. (1998). Condensation-conditional density propagation for visual tracking. *International Journal of Computer Vision*, *29*(1), 5–28. doi:10.1023/A:1008078328650

ISO/IEC JTC1/SC29/WG11/N2467. (1998). *Description of MPEG-7 content set*. Retrieved from http://www.tnt.uni-hannover.de/project/mpeg/audio/public/mpeg7/w2467.html

ITU-T Recommendation G.729-Annex B. (1996). *A silence compression scheme for G.729 optimized for terminals conforming to recomendation V.70*. Retrieved from http://www.itu.int

ITU-T Recommendation P. 910. (1996). *Subjective video quality assessment methods for multimedia applications*. Geneva, Switzerland: International Telecommunication Union.

ITU-T Recommendation P.800. (1996). *Methods for subjective determination of transmission quality*. Geneva, Switzerland: International Telecommunication Union.

Ivanov, Y. A., & Bobick, A. F. (2000). Recognition of visual activities and interactions by stochastic parsing. *IEEE Transactions on Pattern Analysis and Machine Intelligence*, *22*(8), 852–872. doi:10.1109/34.868686

Iwasawa, S., et al. (1997). Real-time estimation of human body posture from monocular thermal images. In *Proceedings of the IEEE Computer Society Conference on Computer Vision and Pattern Recognition*. IEEE.

Jabri, S., et al. (2000). Detection and location of people in video images using adaptive fusion of color and edge information. In *Proceedings of the 15th International Conference on Pattern Recognition*. IEEE.

Jain, R., & Nagel, H. (1979). On the analysis of accumulative difference pictures from image sequences of real world scenes. *IEEE Transactions on Pattern Analysis and Machine Intelligence*, *1*, 206–214. doi:10.1109/TPAMI.1979.4766907

Jian-Zheng, L. (2011). Fully automatic and quickly facial feature point detection based on LK algorithm. In *Proceedings of the International Conference on Networked Computing and Advanced Information Management*, (pp. 190-194). IEEE.

Jia, X., & Richards, J. A. (1999). Segmented principal components transformation for efficient hyperspectral remote-sensing image display and classification. *IEEE Transactions on Geoscience and Remote Sensing*, *37*(1), 538–542. doi:10.1109/36.739109

Jimenez, L. O., & Landgrebe, D. A. (1997). Supervised classification in high-dimensional space: Geometrical, statistical, and asymptotical properties of multivariate data. *IEEE Transactions on Systems, Man, and Cybernetics*, *28*(1), 39–54.

Jing, Z., & Sclaroff, S. (2003). Segmenting foreground objects from a dynamic textured background via a robust Kalman filter. In *Proceedings of the IEEE International Conference on Computer Vision*. IEEE Press.

Ji, X., & Liu, H. (2010). Advances in view-invariant human motion analysis: A review. *IEEE Transactions on Systems, Man, and Cybernetics*, *40*, 13–24. doi:10.1109/TSMCC.2009.2027608

Johns Hopkins. (2012). *Johns Hopkins APL creates system to detect digital video tampering*. Retrieved from http://www.jhu.edu/

Johnson, N. F. (1999). *An introduction to watermark recovery from images*. Fairfax, VA: George Mason University.

Juang, B. (1991). Speech recognition in adverse environments. *Computer Speech & Language*, *5*, 275–294. doi:10.1016/0885-2308(91)90011-E

Kaewpijit, S., Le Moigne, J., & El-Ghazawi, T. (2003). Automatic reduction of hyperspectral imagery using wavelet spectral analysis. *IEEE Transactions on Geoscience and Remote Sensing*, *41*(4), 863–871. doi:10.1109/TGRS.2003.810712

Kamila, K., Mahapatra, S., & Nanda, S. (2005). Invariance image analysis using modified Zernike moments. *Pattern Recognition Letters*, *26*(6), 747–753. doi:10.1016/j.patrec.2004.09.026

Kapur, J. N., Sahoo, P. K., & Wong, A. K. C. (1985). A new method for graylevel picture thresholding using the entropy of the histogram. *Computer Vision Graphics and Image Processing*, *29*, 273–285. doi:10.1016/0734-189X(85)90125-2

Karaulova, I., et al. (2000). *A hierarchical model of dynamics for tracking people with a single video camera*. Paper presented at the European Conference on Computer Vision. London, UK.

Karmann, K., & Brandt, A. V. (1990). Moving object recognition using an adaptive background memory. *Time-Varying Image Processing and Moving Object Recognition*, 2, 289–296.

Kautz, H. (1987). *A formal theory of plan recognition.* (Unpublished Ph.D. Dissertation). University of Rochester. Rochester, NY.

Kim, J.-H., Lee, J. W., Park, R.-H., & Park, M.-H. (2010). Adaptive edge-preserving smoothing and detail enhancement for video processing of H.263. In *Proceedings of the International Conference Consumer Electronics*, (pp. 337–338). IEEE.

Kim, J., & Jeong, J. (2007). Adaptive deblocking technique for mobile video. *IEEE Transactions on Consumer Electronics*, 53(4), 1694–1702. doi:10.1109/TCE.2007.4429272

Kim, S. D., Yi, J., Kim, H. M., & Ra, J. B. (1999). A deblocking filter with two separate modes in block-based video coding. *IEEE Transactions on Circuits and Systems for Video Technology*, 9(1), 156–160. doi:10.1109/76.744282

Kim, W.-Y., & Kim, Y.-S. (2000). A region-based shape descriptor using zernike moments. *Signal Processing Image Communication*, 16, 95–102. doi:10.1016/S0923-5965(00)00019-9

Ko, T., et al. (2008). *Background subtraction on distributions.* Paper presented at the European Conference on Computer Vision. London, UK.

Kovesi, P. D. (1999). Image features from phase congruency. *Videre: Journal of Computer Vision Research*, 1(3).

Kumar, P., Mittal, A., & Kumar, P. (2008). Study of robust and intelligent surveillance in visible and multi-modal framework. *Informatica*, 32, 63–77.

Kumar, S., Ghosh, J., & Crawford, M. M. (2001). Best-bases feature extraction algorithms for classification of hyperspectral data. *IEEE Transactions on Geoscience and Remote Sensing*, 39, 1368–1379. doi:10.1109/36.934070

Kumatani, K., & Stiefelhagen, R. (2006). Mouth region localization method based on gaussian mixture model. In *Proceedings of Advances in Machine Vision, Image Processing, and Pattern Analysis*. IEEE. doi:10.1007/11821045_12

Kuo, B., & Landgrebe, D. A. (2004). Nonparametric weighted feature extraction for classi_cation. *IEEE Transactions on Geoscience and Remote Sensing*, 42(5), 1096–1105. doi:10.1109/TGRS.2004.825578

Lahouti, F., Fazel, A., Safavi-Naeini, A., & Khandani, A. (2006). Single and double frame coding of speech LPC parameters using a lattice-based quantization scheme. *IEEE Transaction on Audio. Speech and Language Processing*, 14(5), 1624–1632. doi:10.1109/TSA.2005.858560

Lakshmi, H. C., & PatilKulakarni, S. (2010). Segmentation algorithm for multiple face detection in color images with skin tone regions using color spaces and edge detection techniques. *International Journal of Computer Theory and Engineering*, 2(4), 552–558.

Lalitha, Y. S., & Mrityunjaya, V. L. (2011). A novel approach noise filtration for MRI images sample in medical image processing. *International Journal of Computer Science and Communication*, 2(2), 359–363.

Lee, J. B., Woodyatt, A. S., & Berman, M. (1990). Enhancement of high spectral resolution remote-sensing data by a noise-adjusted principal components transform. *IEEE Transactions on Geoscience and Remote Sensing, 28*(3), 295–304. doi:10.1109/36.54356

Lennon, M., Mercier, G., Mouchot, M. C., & Hubert-Moy, L. (2001). Curvilinear component analysis for nonlinear dimensionality reduction of hyperspectral images. *Image and Signal Processing for Remote Sensing VII, 4541*, 157–168. doi:10.1117/12.454150

Leon, C. G. (2009). Robust computer voice recognition using improved MFCC algorithm. In *Proceedings of the International Conference on New Trends in Information and Service Science*, (pp. 835-840). IEEE.

Leong, A. T. (2003). *A music identification system based on audio content similarity.* (Thesis of Bachelor of Engineering). The University of Queensland. St. Lucia, Australia.

Liang, C.-Y., Li, A., & Niu, X.-M. (2007). Video authentication and tamper detection based on cloud model. In *Proceedings of the Third International Conference on International Information Hiding and Multimedia Signal Processing (IIH-MSP 2007)*, (pp. 225-228). IIH-MSP.

Liao, L. (2006). *Location-based activity recognition.* (Unpublished Ph.D. Dissertation). University of Washington. Seattle, WA.

Liao, S. X., & Pawlak, M. (1997). Image analysis with zernike moment descriptors. In *Proceedings of IEEE Canadian Conference on Electrical and Computer Engineering*, (vol. 2, pp. 700–703). IEEE Press.

Liao, L. (2007). Hierarchical conditional random fields for GPS-based activity recognition. *Springer Tracts in Advanced Robotics, 28*, 487–506. doi:10.1007/978-3-540-48113-3_41

Liao, S. X., & Pawlak, M. (1996). On image analysis by moments. *IEEE Transactions on Pattern Analysis and Machine Intelligence, 18*(3), 254–266. doi:10.1109/34.485554

Liew, A., Leung, S., & Lau, W. (2000). Lip contour extraction using a deformable model. *International Conference on Image Processing, 2*, 255-258.

Liew, A. W.-C., & Wang, S. (2009). *Visual speech recognition: Lip segmentation and mapping.* Hershey, PA: IGI Global. doi:10.4018/978-1-60566-186-5

Li, M., & Cheng, Y. (2009). Automatic lip localization under face illumination with shadow consideration. *Journal of Signal Processing, 89*(12), 2425–2434. doi:10.1016/j.sigpro.2009.05.027

Lim, J. S. (1990). *Two-dimensional signal and image processing.* Englewood Cliffs, NJ: Prentice Hall.

Lin, C.-Y., & Chang, S.-F. (1999). Issues and solutions for authenticating MPEG video. In *Proceedings of the SPIE Electronic Imaging 1999.* San Jose, CA: SPIE.

Lin, C. T. (1999). A space-time delay neural network for motion recognition and its application to lipreading. *International Journal of Neural Systems, 9*, 311–334. doi:10.1142/S0129065799000319

Lipton, A. J., et al. (1998). Moving target classification and tracking from real-time video. In *Proceedings of the Fourth IEEE Workshop on Applications of Computer Vision.* IEEE.

Compilation of References

List, T., Bins, J., Fisher, R. B., et al. (2005). Two approaches to a plug-and-play vision architecture - CAVIAR and psyclone. In *Proceedings of AAAI Workshop on Modular Construction of Human-Like Intelligence*. AAAI.

List, P., Joch, A., Lainema, J., Bjontegaard, G., & Karczewicz, M. (2003). Adaptive deblocking filter. *IEEE Transactions on Circuits and Systems for Video Technology, 13*(7), 614–619. doi:10.1109/TC-SVT.2003.815175

Liu, X., & Cheung, Y.-M. (2011). A robust li tracking algorithm using localized color active contours and deformable models. In *Proceedings of the IEEE International Conference on Acoustics, Speech and Signal Processing*, (pp. 1197-1200). IEEE Press.

Liu, Y., & Sato, Y. (2008). Recovering audio-to-video synchronization by audiovisual correlation analysis. In *Proceedings of the IEEE 19th International Conference on Pattern Recognition*, (pp. 1-4). IEEE Press.

Liu, H., Wang, Y., & Tan, T. (2004). Multi-modal data fusion for person authentication using improved ENN. *Chinese Journal of Automation, 30*, 78–85.

Liu, J.-Z., & Li, W.-Q. (1993). The automatic thresholding of graylevel pictures via two-dimensional Otsu method. *Acta Automatica Sinica, 19*(1), 101–105.

Liu, M., He, Y., & Ye, B. (2007). Image Zernike moments shape feature evaluation based on image reconstruction. *Geo-Spatial Information Science, 10*(3), 191–195. doi:10.1007/s11806-007-0060-x

Liu, M., Hu, H., & Zhong, M. (2008). Evolutionary computation based optimization of image Zernike moments shape feature vector. *Wuhan University Journal of Natural Sciences, 13*(2), 151–158. doi:10.1007/s11859-008-0206-1

Lu, K., Wu, Y., & Jia, Y. (2010). Visual speech recognition using convolutional VEF snake and canonical correlations. In *Proceedings of the IEEE Youth Conference on Information Computing and Telecommunications*, (pp. 154-157). IEEE Press.

Lu, C., & Ferrier, N. J. (2004). Repetitive motion analysis: Segmentation and event classification. *IEEE Transactions on Pattern Analysis and Machine Intelligence, 26*, 258–263. doi:10.1109/TPAMI.2004.1262196

Lu, C.-S., & Liao, H. Y. M. (2003). Structural digital signature for image authentication: An incidental distortion resistant scheme. *IEEE Transactions on Multimedia, 5*(2), 161–173. doi:10.1109/TMM.2003.811621

Lu, W. L. (2009). Tracking and recognizing actions of multiple hockey players using the boosted particle filter. *Image and Vision Computing, 27*(1-2), 189–205. doi:10.1016/j.imavis.2008.02.008

Madbahushi, A., & Aggwaral, J. (1999). A bayesian approach to human activity recognition. In *Proceedings of 2nd IEEE Intenational Workshop on Visual Surveillance*. IEEE.

Mahmoud, T. M. (2008). A new fast skin color detection technique. In *Proceedings of 43rd World Academy of Science, Engineering and Technology*, (pp. 501-505). IEEE.

Majumder, A., Behera, L., & Subramaniam, V. K. (2011). Automatic and robust detection of facial features in frontal face images. In *Proceedings of the UKSim 13th International Conference on Modelling and Simulation*, (pp. 331-336). UKSim.

Ma, L., Crawford, M. M., & Tian, J. (2010). Local manifold learning-based k-nearest neighbor for hyperspectral image classification. *IEEE Transactions on Geoscience and Remote Sensing, 48*(11), 4099–4109.

Malisia, A. R., & Tizhoosh, H. R. (2006). Image thresholding using ant colony optimization. In *Proceedings of the 3rd Canadian Conference on Computer and Robot Vision*, (pp. 26-29). IEEE.

Mallat, S. G., & Zhang, Z. (19993). Matching pursuits with time-frequency dictionaries. *IEEE Transactions on Signal Processing, 41*(12), 3397–3415. doi:10.1109/78.258082

Manfredotti, C. (2009). Modeling and Inference with relational dynamic Bayesian networks. *Lecture Notes in Computer Science, 5549*, 287–290. doi:10.1007/978-3-642-01818-3_44

Martinian, E., Wornell, G. W., & Chen, B. (2005). Authentication with distortion criteria. *IEEE Transactions on Information Theory, 51*(7). doi:10.1109/TIT.2005.850123

Marzinzik, M., & Kollmeier, B. (2002). Speech pause detection for noise spectrum estimation by tracking power envelope dynamics. *IEEE Transactions on Speech and Audio Processing, 10*(6), 341–351.

Matthews, I., Cootes, T., Bangham, J., Cox, S., & Harvey, R. (2002). Extraction of visual features for lipreading. *IEEE Transactions on Pattern Analysis and Machine Intelligence, 24*, 198–213. doi:10.1109/34.982900

Ma, Z. M., Zhang, G., & Yan, L. (2011). Shape feature descriptor using modified Zernike moments. *Pattern Analysis & Applications, 14*(1), 9–22. doi:10.1007/s10044-009-0171-0

McFedries, P. (2012). *iPhone 4S portable genius.* Indianapolis, IN: John Wiley & Sons, Inc.

McKenna, S. (2000). Tracking groups of people. *Computer Vision and Image Understanding, 80*, 42–56. doi:10.1006/cviu.2000.0870

Melgani, F., & Bruzzone, L. (2004). Classification of hyperspectral remote sensing images with support vector machine. *IEEE Transactions on Geoscience and Remote Sensing, 42*(10), 1778–1790. doi:10.1109/TGRS.2004.831865

Meyer, D., et al. (1997). Model based extraction of articulated objects in image sequences for gait analysis. In *Proceedings of International Conference on Image Processing.* IEEE.

Meyer, D., et al. (1998). *Gait classification with HMMs for trajectories of body parts extracted by mixture densities.* Paper presented at the The British Machine Vision Conference. London, UK.

Milonas, M. M. (1994). Swarms, phase transitions, and collective intelligence. In Langton, C. G. (Ed.), *Artificial Life III.* Reading, MA: Addison Wesley.

Mittal, A., & Paragios, N. (2004). Motion-based background subtraction using adaptive kernel density estimation. In *Proceedings of the 2004 IEEE Computer Society Conference on Computer Vision and Pattern Recognition.* IEEE Press.

Compilation of References

Mobasseri, B. G., & Evans, A. E. (2001). Content dependent video authentication by self water marking in color space. In *Proceedings of Security and Watermarking of Multimedia Contents 3 (Vol. 4314*, pp. 35–46). IEEE. doi:10.1117/12.435437

Mohan, A., Sapiro, G., & Bosch, E. (2007). Spatially coherent nonlinear dimensionality reduction and segmentation of hyperspectral images. *IEEE Geoscience and Remote Sensing Letters*, *4*(2), 206–210. doi:10.1109/LGRS.2006.888105

Monnet, A., et al. (2003). Background modeling and subtraction of dynamic scenes. In *Proceedings of the IEEE International Conference on Computer Vision*. IEEE Press.

Mukundan, R., & Pang, A. (2002). Stereo image analysis: A new approach using orthogonal moment functions. In *Proceedings of Asian Technology Conference in Mathematics*, (pp. 513-522). IEEE.

Murase, H., & Nayar, N. (1995). Visual learning and recognition of 3-D objects from appearance. *International Journal of Computer Vision*, *14*, 5–24. doi:10.1007/BF01421486

Needell, D., & Tropp, J. A. (2009). CoSaMP: Iterative signal recovery from incomplete and inaccurate samples. *Applied and Computational Harmonic Analysis*, *26*(3), 301–321. doi:10.1016/j.acha.2008.07.002

Nemer, E., Goubran, R., & Mahmoud, S. (2001). Robust voice activity detection using higher order statistics in the PLC residual domain. *IEEE Transactions on Speech and Audio Processing*, *9*(3), 217–231. doi:10.1109/89.905996

Nica, A., Caruntu, A., Toderean, G., & Buza, O. (2006). Analysis and synthesis of vowels using matlab. *IEEE Conference on Automation, Quality and Testing. Robotics*, *2*, 371–374.

Niyogi, S., & Adelson, E. (1994). *Analyzing and recognizing walking figures in XYT.* Paper presented at the IEEE Computer Society Conference on Computer Vision and Pattern Recognition. New York, NY.

Nummiaro, K. (2003). An adaptive color-based particle filter. *Image and Vision Computing*, *21*, 99–110. doi:10.1016/S0262-8856(02)00129-4

Nwagboso, C. (1998). *User focused surveillance systems integration for intelligent transport systems.* Boston, MA: Kluwer Academic Publishers.

Oguz, S. H., Hu, Y. H., & Nguyen, T. Q. (1998). Image coding ringing artifact reduction using morphological post-filtering. In *Proceedings IEEE Second Workshop Multimedia Signal Processing*, (pp. 628–633). IEEE Press.

Oliver, N. M. (2000). A bayesian computer vision system for modeling human interactions. *IEEE Transactions on Pattern Analysis and Machine Intelligence*, *22*, 831–843. doi:10.1109/34.868684

Ong, E. P., Yang, X., Lin, W., Lu, Z., Yao, S., & Lin, X. (2006). Perceptual quality and objective quality measurements of compressed videos. *Journal of Visual Communication and Image Representation*, *17*(4), 717–737. doi:10.1016/j.jvcir.2005.11.002

Oren, M., et al. (1997). *Pedestrian detection using wavelet templates.* Paper presented at the IEEE Computer Society Conference on Computer Vision and Pattern Recognition. New York, NY.

Otsu, N. (1979). A threshold selection method from gray level histograms. *IEEE Transactions on Systems, Man, and Cybernetics*, *9*(1), 62–66. doi:10.1109/TSMC.1979.4310076

Pal, N. R., & Pal, S. K. (1989). Object-background segmentation using new definitions of entropy. *IEEE Proceedings*, *136*(4), 284-295.

Palak, A., & Subbalakshmi, P. (2004). Rotation and cropping resilient data hiding with Zernike moments. In *Proceeding of International Conference on Image Processing*, (vol. 4, pp. 2175-2178). IEEE.

Pal, M., & Foody, G. M. (2010). Feature selection for classi_cation of hyperspectral data by SVM. *IEEE Transactions on Geoscience and Remote Sensing*, *48*(5), 2297–2307. doi:10.1109/TGRS.2009.2039484

Pal, N. R., & Pal, S. K. (1991). Entropy: A new definition and its applications. *IEEE Transactions on Systems, Man, and Cybernetics*, *21*(5), 1260–1270. doi:10.1109/21.120079

Pal, N. R., & Pal, S. K. (1993). A review on image segmentation techniques. *Pattern Recognition*, *26*(2), 1277–1294. doi:10.1016/0031-3203(93)90135-J

Pang, H., Andrew, B., & David, L. (2004). Palmprint verification with moments. *Journal of WSCG*, *12*(3), 325–332.

Paragios, N., & Deriche, R. (2000). Geodesic active contours and level sets for the detection and tracking of moving objects. *IEEE Transactions on Pattern Analysis and Machine Intelligence*, *22*, 266–280. doi:10.1109/34.841758

Park, J. M., Chong, E. K. P., & Siegel, H. J. (2002). Efficient multicast packet authentication using signature amortization. In *Proceedings of the IEEE Symposium on Security and Privacy*, (pp. 227-240). IEEE Press.

Pawar, R., Kajave, P. P., & Mali, S. N. (2005). Speaker identification using neural networks. *Proceeding of World Academy of Science, Engineering and Technology, 7*.

Pearson, K. (1901). On lines and planes of closest fit to systems of points in space. *Philosophical Magazine*, *2*, 559–572. doi:10.1080/14786440109462720

Pei, J., Lu, Z., & Xie, W. (2006). A method for IR point target detection based on spatial-temporal bilateral filter. In *Proceedings International Conference Pattern Recognition*, (pp. 846–849). IEEE.

Peng, H. (2002). A semi fragile water marking system for MPEG video authentication. In *Proceedings of ICASSP 2002*. Orlando, FL: ICASSP.

Pérez, P., et al. (2002). *Color-based probabilistic tracking*. Paper presented at the European Conference on Computer Vision. London, UK.

Peterfreund, N. (1999). Robust tracking of position and velocity with Kalman snakes. *IEEE Transactions on Pattern Analysis and Machine Intelligence*, *21*, 564–569. doi:10.1109/34.771328

Pham, T. Q., & Vliet, L. J. (2005). Separable bilateral filtering for fast video preprocessing. In *Proceedings of the IEEE International Conference Multimedia and Expo ICME 2005*, (pp. 454–457). IEEE Press.

Podilchuk, C. I., Jayant, N. S., & Farrardin, N. (1995). Three dimensional sub band coding of video. *IEEE Transactions on Image Processing*, *4*(2), 125–139. doi:10.1109/83.342187

Polana, R., & Nelson, R. (1994). Low level recognition of human motion. In *Proceedings of IEEE Workshop on Nonrigid and Articulate Motion*. IEEE Press.

Potamianos, G., Gravier, G., Garg, A., & Senior, A. W. (2003). Recent advances in the automatic recognition of audio-visual speech. *Proceedings of the IEEE, 91*(9), 1–18.

Potnis, A., Somkuwar, A., & Sapre, S. D. (2010). A review on natural image denoising using independent component analysis (ica) technique. *Advances in Computational Research, 2*(1), 6–14.

Press, O. U. (2001). *Oxford dictionary of English*. Shah Alam, Malaysia: Oxford Fajar Sdn Bhd.

Queluz, M. P. (1998). Toward robust, content based techniques for image authentication. In *Proceedings of the IEEE Second Workshop on Multimedia Signal Processing*, (pp. 297-302). IEEE Press.

Queluz, M. P. (2001). Authentication of digital images and video: Generic models and a new contribution, signal processing. *Image Communication, 16*, 461–475.

Quisquater, J. (1997). Authentication of sequences with the SL2 hash function application to video sequences. *Journal of Computer Security, 5*(3), 213–223.

Rahman, N. A., Wei, K. C., & See, J. (2006). RGB-H-CbCr skin colour model for human face detection. In *Proceedings of The MMU International Symposium on Information & Communications Technologies*. MMU.

Ramírez, J. M. (2007). Voice activity detection: Fundamentals and speech recognition systems robustness. In Grimm, M., & Kroschel, K. (Eds.), *Robust Speech Recognition and Understanding* (pp. 1–22). I-Tech Education and Publishing. doi:10.5772/4740

Rathi, Y. (2007). Tracking deforming objects using particle filtering for geometric active contours. *IEEE Transactions on Pattern Analysis and Machine Intelligence, 29*, 1470–1475. doi:10.1109/TPAMI.2007.1081

Ribeiro, P., & Santos-Victor, J. (2005). Human activities recognition from video: Modeling, feature selection and classification architecture. In *Proceedings of Workshop on Human Activity Recognition and Modeling*. IEEE.

Rijkse, K. (1996). H.263 video coding for low-bit-rate communication. *IEEE Communications Magazine, 34*(12), 42–45. doi:10.1109/35.556485

Ritter, G. X., & Urcid, G. (2011). A latex matrix method for hyperspectral image unmixing. *Information Science, 181*, 1787–1803. doi:10.1016/j.ins.2010.03.022

Robertson, N., & Reid, I. (2006). A general method for human activity recognition in video. *Computer Vision and Image Understanding, 104*(2-3), 232–248. doi:10.1016/j.cviu.2006.07.006

Rohr, K. (1994). Towards model-based recognition of human movements in image sequences. *CVGIP: Image Understanding, 59*(1), 94–115. doi:10.1006/ciun.1994.1006

Romberg, J. K., Hyeokho, C., & Baraniuk, R. G. (2001). Bayesian tree-structured image modeling using wavelet-domain hidden Markov models. *IEEE Transactions on Image Processing, 10*(7), 1056–1068. doi:10.1109/83.931100

Rosenblum, M., et al. (1994). Human emotion recognition from motion using a radial basis function network architecture. In *Proceedings Motion of Non-Rigid and Articulated Obgects Workshop*. IEEE.

Ross, L. A., Saint-Amour, D., Leavitt, V. M., Javitt, D. C., & Foxe, J. J. (2006). Do you see what i am saying? Exploring visual enhancement of speech comprehension in noisy environment. *Oxford Journals Life Sciences & Medicine Cerebral Cortex, 17*(5), 1147–1153. doi:10.1093/cercor/bhl024

Rota, N., & Thonnat, M. (2000). *Activity recognition from video sequences using declarative models*. Paper presented at the European Conference on Artificial Intelligence. London, UK.

Sahoo, P. K., Soltani, S., & Wong, A. K. C. (1988). A survey of threshold techniques. *Computer Vision Graphics and Image Processing, 41*(2), 233–260. doi:10.1016/0734-189X(88)90022-9

Saikia, N., & Bora, P. K. (2007). Video authentication using temporal wavelet transform. In *Proceedings of the 15th International Conference on Advanced Computing and Communications*, (pp. 648-653). ADCOM.

Seeley, T. D. (1995). *The wisdom of the hive*. Cambridge, MA: Harvard University Press.

Seo, J. S., & Yoo, C. D. (2006). Image watermarking based on invariant regions of scale-space representation. *IEEE Transactions on Signal Processing, 54*(4), 1537–1549. doi:10.1109/TSP.2006.870581

Sezgin, M., & Sankur, B. (2004). Survey over image thresholding techniques and quantitative performance evaluation. *Journal of Electronic Imaging, 13*(1), 146–165. doi:10.1117/1.1631315

Sheikh, Y., & Shah, M. (2005). Bayesian modeling of dynamic scenes for object detection. *IEEE Transactions on Pattern Analysis and Machine Intelligence, 27*, 1778–1792. doi:10.1109/TPAMI.2005.213

Shelokar, P. S., Jayaraman, V. K., & Kulkarni, B. D. (2004). An ant colony approach for clustering. *Analytica Chimica Acta, 59*, 187–195. doi:10.1016/j.aca.2003.12.032

Shivappa, S. T., Trivedi, M. M., & Rao, B. D. (2010). Audiovisual information fusion in human-computer interfaces and intelligent environments: A survey. *Proceedings of the IEEE, 98*(10), 1–24. doi:10.1109/JPROC.2010.2057231

Sigal, L., et al. (2004). Tracking loose-limbed people. In *Proceedings of the 2004 IEEE Computer Society Conference on Computer Vision and Pattern Recognition*. IEEE Press.

Sigg, C., Dikk, T., & Buhmann, J. (2012). Speech enhancement using generative dictionary learning. *IEEE Transactions on Audio. Speech and Language Processing, 20*(6), 1698–1712. doi:10.1109/TASL.2012.2187194

Signh, C., Walia, E., & Mittal, N. (2012). Rotation invariant complex Zernike moments features and their applications to human face and character recognition. *Computer Vision, 5*(5), 255–265.

Singh, R., Vatsa, M., & Noore, A. (2006). Intelligent biometric information fusion using support vector machine. In *Soft Computing in Image Processing: Recent Advances* (pp. 327–350). Berlin, Germany: Springer Verlag.

Singh, R., Vatsa, M., Singh, S. K., & Upadhyay, S. (2008). Integrating SVM classification with SVD watermarking for intelligent video authentication. *Telecommunication Systems Journal, 40*(1-2), 5–15. doi:10.1007/s11235-008-9141-x

Compilation of References

Spearman, C. (1904). General intelligence objectively determined and measured. *The American Journal of Psychology, 15,* 206–221. doi:10.2307/1412107

Spears, W. M., Jong, K. A., Baeck, T., et al. (1993). An overview of evolutionary computation. In *Proceeding of European Conference on Machine Learning,* (vol. 667, pp. 442-459). IEEE.

Starner, T., & Pentland, A. (1995). *Real-time american sign language recognition from video using hidden markov models.* Paper presented at the IEEE International Conference on Computer Vision. New York, NY.

Stauffer, C., & Grimson, W. (2000). Learning patterns of activity using real-time tracking. *IEEE Transactions on Pattern Analysis and Machine Intelligence, 22,* 747–757. doi:10.1109/34.868677

Storn, R., & Price, K. (1995). *Differential evolution - A simple and efficient adaptive scheme for global optimization over continuous spaces.* ICSI Technical Report TR-95-012. Retrieved August 16, 2011, from http://www.icsi.berkeley.edu/~storn/TR-95-012.pdf

Su, J. K., & Mersereau, R. M. (2000). Motion estimation methods for overlapped block motion compensation. *IEEE Transactions on Image Processing, 9*(9), 1509–1521. doi:10.1109/83.862628

Sujatha, P., & Krishnan, M. R. (2012). Lip feature extraction for visual speech recognition using hidden Markov model. In *Proceedings of the International Conference on Computing, Communication and Applications,* (pp. 1-5). IEEE.

Sullivan, G. (2001). Recommended simulation common conditions for H.26L coding efficiency experiments on low resolution progressive scan source material. *Document VCEG-N81, 14th Meeting.*

Sumby, W. H., & Pollack, I. (1954). Visual contribution to speech intellligibility in noise. *The Journal of the Acoustical Society of America, 26,* 212–215. doi:10.1121/1.1907309

Sun, Q., Chang, S.-F., & Maeno, K. (2002). A new semi fragile image authentication framework combining ECC and PKI infrastructure. In *Proceedings of the ISCAS 2002.* Phoenix, AZ: ISCAS.

Sun, Q., He, D., Zhang, Z., & Tian, Q. (2003). A secure and robust approach to scalable video authentication. In *Proceedings of ICME 2003.* ICME.

Su, P.-C., Chen, C.-C., & Chang, H. M. (2009). Towards effective content authentication for digital videos by employing feature extraction and quantization. *IEEE Transactions on Circuits and Systems for Video Technology, 19*(5), 668–677. doi:10.1109/TCSVT.2009.2017404

Takahashi, K., et al. (1994). Recognition of dexterous manipulations from time-varying images. In *Proceedings of the 1994 IEEE Workshop on Motion of Non-Rigid and Articulated Obgects Workshop.* Austin, TX: IEEE Press.

Talea, H., & Yaghmaie, K. (2011). Automatic combined lip segmentation in color images. In *Proceedings of the IEEE 3rd International Conference on Communication Software and Networks,* (pp. 109-112). IEEE Press.

Talea, H., & Yaghmaie, K. (2011). Automatic visual speech segmentation. In *Proceedings of the IEEE 3rd International Conference on Communication Software and Networks*, (pp. 184-188). IEEE Press.

Tang, H., Fu, Y., Tu, J., Hasegawa-Johnson, M., & Huang, T. (2008). Humanoid audio–visual avatar with emotive text-to-speech synthesis. *IEEE Transactions on Multimedia*, *10*(6), 969–981. doi:10.1109/TMM.2008.2001355

Tan, T. N., Sullivan, G. D., & Baker, K. D. (1998). Model-based localization and recognition of road vehicles. *International Journal of Computer Vision*, *27*, 5–25. doi:10.1023/A:1007924428535

Tanyer, S., & Özer, H. (2000). Voice activity detection in nonstationary noise. *IEEE Transactions on Speech and Audio Processing*, *8*(4), 478–482. doi:10.1109/89.848229

Tan, Z.-H., & Lindberg, B. (2010). Low-complexity variable frame rate analysis for speech recognition and voice activity detection. *IEEE Journal of Selected Topics in Signal Processing*, *4*(5), 798–807. doi:10.1109/JSTSP.2010.2057192

Tao, W., Jin, H., & Liu, L. (2007). Object segmentation using ant colony optimization algorithm and fuzzy entropy. *Pattern Recognition Letters*, *28*, 788–796. doi:10.1016/j.patrec.2006.11.007

Tashev, I. (2009). *Sound capture and processing practical approaches*. Chippenham, UK: John Wiley and Sons Ltd. doi:10.1002/9780470994443

Teh, C., & Chin, T. (1988). On image analysis by the method of moments. *IEEE Transactions on Pattern Analysis and Machine Intelligence*, *10*(4), 496–513. doi:10.1109/34.3913

Teodorovic, D., & Lucic, P. (2006). Goran bee colony optimization: Principles and applications. In *Proceedings of the 8th Seminar on Neural Network Applications in Electrical Engineering, NEUREL*, (pp. 51-156). NEUREL.

Tereshko, V., & Loengarov, A. (2005). Collective decision-making in honey bee foraging dynamics. *Computing and Information Systems Journal*, 1352-4049.

Tereshko, V., & Lee, T. (2002). How information mapping patterns determine foraging behaviour of a honey bee colony. *Open Systems & Information Dynamics*, *9*, 181–193. doi:10.1023/A:1015652810815

Tian, Y. L., & Brown, L. (2008). IBM smart surveillance system (S3): Event based video surveillance system with an open and extensible framework. *Machine Vision and Applications*, *19*, 315–327. doi:10.1007/s00138-008-0153-z

Tomasi, C., & Manduchi, R. (1998). Bilateral filtering for gray and color images. In *Proceedings of the IEEE International Conference Computer Vision*, (pp. 839–846). IEEE Press.

Toole, A. J., Harms, J., & Snow, S. L. (2005). A video database of moving faces and people. *IEEE Transactions on Pattern Analysis and Machine Intelligence*, *27*, 812–816. doi:10.1109/TPAMI.2005.90

Torgerson, W. S. (1952). Multidimensional scaling I: Theory and method. *Psychometrika*, *17*, 401–419. doi:10.1007/BF02288916

Toyama, K., et al. (1999). Wallflower: Principles and practice of background maintenance. In *Proceedings of the Seventh IEEE International Conference on Computer Vision*. IEEE Press.

Compilation of References

Tran, S. D., & Davis, L. S. (2008). *Event modeling and recognition using Markov logic networks*. Paper presented at the European Conference on Conputer Vision. London, UK.

Tropp, J. A., & Gilbert, A. C. (2007). Signal recovery from random measurements via orthogonal matching pursuit. *IEEE Transactions on Information Theory*, *53*(12), 4655–4666. doi:10.1109/TIT.2007.909108

Tropp, J. A., & Wright, S. J. (2010). Computational methods for sparse solution of linear inverse problems. *Proceedings of the IEEE*, *98*(6), 948–958. doi:10.1109/JPROC.2010.2044010

Truyen, T. T. (2008). *Learning discriminative sequence models from partially labelled data for activity recognition* (pp. 903–912). Lecture Notes in Computer ScienceBerlin, Germany: Springer. doi:10.1007/978-3-540-89197-0_84

Tsuhan Chen, R. R. (1998). Audio-visual integration in multimodal communication. *IEEE Proceedings*, *86*(5), 837-852.

Tucker, R. (1992). Voice activity detection using a periodicity measure. *Proceedings of the Institution of Electrical Engineers*, *139*(4), 377–380.

Tweed, D., Fang, W., Fisher, R., et al. (2005). Exploring techniques for behavior recognition via the CAVIAR modular vision framework. In *Proceedings of Workshop on Human Activity Recognition and Modeling*. IEEE.

Unnikrishnan, R., Pantofaru, C. E., & Hebert, M. (2007). Toward objective evaluation of image segmentation algorithms. *IEEE Transactions on Pattern Analysis and Machine Intelligence*, *29*(6), 929–943. doi:10.1109/TPAMI.2007.1046

Upadhyay, S., Singh, M., Vatsa, M., & Singh, R. (2007). Video authentication using relative correlation information and SVM. In Hassanien, A. E., Kacprzyk, J., & Abraham, A. (Eds.), *Computational Intelligence in Multimedia Processing: Recent Advances*. Berlin, Germany: Springer Verlag.

Vacca, J. (2007). *Biometric technologies and verification systems*. Burlington, VT: Elsevier.

Vail, D. L., et al. (2007). Conditional random fields for activity recognition. In *Proceedings of the International Conference on Autonomous Agents*. IEEE.

Vail, D. L., et al. (2007). *Feature selection in conditional random fields for activity recognition*. Paper presented at the IEEE International Conference on Intelligent Robots and Systems. New York, NY.

Vapnik, V. N. (1995). *The nature of statistical learning theory*. Berlin, Germany: Springer Verlag.

Varadarajan, B., Khudanpur, S., & Tran, T. D. (2011). Stepwise optimal subspace pursuit for improving sparse recovery. *IEEE Signal Processing Letters*, *18*(1), 27–30. doi:10.1109/LSP.2010.2090143

Varga, P., & Moore, R. (1990). Hidden Markov model decomposition of speech and noise. In *Proceedings in International Conference in Acoustic, Speech and Signal Processing*, (pp. 845-848). IEEE.

Viterbi, A. (2006). A personal history of the viterbi algorithm. *IEEE Signal Processing Magazine*, *23*(4), 120–142. doi:10.1109/MSP.2006.1657823

Wang, W., & Farid, H. (2007). Exposing digital forgeries in video by detecting duplication. In *Proceedings of the 9th Workshop on Multimedia & Security*. Dallas, TX: IEEE.

Wang, Z., Bovik, A. C., Sheikh, H. R., & Simoncelli, E. P. (2004). Image quality assessment: From error visibility to structural similarity. *IEEE Transactions on Image Processing, 13*(4), 600-612. Retrieved November 20, 2011, from http://www.ece.uwaterloo.ca/~z70wang/research/ssim/

Wang, J., & Chang, C. (2006). Independent component analysis-based dimensionality reduction with applications in hyperspectral image analysis. *IEEE Transactions on Geoscience and Remote Sensing, 44*(6), 1586–1600. doi:10.1109/TGRS.2005.863297

Wang, L., Hu, W., & Tan, T. (2003). Recent developments in human motion analysis. *Pattern Recognition, 36*, 585–601. doi:10.1016/S0031-3203(02)00100-0

Wang, L., Tan, T., & Ning, H. (2004). Fusion of static and dynamic body biometrics for gait recognition. *IEEE Transactions on Circuits and Systems for Video Technology, 14*, 149–158. doi:10.1109/TCSVT.2003.821972

Wang, S., Lau, W., & Leung, S. (2004). Automatic lip contour extraction from color. *Pattern Recognition, 37*(12), 2375–2387.

Wang, Y., & Mori, G. (2009). Human action recognition by semi-latent topic models. *IEEE Transactions on Pattern Analysis and Machine Intelligence, 31*, 1762–1774. doi:10.1109/TPAMI.2009.43

Wan, S., Mrak, M., Ramzan, N., & Izquierdo, E. (2007). Perceptually adaptive joint deringing-deblocking filtering for scalable video transmission over wireless networks. *Signal Processing Image Communication, 22*(3), 266–276. doi:10.1016/j.image.2006.12.005

Webe, M., Milch, M., & Myszkowski, K. (2004). Spatio-temporal photon estimation using bilateral filtering. In *Proceedings Computer Graphics International 2004* (pp. 120–127). IEEE. doi:10.1109/CGI.2004.1309200

Wedde, H. F., Farooq, M., & Zhang, Y. (2004). BeeHive: An efficient fault-tolerant routing algorithm inspired by honey bee behavior, ant colony, optimization and swarm intelligence. In *Proceedings of the 4th International Workshop*. Brussels, Belgium: ANTS.

WenJuan. Y., YaLing, L., & MingHui, D. (2010). A real-time lip localization and tracking for lip reading. In *Proceedings of the 3rd International Conference on Advanced Computer Theory and Engineering*, (pp. 363-366). IEEE.

Westwood, P. (2007). *Commonsense methods for children with special educational needs* (5th ed.). New York, NY: Routledge.

Wiegand, T., Sullivan, G. J., Bjøntegaard, G., & Luthra, A. (2003). *Draft ITU-T recommendation and final draft international standard of joint video specification*. ITU-T Rec. H.264/ISO/IEC 14496-10 AVC. Retrieved from http://www.itu.int

Wiegand, T., Sullivan, G. J., Bjntegaard, G., & Luthra, A. (2003). Overview of the H.264/AVC video coding standard. *IEEE Transactions on Circuits and Systems for Video Technology, 13*(7), 560–576. doi:10.1109/TCSVT.2003.815165

Wilson, A. D., & Bobick, A. F. (1998). *Recognition and interpretation of parametric gesture*. Paper presented at the IEEE International Conference on Computer Vision. New York, NY.

Winfrey, O. (2009, August 14). *Measuring facial perfection - The golden ratio.* Retrieved April 10, 2012, from http://www.oprah.com/oprahshow/Measuring-Facial-Perfection-The-Golden-Ratio

Wohlmacher, P. (1998). Requirements and mechanism of IT-security including aspects of multimedia security. In *Proceedings of the Multimedia and Security Workshop at ACM Multimedia 1998.* Bristol, UK: ACM Press.

Woo, K., Yang, T., Park, K., & Lee, C. (2000). Robust voice activity detection algorithm for estimating noise spectrum. *Electronics Letters*, *36*(2), 180–181. doi:10.1049/el:20000192

Wren, C. R., Azarbayejani, A., Darrell, T., & Pentland, A. P. (1997). Pfinder: Real-time tracking of the human body. *IEEE Transactions on Pattern Analysis and Machine Intelligence*, *19*, 780–785. doi:10.1109/34.598236

Wu, D., Pan, F., Lim, K. P., Wu, S., Li, Z. G., & Lin, X. (2005). Fast intermode decision in H.264/AVC video coding. *IEEE Transactions on Circuits System Video Technology*, *15*(6), 953–958. doi:10.1109/TCSVT.2005.848304

Wu, H., & Wang, S. (2012). Adaptive sparsity matching pursuit algorithm for sparse reconstruction. *IEEE Signal Processing Letters*, *19*(8), 471–474. doi:10.1109/LSP.2012.2188793

Yaling, L., Wenjuan, Y., & Minghui, D. (2010). Feature extraction based on LSDA for lipreading. In *Proceedings of the International Conference on Multimedia Technology*, (pp. 1-4). IEEE.

Yamato, J., et al. (1992). *Recognizing human action in time-sequential images using hidden markov model.* Paper presented at the IEEE Computer Society Conference on Computer Vision and Pattern Recognition. New York, NY.

Yang, X. S. (2005). Engineering optimizations via nature-inspired virtual bee algorithms. *Lecture Notes in Computer Science*, *3562*, 317. doi:10.1007/11499305_33

Yan, W.-Y., & Kankanhalli, M. S. (2003). Motion trajectory based video authentication. In *Proceedings of ISCAS*, (vol. 3, pp. 810-813). ISCAS. Peng, Y., & Hong, H. Y. (2001). Classification of video tampering methods and countermeasures using digital watermarking. []. SPIE.]. *Proceedings of the Society for Photo-Instrumentation Engineers*, *4518*, 239–246.

Ye, B., & Peng, J. (2002). Improvement and invariance analysis of Zernike moments using as a region-based shape descriptor. *Journal of Pattern Recognition and Image Analysis*, *12*(4), 419–428.

Ye, B., & Peng, J. (2002). Invariance analysis of improved Zernike moments. *Journal of Optics. A, Pure and Applied Optics*, *4*(6), 606–614. doi:10.1088/1464-4258/4/6/304

Yilmaz, A. (2006). Object tracking: A survey. *ACM Computing Surveys*, *38*(4). doi:10.1145/1177352.1177355

Yin, J., et al. (2009). *Spatio-temporal event detection using dynamic conditional random fields.* Paper presented at the the International Joint Conferences on Artificial Intelligence. New York, NY.

Yingjie, M., Haiyan, Z., Yingjie, H., & Jinyang, L. (2011). Lip information extraction based on the fusion of geometry and motion features. In *Proceedings of the 8th International Conference on Fuzzy Systems and Knowledge Discovery*, (pp. 2186-2190). Shanghai, China: IEEE.

Yu, Z., & Zhang, J. (2004). Video deblocking with fine-grained scalable complexity for embedded mobile computing. In *Proceedings of the 7th International Conference on Signal Processing*, (pp. 1173–1178). IEEE.

Yu, B., Ostland, M., Gong, P., & Pu, R. (1999). Penalized discriminant analysis of in situ hyperspectral data for conifer species recognition. *IEEE Transactions on Geoscience and Remote Sensing, 37*(5), 2569–2577. doi:10.1109/36.789651

Yuhas, B. P., Jr. M. H., & Sejnowski, T. J. (1990). Neural network models of sensory integration for improved vowel recognition. *IEEE Proceedings, 78*(10), 1658-1668.

Yu, W., Zou, R., & Yu, Z. (2010). Image segmentation based on local ant colony optimization. *Computer Applications, 30*(5), 1344-2346.

Z., Z., P., M., & S., H. T. (2009). *Emotion recognition based on multimodal information, affective information processing.* London, UK: Springer Verlag.

Zhang, S. (2011). Image denoising using FIR filters designed with evolution strategies. In *Proceedings of the 2011 3rd International Workshop on Intelligent Systems and Applications (ISA)*, (pp. 1-4). IEEE. Hao, Z. F., Guo, G. H., & Huang, H. (2007). A particle swarm optimization algorithm with differential evolution over continuous spaces. In *Proceedings of the International Conference on Machine Learning and Cybernetics*, (vol. 2, pp. 1031-1035). IEEE.

Zhang, T. (2011). Sparse recovery with orthogonal matching pursuit under RIP. *IEEE Transactions on Information Theory, 57*(9), 6215–6221. doi:10.1109/TIT.2011.2162263

Zhao, L., Qi, W., Li, S., Yang, S., & Zhang, H. (2000). Key frame extraction and shot retrieval using nearest feature line (NFL). In *Proceedings of ACM Multimedia 2000*. ACM Press.

Zhao, T., & Nevatia, R. (2003). Bayesian human segmentation in crowded situations. In *Proceedings of the IEEE Computer Society Conference on Computer Vision and Pattern Recognition*. IEEE Press.

Zhao, M., Fu, A. M. N., & Yan, H. A. (2001). Technique of three-level thresholding based on probability partition and fuzzy 3-partition. *IEEE Transactions on Fuzzy Systems, 9*(3), 469–479. doi:10.1109/91.928743

Zhao, T. (2008). Segmentation and tracking of multiple humans in crowded environments. *IEEE Transactions on Pattern Analysis and Machine Intelligence, 30*, 1198–1211. doi:10.1109/TPAMI.2007.70770

Zhao, T., & Nevatia, R. (2004). Tracking multiple humans in complex situations. *IEEE Transactions on Pattern Analysis and Machine Intelligence, 26*(9), 1208–1221. doi:10.1109/TPAMI.2004.73

Zhao, W., Chellappa, R., Philips, P., & Rosenfeld, A. (2003). Face recognition: A literature survey. *ACM Computing Surveys, 35*(4), 399–458. doi:10.1145/954339.954342

Zitova, B., & Flusser, J. (2003). Image registration methods: A survey. *Image and Vision Computing, 21*(11), 977–1000. doi:10.1016/S0262-8856(03)00137-9

Zoric, G. (2005). *Automated lip synchronization by speech signal analysis.* (Master Thesis). University of Zagreb. Zagreb, Croatia.

About the Contributors

Jing Tian received his B.Eng. degree (Electronic and Information Engineering), from School of Electronic and Information Engineering, South China University of Technology, Guangzhou, China, M.Eng. degree (Electronic and Information Engineering), School of Electronic and Information Engineering, South China University of Technology, Guangzhou, China, Ph.D. degree (Electrical and Electronic Engineering), School of Electrical and Electronic Engineering, Nanyang Technological University, Singapore. His research interests include image processing and computer vision.

Li Chen received the PhD degree in Computer Science and Engineering from Nanyang Technological University, Singapore, in 2006. Currently, he is an Associate Professor in the School of Computer Science and Technology, Wuhan University of Science and Technology, Wuhan, China. His research interests include computer vision, visual surveillance, and image processing.

* * *

Dongfang Chen received the PhD degree in Computer Science and Engineering from Anhui University, China, in 2003. Currently, he is a Professor in the School of Computer Science and Technology, Wuhan University of Science and Technology, Wuhan, China. His research interests include information management, visual surveillance, and image processing.

Sheng Ding received the B.S. and M.S. degrees in Computer Sciences from China Center Normal University, Wuhan University of Science and Technology, Wuhan, China, in 1998 and 2005, respectively, and the Ph.D. degree in Sciences and Techniques of Remote Sensing from the School of Remote Sensing and Information Engineering, Wuhan University, in 2010. He is currently Associate Professor in College of Computer Science and Technology, Wuhan University of Science and Technology. His research interests include hyperspectral data analysis, high-resolution image processing, pattern recognition, and remote-sensing applications.

Ming-Hui Du was born in 1964. He received the B.S. degree in 1985 from Fudan University, Shanghai, the M.S. degree and Ph.D. degree in 1991, from South China University of Technology, Guangzhou, China. He is currently a Professor in the School of Electronic and Information Engineering, South China University of Technology, Guangzhou, China. His research interests include biomedical signal processing and image reconstruction.

Xiaowei Fu received her Ph.D degree in Control Science and Engineering from Huazhong University of Science and Technology, Wuhan, China, in 2010. Currently, she is an Associate Professor in Department of Computer Science and Technology, Wuhan University of Science and Technology, China. Her research interests include computer vision, image processing, and quantum signal processing.

Huijun Hu is a Ph.D. candidate in the State Key Lab of Software Engineering of Wuhan University and also a Lecturer in College of Computer Science and Technology of Wuhan University of Science and Technology. She received her M.Sc degree from Wuhan University in Computer Science in 2006. Her current main research interests include optimization theory, image processing, and text processing.

Jingyu Hua was born in Zhejiang Province, China, in 1978. He received the B.S. and M.S. degrees in Radio Engineering from South China University of Technology (SCUT) in 1999 and 2002, and received his Ph.D. degree of Electronic Engineering from Southeast University in 2006. From 2006 to 2007, he was with Zhejiang University of Technology (ZJUT) as an Assistant Professor, now as a Full Professor (tenured). His research interests include mobile communications, statistical signal processing, and digital filter design with applications to communications. Dr. Hua had published more than fifty papers in international journals and conferences, and received the Outstanding Young Teacher Foundation from Zhejiang University of Technology in 2009. He was also a recipient of the 2009 Young Teacher Foundation of Zhejiang Provincial Education Department.

Ji-Hye Kim received the B.S. degree in Electronic Engineering from Myongji University in 2005. She received the M.S. degree in Electronic Engineering from Sogang University, Seoul, Korea, in 2011. She has been an Engineer in Image Development Team in Samsung Electronics, Inc. since 2011. Her current research interests are image processing and image enhancement.

Wankun Kuang was born in Hunan Province, China, in 1987. He received his Bachelor degree of EE from Jishou University in 2010. Currently, he is pursuing his M. Phil. degree of EE from Zhejiang University of Technology. His research interests lie in the area of FIR filter design and image processing. He has published several papers in international journals and conferences.

Ji Won Lee received the B.S. degree in Physics from Sookmyung Women's University in 1999. She received the B.S., M.S., and Ph D. degrees in Electronic Engineering from Sogang University in 2004, 2006, and 2011, respectively. She has been a Senior Research Engineer in Mobile Application Processor Group System IC R&D Lab., LG Electronics Inc. since 2011. Her current research interests are image processing and resolution enhancement.

Jun Li received the B.Eng. degree and M.Eng. degree in Computer Science from the Wuhan University of Technology in 2000 and 2003. Currently, he is a Ph.D candidate in Wuhan University. He is currently Associate Professor in the College of Computer Science and Technology, Wuhan University of Science and Technology. His research interests include pattern recognition.

Ang Li-Minn received the B.Eng (1st class) and PhD from Edith Cowan University, Australia, in 1996 and 2001, respectively. He is currently a research staff at School of Engineering, Edith Cowan University. Prior to joining Edith Cowan University, he was Associate Professor at School of Electrical and Electronic Engineering, Nottingham University. His research interests include the fields of video compression, visual processing, wireless visual sensor networks, and reconfigurable computing.

Maofu Liu is currently an Associate Professor in College of Computer Science and Technology of Wuhan University of Science and Technology. He received his Ph.D, M.Sc, and B.Sc degrees from Wuhan University in Computer Science in 2005, 2002, and 1998, respectively. His main research interests include natural language processing, image processing, and machine learning.

Xiaoming Liu received his Ph.D. degree from Zhejiang University, China, in 2007. He visited the Image Processing and Bio-Imaging Research Laboratory, Alcorn State University, USA, as a Post Doctorate Research Associate in 2008. Currently, he is an Associate Professor in the College of Computer Science and Technology, Wuhan University of Science and Technology, Wuhan, China. His interests include pattern recognition, image processing, and 3-D human body recognition.

Li-Hong Ma received the B.Sc. in Radio Engineering, M.Sc. and Ph.D. degrees both in Communication and Circuit Systems from South China University of Technology, Guangzhou, China, in 1987, 1990, and 1999, respectively. She was a Research Assistant at the Hong Kong Polytechnic University in 2000. She is currently a Professor of the School of Electronic and Information Engineering, South China University of Technology. Her research interests include digital signal transformation, image/video analysis, and coding.

Min-Ho Park received the B.S. degree in Electronic Engineering from Dongguk University, Seoul, Korea, in 2004. He received the M.S. degree in Electronic Engineering from Sogang University, Seoul, Korea, in 2006. In 2006, he joined Video Team in the Research and Development of PIXTREE, Inc. as Senior Engineer. He has been a Senior Software Engineer in SmartTV Platform Team in the Research and Development of LG Electronics Inc. since 2010. His research interests include video processing, analysis, indexing, and compression.

Rae-Hong Park was born in Seoul, Korea, in 1954. He received the B.S. and M.S. degrees in Electronics Engineering from Seoul National University, Seoul, Korea, in 1976 and 1979, respectively, and the M.S. and Ph.D. degrees in Electrical Engineering from Stanford University, Stanford, CA, in 1981 and 1984, respectively. In 1984, he joined the faculty of the Department of Electronic Engineering, Sogang University, Seoul, Korea, where he is currently a Professor. In 1990, he spent his sabbatical year as a Visiting Associate Professor with the Computer Vision Laboratory, Center for Automation Research, University of Maryland at College Park. In 2001 and 2004, he spent sabbatical semesters at Digital Media Research and Development Center (DTV image/video enhancement), Samsung Electronics Co., Ltd. In 2012, he spent a sabbatical year in Digital Imaging Business (R&D Team) and Visual Display Business (R&D Office), Samsung Electronics Co., Ltd. His current research interests are video communication, computer vision, and pattern recognition. He served as Editor for the *Korea Institute of Telematics and Electronics (KITE) Journal of Electronics Engineering* from 1995 to 1996. Dr. Park was the recipient of a 1990 Post-Doctoral Fellowship presented by the Korea Science and Engineering Foundation (KOSEF), the 1987 Academic Award presented by the KITE, the 2000 Haedong Paper Award presented by the Institute of Electronics Engineers of Korea (IEEK), the 1997 First Sogang Academic Award, and the 1999 Professor Achievement Excellence Award presented by Sogang University. He is a co-recipient of the Best Student Paper Award of the IEEE International Symposium on Multimedia (ISM 2006) and IEEE International Symposium on Consumer Electronics (ISCE 2011).

Seng Kah Phooi received the B.Eng (1st class) and PhD from University of Tasmania, Australia, in 1997 and 2001, respectively. She is currently a Professor at Sunway University, Malaysia. Prior to joining Sunway University, she was Associate Professor at the School of Electrical and Electronic Engineering, Nottingham University. Her research interests include the fields of visual processing, multi-biometrics, artificial intelligence, and wireless visual sensor networks.

Jae-Seob Shin received the B.S. and M.S. degrees from Sogang University, Seoul, Korea, in 1985 and 1987, respectively. From 1987 to 2000, he was an Engineer with Digital Signal Processing Laboratories in Samsung Advanced Institute of Technology (SAIT), Gyeonggido, Korea. He conducted a research in the area of image processing and video coding technology. Several kinds of technologies that were developed by his team have been selected as candidates of MPEG-4 International Standard since he joined the ISO/IEC JTC1/SC29/WG11(MPEG) in 1992 as a member of Korean delegation. He also did a chairing position for the Version Management ad-hoc group of MPEG from November 1997 to March 1998. He is now in chairing position of Interoperability Work Group in MPEG Industry Forum and Vice President of MPEG Forum controlled under MIC (Ministry of Information and Communication). He was a Principal Investigator in the MPEG-4 audio-visual coding team in SAIT from 1990 to 2000. During his research period, he applied more than 60 patents and submitted 13 papers as well as more than 60 technical reports in MPEG standard group. In July 2002, he established PIXTREE, Inc., Seoul, Korea, as a CEO/President of the company.

Sanjay K. Singh is Associate Professor in Department of Computer Engineering at Institute of Technology, Banaras Hindu University, India. He is a certified Novel Engineer and Novel Administrator. His research has been funded by UGC and AICTE. He has over 40 publications in refereed journals, book chapters, and conferences. His research interests include computational intelligence, biometrics, video authentication, pattern recognition, and machine learning. Dr. Singh is a member of IET, IEEE, ISTE, CSI.

Shrikant Tiwari received his M.Tech. degree in Computer Science and Technology from University of Mysore, India, in 2009. He is currently working toward the PhD degree at the Institute of Technology, Banaras Hindu University, Varanasi, India. His research interests include biometrics, image processing, and pattern recognition.

Saurabh Upadhyay received the B. Tech. degree in Computer Science and Engineering in 2001, and is currently working toward the Ph.D. degree in Computer Science at U.P. Technical University, India. He is an Associate Professor in the Department of Computer Science and Engineering, Saffrony Institute of Technology, Gujarat, India. He is actively involved in the development of a robust video authentication system that can identify tampering to determine the authenticity of the video. His current areas of interest include pattern recognition, video and image processing, watermarking, and artificial intelligence.

Lee Hao Wei received the Masters in Engineering from the Faculty of Engineering, the University of Nottingham, in 2011. He is a member of Sunway University Intelligent and Visual Computing Research Group, Graduate Member of the Boards of Engineers Malaysia, and a Member of the Institution of Engineering and Technology (IET). His research interest includes the fields of intelligent visual, audio processing, robotics, and automation.

Yonghao Xiao obtained a first class B.Eng degree in 1993 and a Master's degree in 2003 from South China University of Technology, P R China. He received the PhD degree from South China University of Technology in 2011. Currently, he is working in Foshan University, Foshan, China. His main research areas include image processing, pattern recognition, and intelligent computing.

Xin Xu received the BSc degree in Computer Science and Engineering from Shanghai Jiao Tong University, China, in 2004, and the MSc degree in Computer Science and Technology from Wuhan University of Science and Technology in 2006. He is currently working toward the PhD degree in Computer Application at the Department of Computer Science and Engineering, Shanghai Jiao Tong University, Shanghai, China. He is a Lecturer in the School of Computer Science and Technology, Wuhan University of Science and Technology, Wuhan, China. His current research interests include computer vision, pattern recognition, and visual surveillance.

Weiyu Yu received his PhD degree in Electronic and Information Engineering from South China University of Technology in 2005. He is a Lecturer at the School of Electronic and Information in SCUT. His research interests include image processing, video analysis, and pattern recognition.

Chun-Yan Zeng was born in Hubei Province, China, in 1986. She is currently working towards the Ph.D. degree in the School of Electronic and Information Engineering, South China University of Technology, Guangzhou, China. Her research interests include compressive sensing and image processing.

Xiaolong Zhang received the PhD degree in Computer Science and Engineering from Tokyo Institute of Technology, Japan, in 1998. Currently, he is a Professor in the School of Computer Science and Technology, Wuhan University of Science and Technology, Wuhan, China. His research interests include data mining, protein folding, and image processing.

Index